D1500077

1 e4 e6 2 d4 d5 3 ♘d2

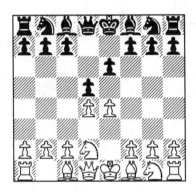

The French Tarrasch

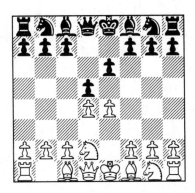

BATSFORD CHESS OPENING GUIDES

Other titles in this series include:

0 7134 8456 X	Budapest Gambit	Bogdan Lalic
0 7134 8451 9	King's Gambit	Neil McDonald
0 7134 8466 7	Scotch Game	Peter Wells
0 7134 8471 3	Spanish Exchange	Andrew Kinsman

For further details for Batsford chess titles, please write to Batsford Chess Books, 583 Fulham Road, London SW6 5BY.

Batsford Chess Opening Guides

The French Tarrasch

John Emms

B.T.Batsford Ltd, London

First published 1998
Copyright © 1998 John Emms

ISBN 0 7134 8461 6

British Library Cataloguing-in-Publication Data.
A catalogue record for this book is
available from the British Library.

All rights reserved. No part of this book may be
reproduced, by any means, without prior permission
of the publisher.

The Batsford Chess Opening Guides were designed
and developed by First Rank Publishing
Typeset and edited by First Rank Publishing, Brighton
Printed in Great Britain by
Redwood Books, Trowbridge, Wilts
for the publishers,
B. T. Batsford Ltd,
583 Fulham Road,
London SW6 5BY

Chess set used in cover photograph courtesy of the
London Chess Centre
Author photograph by Claire Smith

A BATSFORD CHESS BOOK
General Manager: David Cummings
Advisors: Mark Dvoretsky, Raymond Keene OBE,
Daniel King, Jon Speelman, Chris Ward

CONTENTS

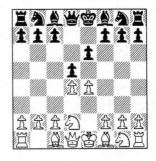

BIBLIOGRAPHY

Books

Encyclopaedia of Chess Openings vol.C, Sahovski Informator 1997
Batsford Chess Openings 2, Kasparov & Keene (Batsford, 1989)
The Complete French, Psakhis (Batsford, 1992)
Winning with the French, Uhlmann (Batsford, 1991)
Mastering the French, McDonald & Harley (Batsford, 1997)
Play the French, Watson (Cadogan, 1984 and 1986)
The Modern French Tarrasch, Gufeld (Cadogan, 1996)

Periodicals

Informator
ChessBase Magazine
New In Chess Yearbook
British Chess Magazine
Chess Monthly

INTRODUCTION

'The problem with playing ♘c3 against the French, is that Black just plays the Winawer, doubles your c-pawns, gangs up and wins your a-pawn, regroups and defends for a bit and then promotes his a-pawn. It's just too easy for Black!' So complained one of my students when he realised that his next opponent was a hardened French Defence player. Well, I must admit to feeling a mixture of smugness and relief at the knowledge that, as an avid Tarrasch devotee, I never have to worry about such things. I briefly showed him a few lines and he was struck by how simple it all looked.

Often when studying a new opening, it can look rather foreign to begin with, but this was not the case here. Perhaps, having played the Tarrasch for virtually all my chessplaying life, I am a little biased, but it is true that the Tarrasch is really quite simple to play for both White and Black. Of course, the real secret is to know how to play it *well*, but that's what this book is all about.

The German grandmaster Siegbert Tarrasch, one of the world's leading chess authorities at the end of the 19th century, introduced this variation into tournament practice in 1890. Since then it has always been a popular way for White and it is still regarded as the soundest approach against the French.

In particular, the Tarrasch has always appealed to players who prefer to start with a sound positional base, and because of this it is unlikely to ever go out of fashion. Its most famous devotee was Anatoly Karpov, who did much to elevate the opening's status in the early seventies, when he used it continuously on his way to the World Championship. More recent exponents include England's World Championship semi-finalist Michael Adams, together with the young Russian stars Peter Svidler (currently ranked in the world's top ten) and Sergei Rublevsky. To this list we can add a whole host of other grandmasters, much too numerous to name individually here!

Positional and Tactical Themes

Before we begin studying the nitty-gritty of the actual theory, it is important to take a brief look at some of the positional and tactical themes associated with the Tarrasch. As the two distinct main lines with 3...♞f6 and 3...c5 constitute at least 90% of the material in this book, I've decided to focus on those two moves here, although you will appreciate that some ideas do overlap with 3...a6, 3...♞c6 and 3...dxe4.

3...♞f6

The exchange of dark-squared bishops

One of White's principal goals in many ...♞f6 variations is to achieve the exchange of the dark-squared bishops. The pawn structure dictates that White has more control of the dark squares, and a trade of these bishops normally only emphasises White's authority. Take the following two positions.

see following diagram

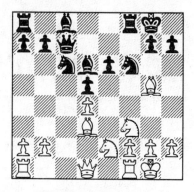

In view of the argument above you will not be surprised to find out that in the first diagram the main theoretical move is 12 ♗f4!, offering the trade. In the second case White's play is more subtle. 12 ♗f4 is impossible as it loses a piece, but White can carry out the exchange with 12 ♗h4, intending ♗g3.

The fight for the dark squares

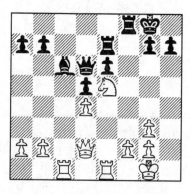

This diagram shows an ideal situation for White. Three sets of minor pieces have been exchanged, leaving White with the classic 'good knight versus bad bishop' situation. Added to this, White's rooks sit very nicely on the open c-file and semi-open e-file. White can choose between attacking Black's weak backward e6-pawn, or piling up on the c-file. In contrast, Black has no constructive plan and can only sit and wait, while White leisurely builds up the pressure. Notice that all of White's pieces stand on dark squares.

Wells-Fries Nielsen
Copenhagen Open 1995

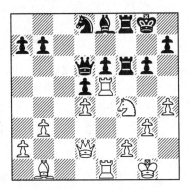

Here's another depressing scenario for Black. Again the dark-squared bishops have been exchanged early in the game. Black has failed to achieve any counterplay and now faces a grim defence. The black e-pawn is extremely weak, while White can also consider a direct attack on the black king starting with 27 h5. Indeed this was Wells's choice in the actual game (see Game 20).

Marjanovic-Timman
Sarajevo 1984

see following diagram

Here's an altogether different situation. White has exchanged off his dark-squared bishop, but only for a knight. Now the dark squares are with Black. His queen is doing a marvellous job on g7, where it protects the black kingside, attacks the weak d4-pawn and prepares a pawn assault starting with 35...g4! See Game 14 for the rest of this very instructive encounter.

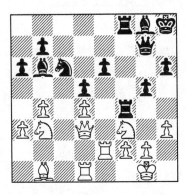

The ...♖xf3 exchange sacrifice
In order to achieve counterplay against the solid white position, Black sometimes employs a common exchange sacrifice which seriously weakens the pawn cover around the white king, while also eliminating a defender of the d4-pawn.

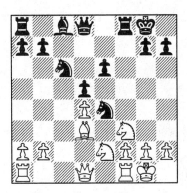

The main option here is 14...♖xf3 15 gxf3 ♘g5, when a very unclear position arises. See Chapter 1, Games 1-4 for a detailed discussion of this line.

The ...e6-e5 break

In many Tarrasch positions the move ...e6-e5 enables Black to free his pieces and thereby solve most of his problems immediately.

Bialas-Uhlmann
Leipzig 1951

After 14...e5! 15 dxe5 ♘xe5 16 ♘xe5 ♗xe5 Black has a very active position, with open lines on which to attack the white king. The rest of this game is a graphic illustration of Black's chances here: 17 ♗c3 ♗xh2+! 18 ♔xh2 ♘g4+ 19 ♔g3 ♖xf2 20 ♗d2 ♘e3 21 ♖xf2 ♕d6+ 22 ♔f3 ♗g4+ 23 ♔xe3 ♕e5+ and White resigned as it is mate next move.

Emms-Poulton
Hastings 1997

see following diagram

Here's an example of Black failing to solve his problems, even after achieving the desired advance. After 14...e5 15 dxe5 ♘xe5 16 ♘xe5 ♕xe5 17 ♕b3 White retains a more comfortable position. In this case Black has no attacking chances against the white king, but has constant problems with his d- and b-pawns.

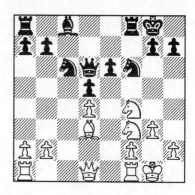

Dismantling the white centre

In the early f2-f4 lines White erects a powerful looking pawn centre, which can often be used to mercilessly crush Black into submission. Because of this, Black players often employ quite violent means to destroy White's pride and joy. Here are a couple of typical examples.

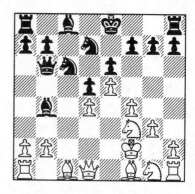

In this position Black has the extraordinary move 10...g5!, which has indeed become the main line here. See Games 32-33 for more details on this variation.

Here's an even more extreme example.

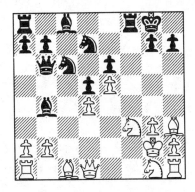

Normal moves would consign Black to a terribly passive position. The brutal solution is 13...♘dxe5!? 14 dxe5 ♘xe5, which gives Black two central pawns and active play for the piece. Note that 15 ♘xe5 allows an immediate catastrophe with 15...♖f2 mate.

3...c5

The ...♕xd5 structure

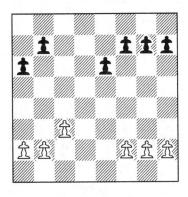

Here is the typical pawn structure arising from the 3...c5 4 exd5 ♕xd5 of the Tarrasch. Black's e-pawn gives him more control over the centre and the island of four pawns provide a valuable shield for the black king. This protection is often vital in repelling early onslaughts from White, who will be attempting to utilise his superior development and activity. Black often has to play the early middlegame very accurately and must be particularly careful not to allow a combinational breakthrough.

Adams-Luther
Oakham 1990

Here the casual 14...♘d7 was punished by 15 ♖xe6! and already Black has a lost position, since 15...fxe6 loses to 16 ♘xe6 ♕b6 (or 16...♗h2+ 17 ♔h1 ♕e5 18 ♘xf8+ ♔xf8 19 ♕h5) 17 ♘xf8+ ♔xf8 18 ♕d5.

The ...♕xd5 lines often liven up when Black chooses the ambitious option of castling queenside. Take the following position, for example.

see following diagram

Black's bishops, knight and queen point menacingly towards the white king, which is enough to give White a lot of headaches.

Black also has some chances of success in an endgame. White owns a useful queenside pawn majority, but the importance of this is often exaggerated. Black also holds some trump cards.

Here is an example of a very successful ...♛xd5 endgame for Black.

Hennigan-Levitt
British Championship 1989

In the ending Black's extra central pawn can be useful in supporting a knight in the centre. Note that Black's kingside pawn phalanx is looking very impressive indeed.

The isolated queen's pawn
After 3...c5 4 exd5 exd5 some sort of isolated queen's pawn (IQP) position is usually reached, and it is worth-

while having a few guidelines for these sorts of positions.

Here we see the IQP as a real strength. Note that it supports the crucial squares e4 and c4, which can be used as outposts for the black knights. As always, piece activity is paramount. In this position Black's minor pieces are superior to their white counterparts and this is enough to give Black the advantage. Notice that if all the minor pieces were taken off the board, then the edge would swing to White, as the weakness of the d-pawn would become more significant. So we can say in general that exchanges of minor pieces normally benefit the side battling against the IQP.

In this position Black's strategy has failed. Two sets of minor pieces have been eliminated and White has the e4- and c4-squares firmly under his control. More importantly, however, the d-pawn is chronically weak and is ready to be picked off at any moment.

Part of White's strategy against the IQP is to exchange the right pieces. In the above diagram there are three possibilities, but only one gives White chances of an advantage. White can exchange a minor piece with 1 ♗xc6 bxc6. However, that change in the pawn structure favours Black, as the d5-pawn is no longer isolated. Another idea is 1 ♗xe7, but after 1...♗xe7 Black gets control of the dark squares and his bishop can be used to support a later ...d5-d4. The best solution is 1 ♗h4!, intending ♗g3, offering a trade of those dark-squared bishops, which would eliminate Black's best piece and increase White's control over the dark squares. Throughout the book you'll find me harping on continuously about the importance of these colour complexes. I apologise in advance, but their importance can never be underestimated!

CHAPTER ONE

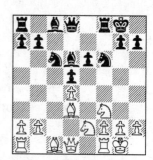

3...♞f6:
Main Line with 11...0-0

1 e4 e6 2 d4 d5 3 ♞d2 ♞f6 4 e5 ♞fd7 5 ♝d3 c5 6 c3 ♞c6 7 ♞e2 cxd4 8 cxd4 f6 9 exf6 ♞xf6 10 ♞f3 ♝d6 11 0-0 0-0

The line starting with 11...0-0 is perhaps the most important variation stemming from 3...♞f6. Black allows his opponent to play the positionally desirable 12 ♝f4 in the hope that the temporary 'looseness' in the white position will allow him to create serious counterattacking chances.

Most of the games in this chapter continue 12 ♝f4 ♝xf4 13 ♞xf4 ♞e4!?, when Black immediately starts operations on the half-open f-file. Games 1-4 are particularly important, as here we will cover the notorious exchange sacrifice (14 ♞e2 ♜xf3), which has breathed new life into Black's position. Some White players have been scared off by the practical difficulties of facing the exchange sacrifice, and in Games 5-8 we shall look at other ways for White to play the position after 13...♞e4. This knight move continues to be the popular choice at all levels,

although there are alternatives (see Game 9). Finally we consider the rarer 12 ♝g5, which often just transposes to lines involving an earlier ...♛c7 or ...♛b6, in Game 10.

Game 1
Rublevsky-Gleizerov
USSR 1991

---

1 e4 e6 2 d4 d5 3 ♞d2 ♞f6 4 e5 ♞fd7 5 ♝d3 c5 6 c3 ♞c6 7 ♞e2 cxd4 8 cxd4 f6 9 exf6 ♞xf6 10 0-0 ♝d6 11 ♞f3 0-0 12 ♝f4 ♝xf4 13 ♞xf4 ♞e4 14 ♞e2

14...♖xf3!?

14...♘g5 is hardly ever seen, but it may well be a playable alternative to the exchange sacrifice. 15 ♘xg5 ♕xg5 16 ♕c1 transposes to Game 5, while 15 ♘e5! is an obvious attempt to claim a more concrete edge. After 15...♘xe5 16 dxe5 White can try to exploit Black's offside knight, although it is not all one-way traffic: 16...♕b6! 17 ♕c2 ♗d7! 18 h4 ♖ac8 19 ♕b1 seems to win a pawn for White, but after either 19...♘f7!? 20 ♗xh7+ ♔h8, when the e5-pawn hangs, or 19...♘e4 20 ♗xe4 dxe4 21 ♕xe4 ♗c6, Black obtains substantial counterplay.

15 gxf3 ♘g5 16 ♔h1

Seemingly leaving the f3-pawn en prise, but White has some tricks based on ♗xh7+. The major alternative 16 f4 will be discussed in Games 3 and 4.

16...e5!

It is imperative for Black to release his light-squared bishop immediately. 16...♘xf3 17 ♗xh7+ ♔xh7 18 ♕d3+ and 19 ♕xf3 just favours White.

17 dxe5 ♘xf3

17...♘xe5 is an underrated alternative to the text. White has two ways to combat this idea, but neither has produced particularly good results:

a) 18 f4? ♗g4! 19 f3 ♗xf3+ 20 ♖xf3 ♘gxf3 21 fxe5 ♕h4 22 ♔g2 ♖f8 23 h3 ♕g5+ 24 ♔h1 ♕xe5 25 ♗xh7+ ♔h8 26 ♘f4 ♕xf4 27 ♕c2 ♕g3 28 ♗f5 ♘d4 29 ♕c5 ♕f3+ 30 ♔h2 ♕f2+ 31 ♔h1 ♖xf5 and White resigned in Donovan-Kinsman, London (Lloyds Bank Masters) 1994. An easy point for Kinsman, who had had the good fortune of playing exactly the same variation two years earlier!

b) 18 ♘g1 ♕f6 19 ♗e2 ♗d7! (19...♗e6 20 ♕d4 with the idea of f3-f4 gives White a clear plus) 20 ♕d2 (20 ♕xd5+ ♔h8 looks critical; Black's compensation for the material is based on ideas involving ...♗c6) 20...♘e6 21 ♖fe1 ♗c6 22 ♗f1 ♘f4 23 ♖ad1!? and here in Emms-L.B.Hansen, Gausdal 1992, we both missed 23...♘xf3! 24 ♘xf3 d4, when Black has a winning position.

18 ♘g1

18 ♗xh7+ will be studied in Game 2.

18...♘fxe5

A characteristic position for this line. In compensation for the exchange, Black has a menacing passed d-pawn and White's king is not altogether safe. Objectively Black probably has enough, and in any case his position is easier to play.

19 ♗c2

Other tries include:

a) 19 ♗e2 ♗f5 20 ♕d2 d4 21 ♖fe1 ♕d5+ 22 f3 d3 23 ♗f1 ♖d8 24 b3 ♘g6 25 ♖ac1 ♘ce5 26 ♖c3 ♕d4 27 ♖cc1?? ♕xg1+! 0-1 Lhagvasuren-Gleizerov, Cheliabinsk 1991. White has to stay very alert in this variation!

b) 19 f4 ♘g4 (19...♘xd3!? also deserves attention) 20 ♕d2 d4 21 ♗e4 ♘e3 22 ♖f3 ♗g4 23 ♖f2 ♕f6? (I like 23...♗f5! here, as after 24 ♗xf5 ♕d5+ 25 ♘f3 ♘xf5 the exchange of bishops emphasises the weaknesses around the white king) 24 ♖c1 ♖f8 25 ♘e2 ♕e6 26 ♘g3 ♕h6 27 ♘f1 ♘f5 28 ♔g1 ♕h4 29 ♕d3 ♕d8? 30 h3! 1-0 Hunt-Hagarova, Yerevan Women's Olympiad 1996.

19...d4 20 ♗e4 ♗e6 21 ♖c1 ♕h4 22 f3 ♖d8 23 ♖e1 ♕f6

Black has completed his development and his pieces stand harmoniously. All in all, he has a very reasonable position.

24 b3 ♗d5 25 b4! d3 26 ♗xd5+ ♖xd5 27 ♕b3 ♕f7 28 ♖ed1 g5! 29 ♖c5 ♖xc5 30 bxc5 ♘d4 31 ♕xf7+ ♔xf7 32 ♘h3! ♘dxf3 33 ♘f2 d2 34 ♔g2 ♔e6 35 ♘e4 ♔d5 36 ♘xd2 ♘xd2 37 ♖xd2+ ♔xc5 ½-½

Here Rublevsky gives 38 ♖f2 ♔d4 39 ♖f5 g4 40 ♖h5 b5 41 ♖xh7 a5 as leading to a draw. Perhaps this should be expanded a little further. For example, 42 ♔g3 a4 43 ♖b7 ♔c4 44 ♔f4 ♘f3! 45 h3 gxh3! 46 ♔xf3 b4 47 ♔e3 ♔c3 48 ♖c7+ ♔b2 49 ♖a7 a3 50 ♖b7

♔xa2 51 ♖xb4 ♔a1 52 ♔d2 h2 53 ♖h4 ♔b2 54 ♖xh2 a2 and finally the draw becomes inevitable.

Game 2
Kramnik-Ulibin
USSR Championship 1991

1 e4 e6 2 d4 d5 3 ♘d2 ♘f6 4 e5 ♘fd7 5 c3 c5 6 ♗d3 ♘c6 7 ♘e2 cxd4 8 cxd4 f6 9 exf6 ♘xf6 10 ♘f3 ♗d6 11 0-0 0-0 12 ♗f4 ♗xf4 13 ♘xf4 ♘e4 14 ♘e2 ♖xf3!? 15 gxf3 ♘g5 16 ♔h1 e5! 17 dxe5 ♘xf3 18 ♗xh7+ ♔h8!

18...♔xh7 19 ♕d3+ ♔g8 20 ♕xf3 ♘xe5 21 ♕g3 is good for White.
19 ♘g1

19...♘cd4!

Other moves do not quite hit the mark:

a) 19...♘xg1? 20 ♕h5 and wins.

b) 19...♘cxe5? 20 ♗e4! also wins for White.

c) 19...♘fxe5 doesn't lose immediately, but after 20 ♗c2 White still has a clear plus.

20 ♘xf3

20 ♖e1 ♗g4 21 ♖e3 ♕h4! gives Black a clear advantage according to Holmov. 22 ♘xf3 ♕xf2 23 ♕xd4! ♗xf3+ 24 ♖xf3 ♕xd4 bears out his opinion. However, White does have another important alternative to 20 ♘xf3 with 20 ♗d3 ♗g4 21 ♕c1!?

a) 21...♘xg1 and now:

a1) 22 ♔xg1? ♘f3+ 23 ♔h1 ♘xe5 with a dangerous attack.

a2) 22 ♕f4! (this clever move refutes 21...♘xg1) 22...♗e2 23 ♖xg1 ♗xd3 24 ♕xd4 ♗e4+ 25 ♖g2 ♖c8 26 ♖d1 and the extra pawn ensures White a plus.

b) 21...♕f8! 22 ♕e3 and now:

b1) 22...g5?! 23 ♘xf3 ♗xf3+ 24 ♔g1 ♕h6 25 e6! ♕f6 (or 25...♕h3 26 ♕e5+ ♔g8 27 ♕xg5+ ♔h8 28 ♕e5+ ♔g8 29 ♕g3+) 26 ♖ae1 ♘c6 27 ♗b1 g4 28 ♕c3 ♘d4 29 ♕c7 ♗e4 30 ♗xe4 1-0 was played in Johnson-Du Pree, correspondence 1993.

b2) Johnson gives 22...♖e8 as an obvious improvement, yet still assesses the position as clearly better for White. In fact, Black seems to have a dangerous initiative.

see following diagram

The threat is ...♖xe5 followed by ...♖h5, so White has to react quickly with 23 h3 and now I've looked at a couple of lines:

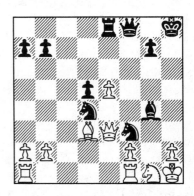

b21) 23...♖xe5? 24 hxg4 ♖xe3 (24...♕f6!? is an improvement, but White is still better after 25 ♔g2 ♖xe3 26 fxe3 ♕g5 27 ♖xf3 ♘xf3 28 ♘xf3 ♕xg4+ 29 ♔f2) 25 fxe3 ♕f6 26 ♘xf3 ♘xf3 27 g5! ♕xb2 28 ♖xf3 ♕xa1+ 29 ♖f1 and White wins.

b22) The calm 23....♗h5! maintains all of Black's attacking chances, e.g. 24 ♘xf3 ♘xf3 25 ♗c2 ♖xe5 26 ♕d3 g6 and the threat of ...♕f4 is looming.

20...♗g4 21 ♘xd4 ♗xd1 22 ♖axd1 ♔xh7

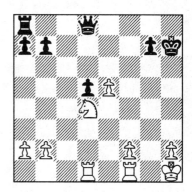

This is a crucial position for the assessment of the whole 14...♖xf3 line. White has obtained a rook, knight and dangerous passed pawn for the queen.

However, White's king is still a little airy and Black can use this to his advantage in the ensuing tactics.

23 f4

Supporting the passed pawn. 23 ♖d3!?, with the idea of ♖g3 and ♖fg1, is another way to play the position.

23...♕b6 24 f5

24 ♖d2!? may be a more serious winning try. Bode-Voigt, Hamburg 1992, continued 24...♕g6 25 ♖e1 ♕h6 26 ♖f2 ♕h4 27 ♖ff1 ♖h8 28 e6 g6?! 29 f5! gxf5? (29...♕xd4 30 f6 ♕c5 31 e7 d4!, when Black has ideas of a perpetual check, is the last chance) 30 ♘xf5 ♕f6 and here 31 ♖f3, threatening ♖h3+, is a killer.

24...♕xb2!

Not so much grabbing a pawn, as paving the way for the rook to travel to c1.

25 ♖d3 ♖c8 26 f6

26 ♖h3+?! ♔g8 27 f6 fails to 27...♕xd4! 28 f7+ ♔f8 29 ♖h8+ ♔e7, when 30 f8♕+ ♖xe8 is slightly better for Black and 30 ♖xc8 runs into 30...♕e4+ 31 ♔g1 ♕g4+ 32 ♔h1 ♕xc8.

26...♖c1

Now everything leads to a perpet-

ual check.

27 ♖h3+ ♔g6 28 ♖g3+ ♔h5 ½-½

White can draw with 29 ♖h3+ or else allow Black the perpetual with 29 ♖xc1 ♕xc1+ 30 ♖g1 ♕e3! 31 fxg7 ♕e4+ 32 ♖g2 ♕e1+.

Game 3
Antonov-Balinov
Djuni 1987

---

1 e4 e6 2 d4 d5 3 ♘d2 ♘f6 4 e5 ♘fd7 5 ♗d3 c5 6 c3 ♘c6 7 ♘e2 cxd4 8 cxd4 f6 9 exf6 ♘xf6 10 ♘f3 ♗d6 11 0-0 0-0 12 ♗f4 ♗xf4 13 ♘xf4 ♘e4 14 ♘e2 ♖xf3!? 15 gxf3 ♘g5 16 f4

The only real alternative to 16 ♔h1.

16...♘f3+!?

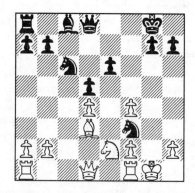

This move adds more fuel to the fire. The safer 16...♘h3+ is discussed in Game 4.

17 ♔g2 ♕h4 18 ♔xf3 ♕h3+ 19 ♘g3 e5 20 ♔e3

The major alternative to Black's threat of ...♗g4 is 20 f5, when after 20...e4+ we have a further split:

see following diagram

a) In Emms-Kinsman, Wuppertal

(rapidplay) 1993, I tried 21 ♔e3 ♛h6+ 22 f4 exd3 23 ♛h5, but after 23...♛xh5 24 ♘xh5 ♗xf5 25 ♘g3 ♖e8+ 26 ♔d2 ♗e4 Black certainly had enough play for the exchange. In hindsight 23 ♛h5 looks to be too accommodating and should be replaced with 23 ♛b3. Even so, it is quite clear that there is no easy solution for White.

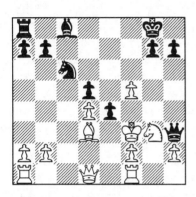

b) 21 ♗xe4 dxe4+ 22 ♔xe4? (22 ♔e3 is safer) 22...♗xf5+! 23 ♘xf5 ♖e8+ 24 ♔f4 ♛g2 25 ♘g3 ♘b4! 26 ♛b3+ ♘d5+ 27 ♔g4 ♖h8 28 ♖ae1 ♖f8!, and White's king has slipped into a mating net. Novotny-Nilsson, European Team Correspondence Championship 1991, concluded 29 h4 ♖f4+ 30 ♔h5 ♖f5+ 31 ♔g4 g6 32 ♖e8+ ♔g7 33 ♛xb7+ ♖f7 34 ♛xf7+ ♔xf7 35 ♖e5 h5+ 36 ♔g5 ♛f3 37 ♔h6 ♛f4+ 0-1, as after 38 ♖g5 ♛xd4 39 ♖xg6 ♘f4 the rook goes or it is mate.

20...exf4+ 21 ♔d2

21 ♔xf4 ♛h6+ 22 ♔f3 ♗h3 23 ♗f5 ♖f8 occurred in De Souza-Ferraro, Zurich 1990, a game that White went onto win. Instead of 23...♖f8, Black should play 23...♛f6!, hitting the d4-pawn. Then 24 ♖e1 ♘xd4+ 25 ♛xd4 ♛xd4 26 ♗xh3 ♖f8+ and 24 ♛d3 ♘e7!

(24...♘xd4+ 25 ♛xd4 ♛xd4 26 ♗xh3 isn't so good now, as f2 is protected) 25 ♖fe1 ♘xf5 26 ♘xf5 ♗xf5 are both very uncomfortable for White.

21...fxg3 22 hxg3 ♛h6+ 23 f4 ♛f6! 24 ♛a4 ♗d7 25 ♖ae1 ♖c8 26 ♗b5 a5!

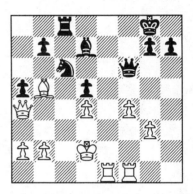

It seems that White is on the verge of consolidation, but Black manages to obtain just enough play to force a draw. 26...a5 prepares ...♘b4, disconnecting White's queen from the defence of the vital d-pawn.

27 ♖c1

After 27 a3 White gets hit with 27...♘b4! (anyway) as 28 ♗xd7 ♛xd4+ 29 ♔e2 ♛d3+ 30 ♔f2 ♖c2+ 31 ♛xc2 ♘xc2 is good for Black.

27...♖e8! 28 ♖fe1 ♘b4! 29 ♖e5

29 ♖xe8+ ♗xe8 30 ♗xe8 ♛xd4+ 31 ♔e2 ♛xb2+ 32 ♔d1 ♛d4+ is also a draw by perpetual check.

29...♖xe5 30 dxe5 ♛b6 31 ♗xd7 ♛f2+ 32 ♔d1 ♛f1+ ½-½

Game 4
Komarov-Barsov
Reims 1994

---

1 e4 e6 2 d4 d5 3 ♘d2 ♘f6 4 ♗d3

c5 5 e5 ♘fd7 6 c3 ♘c6 7 ♘e2 cxd4
8 cxd4 f6 9 exf6 ♘xf6 10 ♘f3 ♗d6
11 0-0 0-0 12 ♗f4 ♗xf4 13 ♘xf4
♘e4 14 ♘e2 ♖xf3!? 15 gxf3 ♘g5 16
f4 ♘h3+

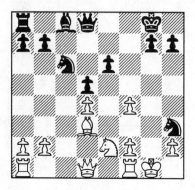

17 ♔h1

17 ♔g2 was thought to be bad due
to 17...♘xf4+ 18 ♘xf4 ♕g5+. After 19
♔h1 (19 ♔f3? ♘xd4+ 20 ♔e3 ♕e5+ is
very good for Black) 19...♕xf4 20
♕h5, however, White can drum up a
powerful initiative before Black has a
chance to co-ordinate, e.g. 20...g6 21
♖g1 ♘xd4!? (very provocative, but
21...♘e7 22 ♕g5! ♕xg5 23 ♖xg5 ♗d7
24 ♖c1 ♘c6 25 ♗b5 ♖f8 26 ♔g2 ♖f4
27 ♖d1 gives White a pleasant endgame) 22 ♗xg6 hxg6 23 ♕xg6+ ♔f8.

Here White's attack seems to be on
the verge of succeeding, but Black has
some surprising counter-chances as
shown, for example, by the following
crazy line: 24 ♕g8+ ♔e7 25 ♖g7+ ♔d6
26 ♖f7 ♘f5 27 ♕d8+ ♔c6 28 ♖c7+
♔b5 29 ♖xc8. Now it is Black's turn
to bat! After 29...♕f3+ 30 ♔g1 ♘h4 31
♕d7+ ♔a6 White has an immediate
draw with 32 ♕a4+ ♔b6 33 ♕b4+ but
nothing better. The winning attempt
32 ♕xe6+!? b6 33 ♕g8 fails to
33...♕h3 34 ♕g3 ♘f3+ 35 ♕xf3 ♕xf3
36 ♖xa8, when it is Black's turn to
deliver perpetual with 36...♕g4+.

In view of the unclear nature of
these variations, Black most practical
choice against 17 ♔g2 is, however,
17...♕h4. After 18 ♗b5 ♗d7 Black
will follow up with ...♖f8 with clear
compensation for the exchange.

**17...♕h4 18 ♕d2 ♘xf2+ 19 ♔g2
♘xd3 20 ♕xd3 ♗d7**

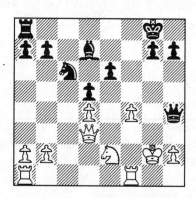

Taking stock, we see that White has
withstood his opponent's initial on-
slaught, but there is still plenty to
fight for. Black has a pawn for the exchange and White still has weaknesses
on f4 and d4. All in all, the position is
very finely balanced.

21 h3!?

Making a slightly safer haven for the king on h2. In contrast 21 f5? failed to hit the mark in Dobosz-Boehsmueller, Loosdorf 1993, which concluded 21...exf5 (why not?) 22 ♘f4 ♖e8 23 ♕b3 ♖e4 24 ♕xd5+ ♗e6 25 ♕d6 ♗c4 26 ♖f2 ♖xd4 27 ♕c7 ♕g4+ 28 ♔h1 ♖xf4 29 ♕c8+ ♔f7 30 ♕xb7+ ♘e7 31 ♖xf4 ♕xf4 and the threat of 32...♗d5+ cannot be parried by 32 ♖d1 as 32...♗d5+ 33 ♖xd5 ♕f1 is mate.

21...♗e8?!

This allows White to open up the position for his two rooks. 21...♖f8 would have been much more natural.

22 f5! e5

In his notes to the game Komarov gives 22...exf5 23 ♕xf5 ♗g6 24 ♕xd5+ ♔h8 25 ♖f4! ♕e7 26 ♘g3 as winning for White and I see no reason to disagree with his assessment.

23 dxe5 ♘xe5 24 ♕d4

24 ♕xd5+ also looks good, although after 24...♘f7 Black can hope for counterplay based on threats along the a8-h1 diagonal.

24...♕g5+ 25 ♘g3 ♘c6 26 ♕f4 ♕f6 27 ♖ae1! ♕xb2+

Grabbing the bait, but 27...♗f7 was wiser, restricting White to a small edge.

28 ♖f2 ♕f6 29 ♖e6 ♕f7 30 ♖d6 ♘a5 31 ♕g5 ♘c4 32 ♖e6 d4 33 f6! h6 34 ♕xg7+ ♕xg7 35 fxg7 ♘e3+ 36 ♔h2 ♔xg7 37 ♖d6

The d-pawn drops and White's rooks rule in the open position. The rest of the game is quite painful for Black.

37...♖c8 38 ♖xd4 ♖c2 39 ♖xc2

♘xc2 40 ♖c4 ♘a3 41 ♖c7+ ♔g6 42 ♖xb7 a5 43 ♖b6+ ♔g5 44 ♖e6 ♗b5 45 ♖e5+ ♔f6 46 ♖h5 ♔g6 47 ♖c5 a4 48 ♘e4 ♗d7 49 ♘c3 ♘c2

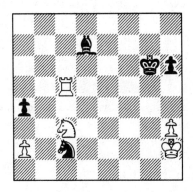

50 ♘xa4! ♗xa4 51 ♖c4 1-0

Game 5
Dvoirys-Ulibin
Cheliabinsk 1990

1 e4 e6 2 d4 d5 3 ♘d2 ♘f6 4 e5 ♘fd7 5 c3 c5 6 ♗d3 ♘c6 7 ♘e2 cxd4 8 cxd4 f6 9 exf6 ♘xf6 10 0-0 ♗d6 11 ♘f3 0-0 12 ♗f4 ♗xf4 13 ♘xf4 ♘e4 14 ♕c1

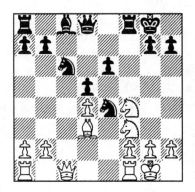

A safe move. The queen keeps an eye on the important dark squares. White now plans ♖e1 to kick the black knight from e4.

14...♘g5!

A positionally sound idea. The exchange of these knights eliminates a defender of the d4-pawn, while also lessening White's control over e5. In contrast the developing 14...♗d7 turns out to be too slow after 15 ♖e1! ♘g5 16 ♘xg5 ♕xg5 17 ♘xe6 ♕xc1 18 ♖axc1 ♗xe6 19 ♖xe6 ♘xd4 20 ♖e7 and White retains a clear advantage in the endgame.

15 ♘xg5 ♕xg5 16 ♘e2

For 16 ♗xh7+!? see Game 6.

16...♕f6 17 ♕e3

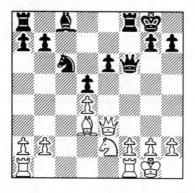

17...♗d7

17...e5 18 dxe5 ♘xe5, immediately releasing the tension in the centre, is the principal alternative. Practical results have favoured White, although with exact play Black may be able to equalise. Tiviakov-Maksimovic, Cheliabinsk 1990, continued 19 ♖ad1 ♘g4 20 ♕c5 ♗e6 21 ♕d4 ♘e5 22 ♗b1 ♖ae8 23 ♘c3 ♖d8 24 ♖fe1 ♘c6 25 ♕xf6 ♖xf6 26 ♖d2 a6 27 ♖ed1 ♘e7 28 ♘e4! ♖h6 29 ♘g5 and Black was already in trouble. Maksimovic suggests 19...♘c4!? as an improvement. It is true that after 20 ♗xc4 dxc4 21 ♘c3

♗g4 22 f3 ♗f5 Black seems to be rid of most of his problems.

18 ♖ad1

18 ♗b5 is another idea, hoping to exchange on c6 and reach a classic 'good knight versus bad bishop' scenario. However, Black can thwart this attempt with the strange looking 18...♘b8!?, when White may have nothing better than to retreat with 19 ♗d3. Instead Heinemann-Kinsman, German Bundesliga 1997, continued 18...♖ac8 19 ♖ac1 (the immediate 19 ♗xc6 ♖xc6 20 ♘c3 initiates White's plan, but after 20...♖c4 21 ♖ad1 ♖fc8 Black can obtain counterplay with ...b7-b5-b4) 19...♘b8 20 ♗d3 ♘c6 (of course this jig with bishop and knight isn't necessary. White can reach the same position with the simple 18 ♖ac1 ♖ac8) 21 ♖c3 ♘e7 22 ♖fc1 ♖xc3 23 ♖xc3 ♗c6 24 ♖c1 ♘c8 25 ♘c3 ♘d6 26 ♖e1 ♖e8 27 ♖e2 a6 28 f4 ♘c4 29 ♕f2 ♖f8 30 b3 ♘d6 31 g3 ♖c8 32 ♖c2 and here Black should have played 32...♗e8, not fearing 33 f5 as 33...♗f7 34 fxe6 ♕xf2+ 35 ♔xf2 ♗xe6 is completely equal.

18...♖ac8 19 ♗b1 ♗e8 20 h3 ♗f7

Not 20...♗g6 21 ♗xg6 and Black has to capture with the pawn, as 21...♕xg6 runs into 22 ♘f4.

21 ♘f4 ♖fe8 22 b3 e5 23 dxe5 ♖xe5 24 ♕c1 d4 25 ♘d3

The ...e6-e5 break has been achieved at a favourable moment, so that Black has enough piece activity to support the passed d-pawn. Notice that 25 ♖xd4? ♘xd4 26 ♕xc8+ ♖e8 loses the knight on f4.

25...♖g5!?

The simple 25...♖5e8 would have

been enough to maintain the balance, but Black decides to go 'all in' with a kingside attack.

26 ♖de1 ♗d5 27 f3 ♖f8 28 ♖f2 ♖g3?! 29 ♔h2 ♕h4? 30 ♕c5 ♖d8

Around here Ulibin must have realised that his kingside offensive had been too ambitious and is forced into an ignominious retreat. The critical line is 30...♗xf3, but after 31 ♖xf3 ♖fxf3 32 ♖e8+ ♔f7 33 ♕f8+ ♔g6 34 ♘f4+ ♔h6 35 ♖e6+ ♖g6 36 ♖xg6+ hxg6 37 ♕h8+ ♔g5 38 ♘e6+ White wins comfortably.

31 ♖fe2 ♗f7 32 ♖e4 ♕g5 33 ♖1e2?

The computer program Fritz immediately spotted 33 ♕c2! ♗d5 34 ♕f2, when the black rook is severely embarrassed!

33...♕xc5 34 ♘xc5 ♖g5! 35 ♘e6

The theme of trapping pieces continues. 35 ♘xb7 ♖d7 36 f4 ♖b5 37 ♖c2 ♗d5 wins for Black.

35...♗xe6 36 ♖xe6 ♖c5

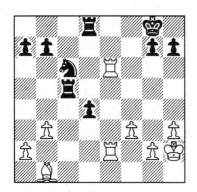

37 ♗e4??

The final and decisive blunder.

37...d3 38 ♖d2 ♔f7!

Now it is White's rook that is trapped! Ulibin's endgame technique proved to be extremely efficient.

39 ♖xc6 bxc6 40 ♖xd3 ♖xd3 41 ♗xd3 ♖c3 42 ♗c4+ ♔f6 43 ♔g3 g5 44 a4 ♖c2 45 a5 ♖b2 46 a6 c5 47 ♗d5 ♔e5 48 ♗f7 h6 49 h4

Or 49 ♗c4 h5 50 ♔h2 h4 and the black king will march into the dark squares.

49...gxh4+ 50 ♔h3 ♔f4 51 ♗d5 ♖a2 52 ♗c4 ♖a1 53 ♔h2

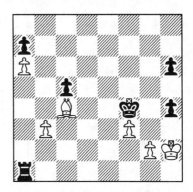

53...h3! 0-1

Game 6
Svidler-Ulibin
Russian Championship 1994

---

1 e4 e6 2 d4 d5 3 ♘d2 ♘f6 4 e5 ♘fd7 5 c3 c5 6 ♗d3 ♘c6 7 ♘e2 cxd4 8 cxd4 f6 9 exf6 ♘xf6 10 0-0 ♗d6 11 ♘f3 0-0 12 ♗f4 ♗xf4 13 ♘xf4 ♘e4 14 ♕c1 ♘g5 15 ♘xg5 ♕xg5 16 ♗xh7+!?

see following diagram

This surprising tactic (possibly a Fritz invention!) nets White a rook and two pawns for two minor pieces. Theoretically speaking, however, this material imbalance should be okay for Black and practical results have reflected this.

16...♔xh7 17 ♘xe6 ♕f5

The main alternative is to head into the endgame immediately with 17...♕xc1 18 ♘xf8+ ♔g8 19 ♖axc1 ♔xf8. Holzke-Kinsman, German Bundesliga 1995, continued 20 ♖fd1 ♗e6 21 ♖d2 ♖e8 22 f3 ♔f7 23 h4! ♔f6 24 ♔f2 g5 25 hxg5+ ♔xg5 26 ♖e1 and the connected pawns on the kingside gave White an edge, although the game was eventually drawn. Kinsman suggests that Black should aim to play ...g7-g5 before White has a chance to play h2-h4, thus making it more difficult for White to utilise the pawn majority. So 22...g5 is more accurate than 22...♔f7; and likewise 22 h4! may be stronger than 22 ♖d2. Taking this to the very limit, it is possible that Black should consider 20...g5!?

18 ♘xf8+ ♕xf8 19 ♕g5 ♕f5

Black has also secured reasonable results with 19...♗f5. Emms-Vareille, Paris 1994, continued 20 ♖fe1 ♖d8 21 ♖e3 ♖d6! (the rook patrols the third rank, along which it can repeatedly annoy the white queen) 22 ♖f3 ♖f6 23 ♖e1 ♔g8 24 ♖g3 ♗e4 and Black had equalised. Notice that 25 f3 can be answered with 25...♘xd4!, as 26 fxe4?

♘e2+ forces mate.

20 ♕xf5+ ♗xf5 21 ♖fe1 ♔g6

It is only good for Black to snatch the d4-pawn if he can retain his own d-pawn. Here 21...♘xd4 only succeeds in opening paths for the white rooks after 22 ♖ad1 ♘c2 23 ♖e5.

22 f3 ♔f6

22...♘xd4? still fails due to 23 ♖ad1 ♘c2 24 ♖e2 with threats of g2-g4 and ♖xd5. Now, however, Black is threatening to grab the pawn.

23 ♖ad1 g5!

We touched upon the importance of this move earlier. The lunge h2-h4 has been prevented.

24 g4 ♗d7! 25 ♔f2 ♖h8! 26 ♔g3 ♘e7!

Heading for f4. It is now White who must play accurately to maintain the balance.

27 ♖e5 ♘g6! 28 ♖xd5 ♗e6 29 ♖b5!

Not 29 ♖d6? ♔e7, trapping the rook.

29...♘f4

30 d5!

It is a good time to bail out. If White continues in pawn grabbing fashion with 30 ♖xb7 then 30...♖h3+ 31 ♔f2 ♗d5! 32 ♖xa7 ♖xh2+ 33 ♔e1

♖e2+ 34 ♔f1 ♖xb2 and it is Black who is doing the pushing.

30...♖h3+ 31 ♔f2 ♗xd5 ½-½

32 ♖dxd5 ♘xd5 33 ♖xd5 ♖xh2+ 34 ♔g3 ♖xb2 leads to a totally drawn rook and pawn endgame.

Game 7
Henao-Sequera
Merida 1992

---

1 e4 e6 2 d4 d5 3 ♘d2 ♘f6 4 e5 ♘fd7 5 c3 c5 6 ♗d3 ♘c6 7 ♘e2 cxd4 8 cxd4 f6 9 exf6 ♘xf6 10 ♘f3 ♗d6 11 0-0 0-0 12 ♗f4 ♗xf4 13 ♘xf4 ♘e4 14 ♘h5

The knight heads for g3, where it will confront its black counterpart on e4. This is a perfectly logical, albeit rather time-consuming plan.

14...g6 15 ♘g3 ♘xg3 16 hxg3

Now White threatens ♗b5, exchanging on c6 and establishing a massive bind on the dark squares. Needless to say, Black has to remain very active.

16...♕b6! 17 ♕a4 a6

17...♕xb2!? is meant to be unplayable due to 18 ♗b5, threatening to trap the black queen with ♖ab1 and

♖fc1. This is far from the end, however, as Black can play 18...♖xf3 19 gxf3 ♘xd4 with a very messy position.

18 ♖ad1 ♗d7 19 ♕a3 ♘xd4 20 ♘xd4 ♕xd4 21 ♗xg6 ♕f6 22 ♗b1 ♗b5 23 ♗d3

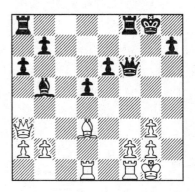

23...♗c6!

Ulibin's suggested improvement over 23...♗xd3, which he labels as a 'strategic howler'. Spasov-Ulibin, Tunja 1989, continued 24 ♖xd3 ♖ac8 25 ♖f3 ♕g7 26 ♖e1 ♖c6 27 ♕b4 b5 28 b3 ♖fc8 29 ♖fe3 ♖e8 30 ♖e5 and Black's shaky king position had become the overriding feature of the position. The idea behind 23...♗c6 is to preserve the bishop in order to support the central pawn mass.

24 ♕b3 ♔h8 25 ♗b1 e5 26 ♖d2 ♖f7 27 ♖e1 ♖g8 28 ♕c3 ♖g5 29 ♗c2 h5

In contrast with the Spasov-Ulibin game, the principal features here are Black's centre and active pieces. Black now has no problems at all.

30 ♗b3 d4 31 ♕c4 ♖e7 32 ♕c5 ♖eg7 33 ♗d1 h4 34 g4 h3 35 gxh3

---
see following diagram

35...♖xg4+ 36 hxg4?

After 36 ♗xg4 ♕f3 37 ♔f1 Black

has only the choice of perpetuals with 37...♗b5 38 ♕xb5 ♕h1+ 39 ♔e2 ♕e4+ 40 ♔d1 ♕b1+ 41 ♔e2 ♕e4+ or 37...♖xg4 38 hxg4 ♕h3+ 39 ♔e2 ♕f3+ 40 ♔f1. Now White is forced to give up the queen.

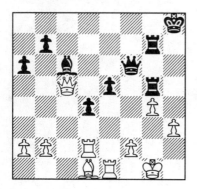

36...♕h4 37 ♕xc6 bxc6 38 ♖xe5 ♖h7 39 ♖e8+ ♔g7 40 ♗f3 ♕h2+ 41 ♔f1 ♕f4

A vigorous technical phase lies ahead, but White's resistance was not up to much.

42 ♖d3 ♕c1+ 43 ♖e1 ♕c4 44 ♖ed1 c5 45 b3 ♕b5 46 a4 ♕b6 47 ♖e1 ♕d6 48 ♖e8 ♕g6 49 ♖e4 ♖h8 50 b4? ♖e8! 0-1

After 51 ♖xe8 ♕xd3+ 52 ♔g2 cxb4 the two passed pawns prove to be decisive.

Game 8
Stigkin-Basin
St Petersburg 1992

---

1 e4 e6 2 d4 d5 3 ♘d2 ♘f6 4 e5 ♘fd7 5 ♗d3 c5 6 c3 ♘c6 7 ♘e2 cxd4 8 cxd4 f6 9 exf6 ♘xf6 10 0-0 ♗d6 11 ♘f3 0-0 12 ♗f4 ♗xf4 13 ♘xf4 ♘e4 14 g3

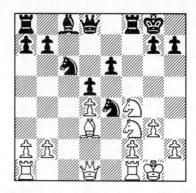

14...g5

The most ambitious reply to 14 g3, but perhaps not the best. Other ideas include:

a) 14...♕f6 (perhaps the most testing response) 15 h4 h6 16 ♗xe4 dxe4 17 ♘e5 ♖d8 18 ♘xc6 bxc6 19 ♕c2 g5 20 hxg5 hxg5 21 ♘e2 ♕f3 22 ♕d2? ♔f7 23 ♕xg5 ♖h8 24 ♕f4+ ♔e7 25 ♕xf3 exf3 26 ♘f4 ♖h6 27 ♘d3 and White resigned in Kotronias-Ulibin, Chalkidiki 1992. Ulibin gives 22 ♘c3 as an improvement for White and assesses 22...♗a6 23 ♖fe1 ♗d3 24 ♕d2 ♕f5 as unclear. There is plenty of scope for home analysis on this position!

b) 14...♘g5 15 ♘e5 ♘xe5 16 dxe5 ♖xf4!? 17 gxf4 ♘h3+ 18 ♔h1 ♘xf4 19 ♖g1 ♗d7 20 ♕g4 ♕f8 21 ♖g3 ♗c6 22 ♖d1 d4+ 23 ♔g1 ♕f7 and here the players agreed a draw in Geller-Züger, Bern 1988, just when the position was getting interesting. Clearly Black has substantial compensation for the exchange in the final position, so White should look for improvements earlier on.

15 ♘h5 e5 16 ♘xe5! ♘xd4

16...♗h3 falls short after 17 ♗xe4

♗xf1 18 ♗xh7+! ♔xh7 19 ♕c2+ ♔h8 20 ♘g6+ ♔g8 21 ♘xf8 with a winning position, while 16...♘xe5 17 dxe5 ♗h3 18 ♗xe4 is no better.

17 ♕a4!

Ulibin has suggested 17 f3, but after 17...♕b6 18 fxe4 ♗h3! 19 ♖xf8+ ♖xf8 Black has a very dangerous attack for the piece. For example, 20 ♔h1 ♖f2, when the threat of ...♗g2+ is extremely difficult to meet.

17...♕b6 18 ♖ad1 ♘xf2 19 ♖xf2 ♘e2+ 20 ♔h1 ♕xf2

20...♖xf2 leads to disaster after 21 ♕e8+ ♖f8 22 ♗xh7+ ♔xh7 23 ♕e7+ ♔h6 24 ♕xf8+ ♔h5 25 ♕e8+ ♔h6 26 ♕h8 mate.

21 ♕c2!

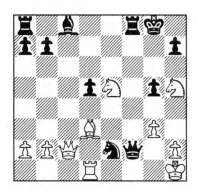

The final word in this tactical sequence. White restores some material balance and can look forward to a favourable endgame.

21...♘xg3+

Other moves lose quickly:

a) 21...♗f5 22 ♕c7!

b) 21....♗h3 22 ♗xh7+ ♔h8 23 ♘g6+ ♔xh7 24 ♘xf8+ ♔g8 25 ♕h7+ ♔xf8 26 ♕g7+ ♔e8 27 ♘f6+ ♔d8 28 ♖xd5+ ♔c8 29 ♕f8+ ♔c7 30 ♕d6+ ♔c8 31 ♕d8 mate.

22 ♘xg3 ♕xc2 23 ♗xc2

Materially speaking, Black is doing okay, but White's active pieces and his opponent's weak pawns add up to an edge for White.

23...♗e6 24 ♔g2 ♖ad8 25 ♗b3 ♔g7 26 ♖d4 h6 27 h4 gxh4 28 ♘h5 ♔g8 29 ♖xh4 a5 30 ♖d4?!

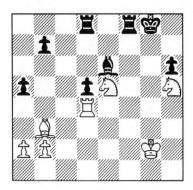

Throwing away the advantage. 30 ♘f4 was the right course.

30...b5?

Missing a chance. After 30...♖f5 31 ♖g4+ ♖g5 Black is not worse, but now White simply rounds up the d-pawn.

31 ♘g6 ♖f7 32 ♘gf4! 1-0

In fact Black can still struggle on with 32...♗f5 33 ♗xd5 ♔h7, but perhaps Basin didn't fancy being tortured.

Game 9
Alvarado-Matamoros
Telde 1993

---

1 e4 e6 2 d4 d5 3 ♘d2 ♘f6 4 e5 ♘fd7 5 ♗d3 c5 6 c3 ♘c6 7 ♘e2 cxd4 8 cxd4 f6 9 exf6 ♘xf6 10 ♘f3 ♗d6 11 0-0 0-0 12 ♗f4 ♗xf4 13 ♘xf4 ♕d6

A useful alternative to the main line, especially if Black wants to avoid the reams of theory that follow after 13...♘e4. Note that 13...♕c7 14 g3 transposes to Chapter 2, Game 15. However, 13...♗d7, while looking like a perfectly useful move, is in fact too pedestrian for the demands of this position. After 14 ♖e1 White can claim a comfortable edge.

14 g3

Not 14 ♕d2?? ♘e4 and White drops a piece, but 14 ♘e2 can be considered.
14...♘g4

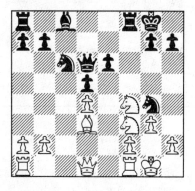

15 ♗xh7+!?

A very tempting idea, but Black has some deeply hidden resources! It is safer to play 15 ♕d2, when we have two main alternatives:

a) 15...e5 16 dxe5 ♕h6 17 h4 was clearly better for White in Zapata-Matamoros, Seville 1992.

b) 15...♗d7 is more subtle, reserving the inevitable ...e6-e5 until an opportune moment arises. Now 16 ♖fe1 ♖ae8 17 h3 e5! carries more punch, as White has weakened himself with h2-h3. For example, 18 dxe5 ♘gxe5 19 ♘xe5 ♘xe5 20 ♗e4 d4 21 ♗xb7?! ♗c6! and Black has excellent play along the a8-h1 diagonal. White can also opt for the waiting 17 ♖ad1

(instead of 17 h3). Erald-Kobalija, World U-18 Championship, Cala Galdana 1996, continued 17...e5!? 18 dxe5 ♘cxe5 19 ♗e4 ♔h8 20 ♘xe5 ♖xe5 21 ♗xd5 ♖xe1+ 22 ♕xe1 ♖xf4 and now instead of 23 ♗f3? ♘e5 White has to take the bait with 23 gxf4! ♕xf4. It looks as if there is no way out, but Fritz has pointed out the brilliant defence 24 ♗c6!!, when White defends after 24...♕xh2+ 25 ♔f1 bxc6 26 ♖xd7 ♕h1+ 27 ♔e2 ♕e4+ 28 ♔d2 ♕f4+ 29 ♕e3!

15...♔xh7 16 ♘g5+ ♔g8 17 ♕xg4 e5 18 dxe5

Another Matamoros encounter went 18 ♕h4 ♕h6 19 ♘xd5 ♕xh4 20 gxh4 exd4 21 ♖ad1 ♗f5 22 ♘c7 ♖ac8 23 ♘ce6 ♗xe6 24 ♘xe6 ♖f6 25 ♘xd4 ♘xd4 26 ♖xd4 ♖c2 27 ♖b4 ♖g6+ 28 ♔h1 ♖b6 29 ♖xb6 ½-½ Godena-Matamoros, Cannes 1996. In the final position Black immediately regains a pawn, when White's wrecked pawns don't offer any winning chances.

18...♕h6 19 ♕h5 ♖xf4 20 ♕xh6 gxh6 21 gxf4 hxg5 22 fxg5 ♗f5!

This is much stronger than 22...♘xe5, which allows White to roll the passed pawns with 23 f4 ♘c4 24 f5.

After 24...♘e3 25 ♖f3! ♘xf5 26 ♖af1 ♘d6 27 ♖f8+ ♔g7 28 h4 White has a winning position. The text move 22...♗f5 leads to a very unusual position. White has four connected passed pawns, but they are all well blockaded and in fact it is Black's lone passed d-pawn that wins the day.

23 f4 ♔f7 24 ♖fd1 ♔e6 25 ♖d2 ♖h8! 26 ♖c1 ♖h4 27 ♖f2 d4 28 ♔f1 ♘b4 29 ♖c7 ♘d3 30 ♖xb7

Giving up an exchange, but after 30 ♖f3 ♘xf4 White's position collapses.

30...♘xf2 31 ♔xf2 ♖xf4+ 32 ♔e1 ♔xe5 33 ♖xa7 ♔e4 34 ♖e7+ ♔d3 35 ♖a7 ♔e3 36 b4 d3 0-1

The d-pawn will soon advance to promotion.

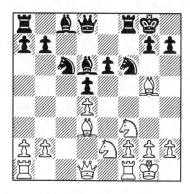

Game 10
Rozentalis-Hergott
Montreal 1995

---

1 e4 e6 2 d4 d5 3 ♘d2 ♘f6 4 e5 ♘fd7 5 ♗d3 c5 6 c3 ♘c6 7 ♘e2 cxd4 8 cxd4 f6 9 exf6 ♘xf6 10 ♘f3 ♗d6 11 0-0 0-0 12 ♗g5

This is probably the most significant alternative to 12 ♗f4, although it does contain many transpositional

possibilities. Other ideas include:

a) 12 h3 (this quiet line should cause Black no problems whatsoever) 12...♗d7 13 ♗e3 ♕e7 14 ♖c1 a6 15 a3 ♔h8 16 ♖e1 ♗e8 17 ♘g3 ♘h5 18 ♘xh5 ♗xh5 19 g4 ♗e8 20 ♔g2 ♕f6 21 ♗g5 ♕f7 22 ♗b1 ♘xd4! and Black had won a pawn in Zaichik-Panchenko, Lvov 1987, as 23 ♘xd4 ♕xf2+ 24 ♔h1 ♕h2 is mate.

b) 12 ♘c3 a6 (12...♕b6 transposes to Chapter 2, Games 16-18) 13 ♗e3 (13 ♗g5!?) 13...♗d7 14 ♖c1 ♕e7 (naturally c7 and b6 are also possible squares for the queen, but here Black opts for the kingside) 15 ♖e1 ♘g4 16 ♗g5 ♕f7 17 h3 h6!? 18 ♗h4 ♘f6 19 ♗g3 ♗xg3 20 fxg3 ♕e7 21 a3 ♕d6 22 ♔h2 ♗e8 23 ♕e2 ♗h5 24 ♕xe6+ ♕xe6 25 ♖xe6 ♗xf3 26 gxf3 ♘xd4 27 ♖e7 ♖f7 with an equal endgame in Rovid-Ulibin, Cappelle la Grande 1994.

c) After the tricky 12 ♖e1!? Black's best bet looks to be a transposition to Chapter 2 with either 12...♕b6 or 12...♕c7, as both 12...♗d7 and 12...♕e8 may be answered by 13 ♗f4, which gives White an edge.

12...♕e8

The only other independent idea is 12...♗d7!?, keeping Black's options open. After 13 ♗h4 ♗e8 14 ♕b1 h6 15 ♗g6 ♗xg6 16 ♕xg6 ♕e8 17 ♕xe8 ♖axe8 18 ♗g3 ♘e4 19 ♗xd6 ♘xd6 20 ♖fd1 ♘e4 21 ♘g3 ♘xg3 22 hxg3 ♖c8 23 ♖d2 ♔f7 24 ♖e1 ♔e7 the players agreed a draw in T.Horvath-Kindermann, Germany 1996. Once again Black also has 12...♕b6 and 12...♕c7.

13 ♗f4!

A clever switchback! Rozentalis believes that the black queen is worse off on e8 than on d8 and after this game it is difficult to argue with his assessment.

13...&xf4 14 &xf4 &e4

Or 14...e5 15 dxe5 &xe5 16 &e2 &f7 17 &e1 &d8 18 &d4 and White's control over d4 and pressure against the d-pawn was sufficient for an advantage in Brodsky-Lipka, Karvina 1992.

15 &c1

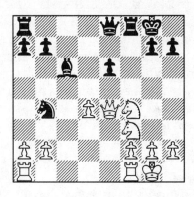

19 d5

This is stronger than 19 &xe6+ &h8!, when 20 d5 fails to 20...&xf4! and 20 &xe8 &axe8 gives Black plenty of play.

19...&xd5 20 &xe6+ &f7! 21 &xe8+ &xe8 22 &xd5 &xd5 23 &d4 &d7 24 &f5 &e2 25 b3 &e6?! 26 &g3 &c2 27 &fe1 &f7 28 &e3 &dd2?

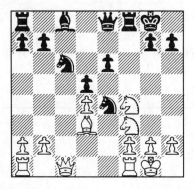

15...&d7

Aggressive measures only backfire for Black. For example, 15...g5 16 &xe4 &xf4 17 &xh7+ &xh7 18 &xg5+ wins, while 16...gxf4 17 &d3 leaves Black's pawn structure in a real mess. Black's 'extra move' ...&e8 also means that the positionally desirable ...&g5 is impossible. All in all, it would appear that White can retain a significant edge.

16 &e3 &b4 17 &xe4?!

After this move Black obtains some unexpected counterplay. Rozentalis gives 17 &e5 &xd3 18 &fxd3 &b5 19 &fe1 &xd3 20 &xd3 as an improvement.

17...dxe4 18 &xe4 &c6!

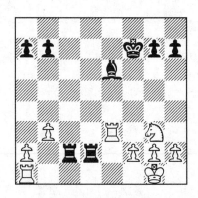

After 28...&d5! Black's active pieces ensure good drawing chances.

29 &e4! &e2 30 &g5+ &e7 31 &xe2 &xe2 32 &f1 &g4

After 32...&c2 33 &e1 or 32...&e5 33 &xe6 &xe6 34 &e1 White can achieve a won king and pawn endgame. Now, however, Black loses the exchange.

33 h3 &e5 34 f4 1-0

Summary

Despite rigorous tests, the 12 ♗f4 ♗xf4 13 ♘xf4 ♘e4 14 ♘e2 ♖xf3 exchange sacrifice continues to annoy White, although it is clear that both players need to know their stuff before they venture into these critical lines. White players wanting an easier life will probably prefer 14 ♕c1, which is certainly a super-solid option. It will be interesting to see whether 14 ♘h5 or 14 g3 become more popular.

1 e4 e6 2 d4 d5 3 ♘d2 ♘f6 4 e5 ♘fd7 5 ♗d3 c5 6 c3 ♘c6 7 ♘e2 cxd4 8 cxd4 f6 9 exf6 ♘xf6 10 ♘f3 ♗d6 11 0-0 0-0

12 ♗f4
    12 ♗g5 – *Game 10*
12...♗xf4 13 ♘xf4 ♘e4 (D)
    13...♕d6 – *Game 9*
14 ♘e2
    14 ♕c1 ♘g5 15 ♘xg5 ♕xg5 (D)
        16 ♘e2 – *Game 5*
        16 ♗xh7+ – *Game 6*
    14 ♘h5 – *Game 7*
    14 g3 – *Game 8*
14...♖xf3 15 gxf3 ♘g5 16 ♔h1
    16 f4 *(D)*
        16...♘f3+ – *Game 3*
        16...♘h3+ – *Game 4*
16...e5 17 dxe5 ♘xf3 18 ♘g1
    18 ♗xh7+ – *Game 2*
18...♘fxe5 – *Game 1*

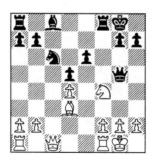
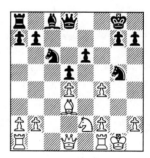

 13...♘e4   15...♕xg5   16 f4

CHAPTER TWO

3...♘f6: Main Line with 11...♕c7 and 11...♕b6

1 e4 e6 2 d4 d5 3 ♘d2 ♘f6 4 e5 ♘fd7 5 ♗d3 c5 6 c3 ♘c6 7 ♘e2 cxd4 8 cxd4 f6 9 exf6 ♘xf6 10 ♘f3 ♗d6 11 0-0

In this chapter we shall look at lines involving an early ...♕c7 or ...♕b6, both of which discourage White from playing the desirable ♗f4. In contrast to the previous chapter, play tends to be more positional, with both colours battling for control over the all-important dark squares in the centre.

Games 11-15 deal with 11...♕c7, which directly prevents 12 ♗f4. This line reached its height of popularity in the 1980s, when it was used successfully by top players such as Jan Timman, Mikhail Gurevich and Sergei Dolmatov. Although new methods have been discovered for White that have rendered 11...♕c7 less fashionable than 11...0-0, it remains a very important line.

In Games 16-20 we look at 11...♕b6. Originally this was the most usual move, but it has been gradually superseded by 11...♕c7 and then 11...0-0. However, there was no concrete reason for its decline in popularity, and it remains a fundamentally sound variation.

Game 11
Emms-Menoni
Montecatini Terme 1996

---

1 e4 e6 2 d4 d5 3 ♘d2 ♘f6 4 ♗d3 c5 5 e5 ♘fd7 6 c3 ♘c6 7 ♘e2 cxd4 8 cxd4 f6 9 exf6 ♘xf6 10 ♘f3 ♗d6 11 0-0 ♕c7 12 ♗g5

The most popular move. 12 g3 is considered in Game 15.

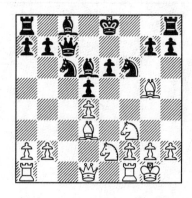

12...0-0 13 ♗h4

Again this is the most fashionable move. 13 ♖c1 and 13 ♘c3 a6 are the subjects of Games 13 and 14 respectively.

13...e5

We shall look at 13...♘h5 in Game 12.

14 dxe5 ♘xe5 15 ♘xe5 ♗xe5 16 ♗g3 ♗xg3 17 ♘xg3

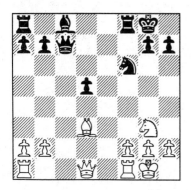

In practice White has scored very well from this position. Indeed, in searching through over twenty games I was unable to find a Black victory. Although his position looks quite sound, Black has no real attacking prospects; White has no weaknesses whatsoever and this makes it difficult for Black to achieve any counterplay along the f-file. Furthermore, the d-pawn often becomes a liability, while Black's king also sometimes suffers from its slight lack of cover. The real problem is that White's edge often persists well into the endgame. From a purely theoretical standpoint Back must be quite close to equality, but it is not surprising that many Black experts avoid this position.

17...♕b6 18 ♕d2 ♗d7 19 ♖ad1

♖ae8 20 h3 ♖e7

20...♗b5 21 ♕b4 ♗xd3 22 ♕xb6 axb6 23 ♖xd3 still leaves White with an edge, due to the pawn weaknesses in the black camp.

21 ♖fe1 ♖fe8 22 ♖xe7 ♖xe7 23 ♗c2 ♗b5 24 ♕g5 h6 25 ♕d2 a5 26 ♗b1 ♖d7

If 26...d4 then not 27 ♕xd4 ♕xd4 28 ♖xd4 ♖e1+, but 27 ♗f5! and Black has problems defending the d4-pawn.

27 ♘f5 ♘e4 28 ♕d4 ♕e6

28...♕xd4 29 ♘xd4 ♗a6 30 ♘b3 wins a pawn for White, as e4 and a5 are attacked.

29 ♘e3 ♗c6 30 a3 ♕f6 31 f3 ♕xd4 32 ♖xd4 ♘f6 33 ♔f2

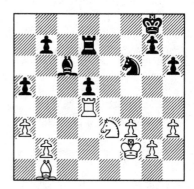

White's agreeable position continues into the endgame. White has a simple plan of advancing the kingside pawn majority to gain more space, while the d5-pawn remains a permanent worry for Black.

33...♔f7 34 h4 h5 35 ♔g3

35 g4! is more direct, e.g. 35...hxg4 36 fxg4 ♘e4+ 37 ♗xe4 dxe4 38 ♖xd7+ ♗xd7 39 ♔g3 ♗c6 40 ♔f4.

35...♘e8 36 ♘f5 g6 37 ♘e3 ♘c7 38 ♖d2 ♔f6 39 ♔f2 ♘e6 40 g4 ♘c5?!

40...g5! would have offered good

drawing chances.

41 g5+ ♔f7 42 ♗a2! ♔e6 43 b4 axb4 44 axb4 ♘a6

45 b5! ♗xb5 46 ♘xd5!

46 ♖xd5 ♖xd5 47 ♗xd5+ ♔e7 48 ♗xb7 also maintains reasonable winning chances, but I was tempted by a mating net.

46...♔f5 47 ♖b2!? ♗c6 48 ♘f6 ♖g7 49 ♖e2 ♘c5?

49...♔f4 was the last chance. Now the web closes around the black king.

50 ♔g3! ♗b5 51 ♗b1+ ♗d3

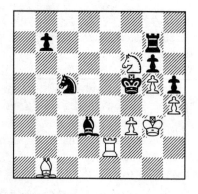

52 f4!

Needless to say, I was very satisfied with the conclusion of this game, but in fact it turns out White has an alternative finish with 52 ♗xd3+ ♘xd3 53

♘g4! (53...hxg4 54 fxg4 mate is quite visual) 53...♖h7 54 ♖e8 and ♘e3 mate.

52...♘e4+ 53 ♘xe4! ♗xe2 54 ♘c5+ 1-0

It is mate next move.

Game 12
Yemelin-Kostenko
Szeged 1994

---

1 e4 e6 2 d4 d5 3 ♘d2 ♘f6 4 e5 ♘fd7 5 c3 c5 6 ♗d3 ♘c6 7 ♘e2 cxd4 8 cxd4 f6 9 exf6 ♘xf6 10 ♘f3 ♗d6 11 0-0 ♕c7 12 ♗g5 0-0 13 ♗h4 ♘h5

The major alternative to 13...e5, although the uncommon 13...♗d7 also looks quite playable.

14 ♕c2

The most questioning reply. Other moves do nothing to prevent Black's standard plan of ...g7-g6 and ...♕g7.

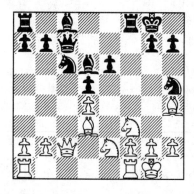

14...h6

The natural 14...g6 falls short after 15 ♗xg6! and now:

a) 15...hxg6 16 ♕xg6+ ♘g7 17 ♘g5 and wins.

b) 15...♖xf3 16 ♗xh5 ♗xh2+ 17 ♔h1 ♖f5 18 ♗g4 ♖f8 19 g3 and the bishop is lost.

15 ♗g6 ♘f4

After this move White tends to obtain a clear advantage, so perhaps Black players should look into 15...♖xf3!?, which hasn't been witnessed much but is a trickier move. After 16 gxf3 ♗xh2+ 17 ♔h1 ♘f4 18 ♘g3 Black has two ways to play:

a) Akopian gives 18...♘xg6 19 ♕xg6 ♗xg3 20 ♗xg3 ♕f7 21 ♕xf7+ ♔xf7 22 ♖fd1 with only a minute advantage for White in the endgame. Indeed Black's position does seem quite difficult to breach.

b) Altgelt-Stamenkovic, Sofia 1994, saw instead 18...♗xg3 19 ♗xg3 ♗d7 20 ♕d2 ♖f8 with some compensation for the exchange. Indeed, Black went on to win this game.

16 ♘xf4 ♗xf4 17 ♖ad1

Black's predicament lies with the shaky light squares around his king. White has a very simple plan of switching the roles of bishop and queen along the b1-h7 diagonal and playing for checkmate. It is difficult to find a suitable antidote to this idea.

17...♗d7 18 ♕e2! a6 19 ♖fe1 ♘d8 20 ♘e5 ♗xe5 21 dxe5 ♖c8 22 b3 ♗e8 23 ♗b1 g5

Extremely committal, but Black feels obliged to cover h7.

24 ♗g3 ♕g7 25 ♕d3 ♖f7 26 ♕d2 ♖fc7

see following diagram

27 f4!

The start of a decisive breakthrough **27...♗g6 28 f5! exf5 29 ♕xd5+ ♔h7 30 e6 f4 31 e7 ♖xe7 32 ♗xg6+ ♔xg6 33 ♕d6+ ♕f6 34 ♖xe7 fxg3 35 ♕xf6+ ♔xf6 36 ♖e8 1-0**

Game 13
Smagin-Dolmatov
USSR Championship 1986

1 e4 e6 2 d4 d5 3 ♘d2 ♘f6 4 e5 ♘fd7 5 ♗d3 c5 6 c3 ♘c6 7 ♘e2 cxd4 8 cxd4 f6 9 exf6 ♘xf6 10 0-0 ♗d6 11 ♘f3 ♕c7 12 ♗g5 0-0 13 ♖c1

An alternative way to proceed. The objective is to dissuade ...e6-e5 before proceeding with the ♗h4-g3 plan. Of course the tempo spent achieving this idea gives Black more time to start a counterattack.

13...♘g4!

Cutting across White's main goal. Now 14 h3 allows 14...♖xf3!, when 15 gxf3 ♘h2 and 15 hxg4 ♖f7 are both fine for Black.

14 ♘g3 g6 15 ♘h4

15 ♘d2!? is a fairly new move of Tiviakov's which certainly deserves attention. After 15...♘f6 16 ♘b3 ♕g7 17 ♕d2 ♗b4 18 ♕e3 ♘g4 19 ♕e2 ♘h6 20 ♗b5 ♗d7 21 ♗xc6 bxc6 22 ♘c5 ♗xc5 23 ♗xh6 ♕xh6 24 ♖xc5 Black's bad bishop condemned him to a pas-

sive position in Tiviakov-Komarov, Kherson 1991.

15...e5

Also possible is 15...♘f6 16 ♕d2 and then:

a) 16...♕b6? walks into a nasty attack with 17 ♗h6 ♕xd4 18 ♘f3 ♕b6 19 ♕g5! ♘e4 20 ♘xe4 ♗f4 21 ♘f6+ ♖xf6 22 ♕xf6 ♗xh6 23 ♗xg6 hxg6 24 ♕xg6+ ♗g7 25 ♘g5 ♕d8 26 ♕f7+ ♔h8 27 ♕h5+ ♔g8 28 ♖c3 ♘e5 29 f4 1-0, Geller-Ravi, Coimbatore 1987.

b) 16...♘g4!? 17 ♕d1 ♘f6 18 ♕d2 ♘g4 19 ♕e2 (19 ♕d1 ♘f6 would be a threefold repetition) 19...♘f6 20 ♗e3 (20 ♗h6! ♖f7 21 ♗e3 is stronger, as it prevents the ...♕g7 plan) 20...♕g7! 21 f4? (21 ♘f3 is equal) 21...♕h6!, winning a pawn in Emms-Klingelhöfer, Hamburg 1992.

16 ♗e2 ♘f6 17 dxe5 ♗xe5 18 b4 ♗f4 19 ♗xf4 ♕xf4 20 b5

---

see following diagram

20...♘d4!

A big improvement over 20...♘b4 21 ♘xg6! hxg6 22 a3, winning back the knight with an excellent position in Geller-Dolmatov, Russia 1985. After 20...♘d4 White's advantage is

small enough for Black not to have any real problems.

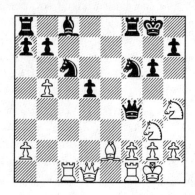

21 ♘f3 ♘xe2+ 22 ♘xe2 ♕d6 23 ♘ed4 ♗d7 24 ♖e1 a6 25 a4 axb5 26 axb5 ♖ae8 27 ♕b3 ♖xe1+ 28 ♖xe1 ♖e8 29 ♖xe8+ ♗xe8 30 h3 ♗d7 31 ♕e3 ♘e4 ½-½

Game 14
Marjanovic-Timman
Sarajevo 1984

---

1 e4 e6 2 d4 d5 3 ♘d2 ♘f6 4 e5 ♘fd7 5 c3 c5 6 ♗d3 ♘c6 7 ♘e2 cxd4 8 cxd4 f6 9 exf6 ♘xf6 10 0-0 ♗d6 11 ♘f3 ♕c7 12 ♘c3

The old line. The white knight heads for the queenside, gaining a tempo because of the threat of ♘b5. White's plans include ♖c1 and ♘a4-c5, which would put the knight on a very useful square. The flip side is that Black has a freer role to operate on the kingside, now that the squares f4 and g3 have less protection.

12...a6 13 ♗g5 0-0

This position also often arises from the alternative move order 12 ♗g5 0-0 13 ♘c3 a6.

14 ♗h4 ♘h5

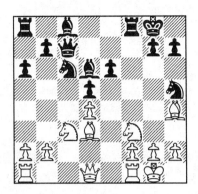

15 ♖c1

15 ♕c2 can be answered with 15...g6! here, as 16 ♗xg6? runs into the surprising 16...♘f4! 17 ♗d3 ♘b4 and Black wins a piece. This is one of the disadvantages of 12 ♘c3.

15...g6 16 ♗b1

16 ♘a4 ♗d7 17 ♘c5 ♖xf3! 18 ♕xf3 ♘xd4 19 ♕g4 ♗xc5 occurred in Grünfeld-Shachar, Israeli Championship 1994. Here White's best is 20 ♕xd4, but after 20...♕xh2+! 21 ♔xh2 ♗xd4 Black is certainly no worse.

16...♕g7 17 ♔h1?!

This seems a little slow. White can also try:

a) 17 ♘a4 ♖xf3!? (17...♖b8!?) 18 gxf3 ♗d7 19 ♘c5 ♖f8 20 ♗g3 ♗xc5 21 dxc5 ♕xb2 22 ♖e1 ♕f6 23 ♔h1 ♘d4 24 ♗e5 ♕xf3+ 25 ♕xf3 ♘xf3 was clearly better for Black in Womacka-Pähtz, East German Championship 1985, but I think that White's play can be improved upon.

b) 17 ♗g5!?, returning to the c1-h6 diagonal, is an interesting idea. The point is that with the knight on h5, the bishop has no real future on h4, so it returns to its original diagonal. I believe that Karpov was the first to use this plan, in a game against Jonathan Mestel. A more recent example went 17...♗d7 18 ♖e1 ♖ae8 19 ♘a4 ♗f4 20 ♗xf4 ♖xf4 21 ♘c5! ♘xd4 22 ♘e5 ♗b5 23 a4 b6 24 axb5 bxc5 25 bxa6 ♕a7 26 ♘d3 and White was better in Unzicker-Rozentalis, Germany 1995.

17...♗d7 18 ♖e1 ♖f7 19 ♘e2 ♔h8 20 a3 ♖af8

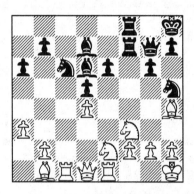

While White is groping for an active plan, his opponent can steadily improve his position before expanding on the kingside. Already Black's position is easier to play.

21 ♖c3 h6 22 ♗g3

An admission of defeat. White exchanges his dark-squared bishop, but only gets a knight in return – a poor swap.

22...♘xg3+ 23 ♘xg3 ♖f4 24 ♘e2 ♖4f6 25 ♘g3 ♗e8 26 ♖ce3 ♗f7 27 ♔g1 ♗g8 28 ♕d3 ♗f4 29 ♖3e2 ♕f7 30 b4 g5 31 h3 ♗c7 32 ♘f1 ♗b6 33 ♘1d2 ♕g7 34 ♘b3 ♖f4 35 ♖d1 g4!

This thrust represents the culmination of Black's strategy. The d4-pawn is very sensitive, while Black also dominates proceedings on the kingside.

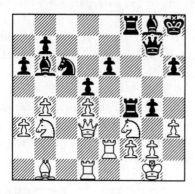

36 ♘h4

After 36 hxg4 ♖xg4 37 g3 e5 White's position falls apart, as 38 dxe5 allows 38...♖xg3+.

36...♘e7 37 g3?

White chooses the path of least resistance. 37 ♘g6+ ♘xg6 38 ♕xg6 would have offered more hope.

37...gxh3 38 ♔h1? ♖xh4 39 f4

Or 39 gxh4 ♕g2 mate.

39...♖g4 40 ♔h2 ♘f5 0-1

A model game from Timman.

Game 15
Kr.Georgiev-Dolmatov
Sofia 1985

---

1 e4 e6 2 d4 d5 3 ♘d2 ♘f6 4 e5 ♘fd7 5 ♗d3 c5 6 c3 ♘c6 7 ♘e2 cxd4 8 cxd4 f6 9 exf6 ♘xf6 10 0-0 ♗d6 11 ♘f3 ♕c7 12 g3

This introduces another procedure for exchanging the dark-squared bishops.

12...0-0 13 ♗f4

see following diagram

13...♗d7

13...♗xf4 14 ♘xf4 ♕b6!? is a different idea. Great complications may arise after 15 b3 (15 ♕d2!?) 15...♔h8 16 ♘g5 e5! 17 ♘xh7 ♘xh7 18 ♕h5 e4 19 ♘g6+ ♔g8 20 ♕xd5+ ♖f7 21 ♗c4 ♘d8 22 ♘e7+ ♔f8. Here White can take a draw with 23 ♘g6+. Instead in Dvoirys-M.Gurevich, USSR Championship 1986, White played on with 23 ♘xc8, but after 23...♖xc8 24 ♕xe4 ♘g5 25 ♕g4 ♘f3+ 26 ♔g2 ♕c6 27 d5 ♕h6 28 h4 ♖b8 matters were still far from clear, and Black eventually won the game.

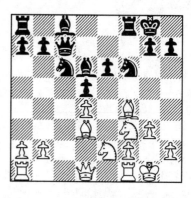

14 ♖c1 ♘h5!? 15 ♘g5?!

This attempt to complicate only gives Black the chances. It would have been better to play 15 ♗xd6 ♕xd6 16 ♘c3 g6 and now:

a) 17 ♖e1 a6 18 ♘e5 ♘xe5 19 ♖xe5

♕b6 20 ♖c2 ♘g7! (the knight performs a very useful defensive role here) 21 ♕g4 ♗b5 22 ♘xb5 axb5 23 b3 ♖ac8 24 ♖ce2 ♖c3 25 ♖5e3 b4 26 h4 ♕d8 27 ♕g5 ♕f6 28 ♕xf6 ♖xf6 29 ♗b5 ♖c7 30 ♔g2 ♔f7 31 ♖d2 ♔e7 with an equal position in Dvoirys-Dolmatov, USSR Championship 1986.

b) Psakhis recommends 17 ♗b5, giving White a small, secure advantage, but the sacrifice 17...♖xf3! is very unclear. Indeed, after 18 ♕xf3 ♘xd4 19 ♕d3 ♘xb5 20 ♘xb5 ♕a6 21 a4 ♕xa4 I prefer Black, who has two pawns and some light-squared control for the exchange. In Malevinsky-Komarov, Leningrad 1989, White tried 18 ♗xc6, only to be shocked by 18...♖xc3! 19 ♗xd7 ♖xc1 20 ♗xe6+ ♕xe6 21 ♕xc1 ♖c8 and Black already had a winning position.

15...h6 16 ♗xd6 ♕xd6 17 ♘h7 ♖f3! 18 ♗b1

Or 18 ♔g2 ♖f5! 19 ♘c3 g6 and the knight on h7 is dead and buried.

18...e5 19 ♖xc6 bxc6 20 dxe5 ♕xe5 21 ♘d4 ♖f7 22 ♖e1

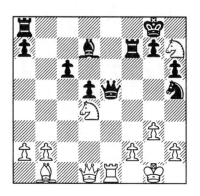

22...♗g4! 23 f3 ♕d6! 24 fxg4 ♘xg3 25 ♘e6 ♖e8 26 ♗g6 ♖xe6 27 ♗xf7+

♔xf7 28 ♖xe6 ♕xe6 29 hxg3 ♔g8 30 ♕d3 ♕xg4

The knight can be picked up at Black's leisure, while the most White can hope for in return is a pawn. Dolmatov, renowned for his immaculate technique, doesn't let it slip.

31 ♔f2 ♕e6 32 ♕c2 g6 33 ♕c5 ♕f7+ 34 ♔g2 ♔xh7 35 ♕xc6 h5 36 b4 d4 37 a4 ♕e7 38 b5 d3 39 ♕d5 ♕e2+ 40 ♔h3 ♕f1+ 41 ♔h2 ♕f2+ 42 ♔h1 d2 0-1

```
Game 16
Nijboer-Farago
Dieren Open 1988
```

1 e4 e6 2 d4 d5 3 ♘d2 ♘f6 4 e5 ♘fd7 5 c3 c5 6 ♗d3 ♘c6 7 ♘e2 cxd4 8 cxd4 ♕b6 9 ♘f3 f6 10 exf6 ♘xf6 11 0-0 ♗d6

see following diagram

This is the standard starting position of the 11...♕b6 variation. Now 12 ♘c3 is White's most popular move, while 12 ♘f4 and 12 b3 are dealt with in Games 19 and 20.

12 ♘c3 0-0 13 ♗g5

13 ♗e3 is seen in Game 18.

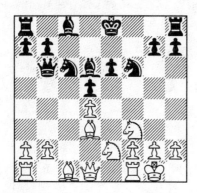

13...♗d7

13...♔h8!? is the subject of the next game.

14 ♖e1

Alternatively White can reach this position via the 13 ♖e1 ♗d7 14 ♗g5 move order.

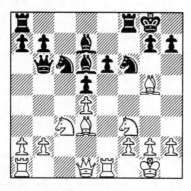

14...♘g4

The other key line is 14...♔h8, which has actually been scoring quite well for Black. White can answer with:

a) 15 ♘a4 (this is common, though I'm not sure why) 15...♕a5! (I prefer this to 15...♕c7, which, however, is also fully playable) and now:

a1) 16 a3 ♘g4 (16...♘xd4 17 ♘xd4 ♗xa4 18 b3 ♕c3 19 ♗c2 ♗d7 20 ♘xe6

is equal) 17 ♗c2 e5 18 dxe5 ♘cxe5 19 ♘xe5 ♗xe5 20 ♖xe5 ♘xe5 21 ♗e7 ♗xa4 22 ♗xa4 ♖f4 with a clear advantage to Black in Marciano-Jonsson, Reykjavik 1993.

a2) 16 ♗d2 ♕d8 17 ♖c1 ♘g4 18 ♗g5? ♕b8! 19 ♗h4 (19 h3 ♗h2+ 20 ♔f1 ♘xf2!! 21 ♔xf2 ♘xd4 is an acute example of Black's attacking potential in this line) 19...♗xh2+ 20 ♔f1 ♕f4, as in Fernandez Garcia-Illescas, Spain 1986.

b) 15 ♘e5!? (I believe that this causes Black more problems):

b1) 15...♗e8 16 ♘xc6 ♕xc6 and now 17 ♖c1 can be answered with 17...♗h5 18 ♕d2 ♘g4, so perhaps White should play the prophylactic 17 h3.

b2) 15...♕xd4!? 16 ♘b5 ♕xe5 17 ♖xe5 ♗xe5 grants Black compensation for the queen in Tolnai-Züger, Budapest 1988, although after 18 f4 (instead of Tolnai's 18 ♘c3) I still prefer White.

15 ♗h4 ♘h6 16 ♗g3 ♗e7 17 ♘a4 ♕a5 18 ♗c2 ♘f5

After 18...♖xf3?! 19 gxf3 ♖f8 20 a3 ♘f5 21 ♗xf5 ♖xf5 22 b4 ♕d8 23 b5 ♘a5 24 ♘c5 Black had no compensation for the exchange in Howell-Ryan, Isle of Man 1994. The American IM John Watson, who has done much to popularise Black's cause in his excellent *Play the French* books, suggests 18...♗e8 19 ♖xe6 ♗h5, but here White should play 20 a3 (not 20 ♕d3 ♘f5 21 ♘e5 ♘cxd4) when I don't believe that Black has enough compensation for the pawn.

19 a3 ♘xg3

19...♖ae8 20 b4 ♕d8 21 ♘c5 gives

White a clear edge, while 19...b6 has been suggested by Watson, though I don't trust that at all after 20 ♕d3 (threatening b2-b4) as 20...♘cxd4 fails to 21 ♘xd4 ♗xa4 22 ♘xf5 ♖xf5 23 ♗xa4 ♕xa4 24 ♖xe6 ♖f7 25 ♖xe7 ♖xe7 26 ♕xd5+.

20 hxg3 ♕c7 21 ♖c1!

Despite the absence of the dark-squared bishop, White still retains control of many of the important dark squares. In particular, both rooks and both knights are actively posted. Overall White holds a significant plus.

21...g6 22 b4 a6 23 ♘c5 ♖f6 24 ♗a4 b5 25 ♗b3 ♗xc5 26 ♖xc5 ♕b6 27 ♘e5 ♘xe5 28 dxe5 ♖f7 29 ♕d4 ♕a7 30 ♖e3 a5 31 bxa5 ♕xa5

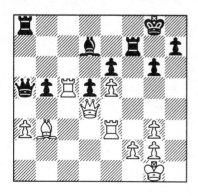

32 ♖xd5!? exd5 33 ♗xd5 ♕a7!

Other moves lose. Nijboer gives the following lines:

a) 33...♗e8 34 e6 ♖e7 35 ♖f3!, intending ♖xf8+ and ♕h8 mate.

b) 33...♖f5 34 g4.

c) 33...♖d8 34 ♗xf7+ ♔xf7 35 ♖d3.

34 ♗xf7+ ♔xf7 35 ♕d6 ♖e8?

35...♔g8 isn't mentioned by Nijboer and seems like a tougher defence. After 36 e6 ♗e8 37 ♖f3 h6 38 ♖f8+ ♔h7 39 e7 (intending ♕f6) 39...♕xa3 40 ♕xa3 (40 ♕f6 ♕a1+) 40...♖xa3 41 ♖xe8 ♖a1+ 42 ♔h2 ♖e1 Black can hold the rook and pawn endgame. After 35...♖e8? it is all quite straightforward for White.

36 ♖c3 ♖c8

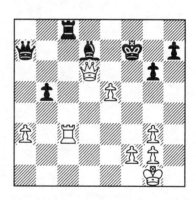

37 ♕f6+ ♔g8 38 ♖xc8+ ♗xc8 39 ♕d8+ ♔f7 40 ♕xc8 ♕xa3 41 ♕d7+ ♔f8 42 ♔h2! ♕b2 43 f4 ♕e2 44 g4 ♕c4 45 ♕d8+ ♔f7 46 ♕f6+ ♔g8 47 e6 ♕c7 48 e7 ♕c8 49 f5 ♕b8+ 50 ♔h3 ♕e8 51 ♕e6+ ♔h8 52 f6 1-0

Game 17
Majer-Ruzicka
Correspondence 1993

---

1 e4 e6 2 d4 d5 3 ♘d2 ♘f6 4 e5

♘fd7 5 ♗d3 c5 6 c3 ♘c6 7 ♘e2 cxd4 8 cxd4 f6 9 exf6 ♘xf6 10 ♘f3 ♗d6 11 0-0 0-0 12 ♗g5 ♕b6 13 ♘c3

This position could also be reached via the move order 11...♕b6 12 ♘c3 0-0 13 ♗g5.

13...♔h8!?

This has some advantages over the often-played 13...♗d7, as Black retains the option of transferring the queen to the kingside via c7-f7. Note that 13...♕xb2 is a little too ambitious: 14 ♘b5! leaves the black queen struggling to find a retreat.

14 ♘a4 ♕c7 15 ♖c1

15...♕f7

15...♘g4!? is another enticing alternative, leading to extremely intense positions. After 16 h3 ♘h2 we have:

a) 17 ♘e5!? ♗xe5 18 dxe5 ♘xf1 19 ♕h5 h6 20 ♗f6 gxf6 21 ♕xh6+ ♔g8 22 exf6 ♖xf6 23 ♕xf6 ♕h2+ 24 ♔xf1 ♕h1+ 25 ♔e2 ♕xc1 26 f4 ♕g1 27 ♗h7+ ½-½ Akopian-Ulibin, Minsk 1990. A crazy miniature.

b) 17 ♘xh2 ♗xh2+ 18 ♔h1 ♗f4! 19 ♕h5 g6 20 ♗xf4 ♖xf4 21 ♗xg6 ♕e7 22 ♗d3 ♖h4 23 ♕e2 e5 and Black had an unexpected attack for the pawn in

Kosashvili-Ulibin, Santiago 1990. The game concluded 24 ♕e3 ♗g4 25 ♘c3 ♖g8 26 ♔h2 e4 27 ♗e2 ♗xh3 28 gxh3 ♕d6+ 29 ♔h1 ♕d7 30 ♔h2 ♕d6+ 31 ♔h1 ♕e6 32 ♔h2 ♘e5 33 f4 exf3 34 ♖xf3 ♘g4+ and White was forced to resign.

16 ♘c3?!

I don't like this move at all. What's the point of sticking the knight on a4, only for it to return, tail between its legs, a few moves later? Here are two other possibilities:

a) 16 ♗h4!? is positionally well motivated, but after 16...♕h5 17 ♗g3 ♗xg3 either recapture allows 18...♘g4 with annoying pressure on the kingside.

b) 16 ♖e1 looks quite natural. The game Andrade-Pettinger, Rimavska Sobota 1996, continued 16...♕h5 17 h3 e5, when instead of 18 dxe5 White should play 18 ♖xc6!, as 18...bxc6 19 dxe5 ♗b4 20 exf6 ♗xe1 21 fxg7+ ♔xg7 22 ♕xe1 clearly favours White. 17...♘xd4 is stronger, and after 18 ♘xd4 ♕xg5 19 ♘xe6 ♗xe6 20 ♖xe6 ♖ad8 we reach a level position.

16...♕h5 17 ♗xf6

17 h3? ♘xd4 18 ♘xd4 ♕xg5 led to a quick Black victory in Hossain-Wiedenkeller, London 1987. 17 ♗xf6 avoids this trick but renounces any claim for an advantage. Indeed, I already like the look of Black's position. The rest of the game is very one-sided and sees White putting up very little resistance to the inevitable kingside attack.

17...♖xf6 18 h3 ♗d7 19 ♗e2 ♖af8 20 ♘e5 ♕e8 21 ♘xd7 ♕xd7 22 ♗g4? ♕f7 23 ♗f3

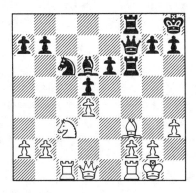

23...♖g6! 24 ♗g4 h5! 0-1

25 ♗xh5 ♕f4 26 g3 ♖xg3+ 27 fxg3 ♕xg3+ 28 ♔h1 ♕h2 is mate.

Game 18
Sowray-B.Martin
London 1996

---

1 e4 e6 2 d4 d5 3 ♘d2 ♘f6 4 e5 ♘fd7 5 c3 c5 6 ♗d3 ♘c6 7 ♘e2 cxd4 8 cxd4 ♕b6 9 ♘f3 f6 10 exf6 ♘xf6 11 0-0 ♗d6 12 ♘c3 0-0 13 ♗e3 ♗d7

13...♕xb2 is again met by 14 ♘b5.

14 a3 ♗e8

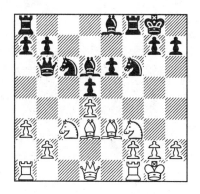

Note that 14...♕xb2 drops the queen immediately to 15 ♘a4!

15 ♘g5

Many moves have been played in this position, but no route to an advantage has been found for White, e.g.

a) 15 ♕c2 ♘e7 16 h3 ♗g6 17 ♖fe1 ♖ae8 18 ♗g5 ♗xd3 19 ♕xd3 ♘g6 20 ♕d2 ♘h5 21 ♘a4 ♕b5 and the exchange of light-squared bishops had eased Black's position in Grinfeld-N.Pert, Hastings 1996.

b) 15 ♕d2 ♗h5 16 ♘e5 ♘g4 17 ♘xg4 ♗xg4 18 ♖ac1 ♕d8 19 ♘e2 ♗f5 20 ♗xf5 ♖xf5 21 ♘g3 ♖f7 22 ♖fe1 ♕b6 23 ♖c3 ♖af8 and once again Black had no problems in I.Gurevich-Gdanski, Santiago 1990.

c) 15 ♘e5 ♗xe5 16 dxe5 ♕xb2 17 exf6 ♕xc3 18 fxg7 ♕xg7 leaves White with insufficient play for the pawn.

15...♘e7 16 ♘a4

This gives Black a comfortable game, but it is difficult to suggest an improvement. After 16 h3 ♗c7 17 ♕c2 h6 18 ♘f3 ♘h5 the knight heads for f4 and Black can once more look to the future with confidence.

16...♗xa4 17 ♕xa4 h6!

17...♘f5 has also been played, but I like the forcing nature of this move.

18 ♘xe6 ♗xh2+ 19 ♔xh2 ♕xe6

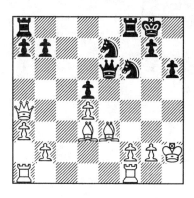

White has the token advantage of

the bishop pair, but it soon becomes obvious that the most important aspect of the position is his shaky king.

20 ♖ae1 ♘g4+ 21 ♔g1 ♕d6 22 g3 ♖f3 23 ♔g2

23 ♗f4 ♖xf4! 24 gxf4 ♕xf4 25 ♔g2 ♖f8 is the end.

23...♖af8 24 ♕b4 ♕f6 25 ♗e2

25...♖xg3+!! 26 ♔xg3 ♘f5+ 27 ♔g2

27 ♔xg4 ♕h4+ 28 ♔f3 ♕e4 is mate.

27...♕g6 28 ♗f3

Other moves also wind up in checkmate, e.g. 28 ♖g1 ♘gxe3+ 29 ♔h2 ♕f6 30 fxe3 ♕h4+ 31 ♔g2 ♘xe3 and 28 ♗xg4 ♕xg4+ 29 ♔h2 ♘h4 30 ♖g1 ♘f3+ 31 ♔h1 ♕h3.

28...♘h4+ 29 ♔g3 ♖xf3+ 30 ♔xh4 ♕f6+ 0-1

31 ♔xg4 ♕f5+ 32 ♔h4 ♖h3 is mate. A convincing display from Martin.

Game 19
Muratov-Bata
Correspondence 1967

1 e4 e6 2 d4 d5 3 ♘d2 ♘f6 4 e5 ♘fd7 5 ♗d3 c5 6 c3 ♘c6 7 ♘e2 ♕b6 8 ♘f3 cxd4 9 cxd4 f6 10 exf6 ♘xf6 11 0-0 ♗d6 12 ♘f4

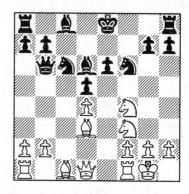

Initially a critical choice, this line has virtually disappeared from tournament chess, as it merely seems to give Black all the chances.

12...0-0 13 ♖e1 ♗d7! 14 ♘xe6 ♖fe8 15 ♗f5 ♗b4 16 ♗d2 ♗xd2 17 ♕xd2 ♘e7!

18 g4?

This makes matters worse. It would have been better to play either 18 ♘xg7!? or 18 ♗h3:

a) 18 ♘xg7!? ♔xg7 19 ♕g5+ ♘g6 20 ♗xd7 ♘xd7 21 h4 h6 22 ♕xd5 ♘f6 23 ♕f5 ♖ad8 and Black's extra piece is worth more than the three pawns.

b) 18 ♗h3 ♘e4 19 ♖xe4 dxe4 20 ♘fg5 ♘d5 21 ♘xg7 ♗xh3 22 ♘xe8 ♗f5 23 ♘f7 e3 24 fxe3 ♖xe8 25 ♘e5 ♕h6, with advantage to Black in Suster-Prokopp, correspondence 1984.

18...♘xf5 19 gxf5 ♘e4 20 ♕e3 ♗xe6 21 fxe6 ♖xe6

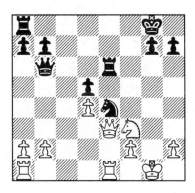

The airy kingside gives Black a decisive advantage. The rest is very painful, but for one side only!

22 ♖e2 ♖f8 23 ♘e5 ♕d8 24 f3 ♘g5 25 f4 ♖xf4! 26 ♖c2 h6 27 ♖ac1 ♕f6 28 ♔h1 ♕f5 29 ♖c3 ♖xe5! 30 dxe5 d4 31 ♖c8+ ♔h7 32 ♕g3 ♖g4 0-1

Game 20
Wells-Fries Nielsen
Copenhagen Open 1995

---

1 e4 e6 2 d4 d5 3 ♘d2 ♘f6 4 e5 ♘fd7 5 c3 c5 6 ♗d3 ♘c6 7 ♘e2 cxd4 8 cxd4 ♕b6 9 ♘f3 f6 10 exf6 ♘xf6 11 0-0 ♗d6 12 b3

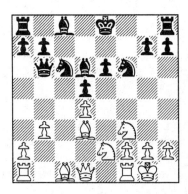

Seemingly planning a fianchetto, but in fact White has a different scheme in mind. The immediate 12 ♗f4 is also possible, when after 12...♗xf4 13 ♘xf4 ♕xb2 14 ♘g5!? White has some compensation for the pawn.

12...0-0 13 ♗f4!? ♗xf4

13...♘xd4 is a playable alternative, e.g. 14 ♘fxd4 e5 15 ♗e3 exd4 16 ♗xd4 ♕d8 17 ♘g3 ♗d7 and Black was okay in Wahls-Zhang Gong, Beijing 1993.

14 ♘xf4 ♗d7

14...♔h8 and 14...g6!?, both renewing the threat against the d4-pawn, also merit consideration. 14...♘xd4?!, however, cannot be recommended. After 15 ♘xd4 e5 16 ♘xd5 Black has two captures but neither lead to equality:

a) 16...♘xd5 17 ♕h5! ♘f6 18 ♕xe5 and White was simply a clear pawn up in Emms-Kinsman, England 4NCL 1995.

b) 16...♕xd4 17 ♗c4! ♕xd1 (17...♔h8 18 ♕xd4 exd4 19 ♘c7 ♖b8 20 ♖fd1 wins a pawn; and although 17...♗e6!? is stronger, after 18 ♘e7+ ♔f7 19 ♗xe6+ ♔xe6 20 ♕xd4 exd4 21

♖fe1+ ♔f7 22 ♘f5! White is still better) 18 ♖fxd1 ♔h8 19 ♖e1 b5? (19...♘xd5 20 ♗xd5 is clearly better for White) 20 ♘c7 bxc4 21 ♘xa8 ♗d7 22 ♘c7 ♖c8 23 ♘a6 ♗b5 24 ♘b4 a5 25 ♖xe5 1-0 Emms-M.Anderton, Maidstone 1995.

15 ♖c1!

An important move. The bishop on d3 will have to move so that the queen can support the d4-pawn, and since b1 is the natural retreat square, it is wise to activate the queen's rook first.

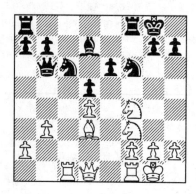

15...g6

Two other moves have also been witnessed from this position:

a) 15...♘e4 16 g3 ♖f5!? 17 ♘h4 ♖f7 18 ♘f3 ♖f5 19 ♘h4 ♖f7 20 ♘f3 and the players agreed a draw in Wahls-Kindermann, Dudweiler 1996. 17 ♖e1!?, hassling the knight on e4, looks more critical.

b) 15...♖ae8 16 ♗b1 ♘xd4 17 ♕xd4 ♕xd4 18 ♘xd4 e5 19 ♘fe2 exd4 20 ♘xd4 with a small edge for White in Rausis-Farago, Germany 1996.

16 ♗b1 ♘e4 17 g3 ♖ac8 18 ♖e1 ♘d6

This retreat represents a concession, but 18...g5 19 ♗xe4 gxf4 20 ♗b1 fxg3 21 hxg3 looks better for White, as the black king remains unsafe.

19 ♘e5 ♘xe5 20 ♖xe5 ♖f6 21 ♕d2 ♖cf8 22 h4!

White has established an ideal position.

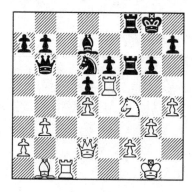

22...♘f7 23 ♖e2 ♗b5 24 ♖e3 ♕d6 25 ♖ce1 ♘d8 26 ♖e5 ♗e8 27 h5 ♕d7 28 hxg6 hxg6 29 ♖g5 ♖xf4 30 gxf4 ♖f6 31 ♕e3 ♗f7 32 ♔g2 ♘c6 33 ♖h1 ♗e8 34 ♖h3 ♕g7 35 f5 ♗f7 36 fxg6 1-0

Summary

The plan of ♗g5-h4-g3, in conjunction with leaving the knight on e2, continues to be the most dangerous plan against 11...♕c7. Black has to play extremely carefully to avoid drifting into a lifeless position in this line. On the other hand it is still unclear how White should proceed against 11...♕b6. Many different ways have been tried but Black seems to have enough resources in each variation.

1 e4 e6 2 d4 d5 3 ♘d2 ♘f6 4 e5 ♘fd7 5 ♗d3 c5 6 c3 ♘c6 7 ♘e2 cxd4 8 cxd4 f6 9 exf6 ♘xf6 10 ♘f3 ♗d6 11 0-0

11...♕c7
      11...♕b6
            12 ♘c3 0-0 *(D)*
                 13 ♗g5
                       13...♗d7 – *Game 16*
                       13...♚h8 – *Game 17*
                 13 ♗e3 – *Game 18*
             12 ♘f4 – *Game 19*
             12 b3 – *Game 20*
12 ♗g5 *(D)*
      12 ♘c3 – *Game 14*
      12 g3 – *Game 15*
12...0-0 13 ♗h4 *(D)*
      13 ♖c1 – *Game 13*
13...e5
      13...♘h5 – *Game 12*
14 dxe5 – *Game 11*

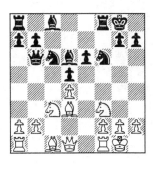
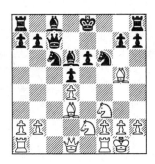
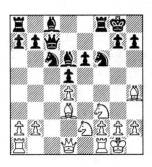

12...0-0   *12 ♗g5*   *13 ♗h4*

CHAPTER THREE

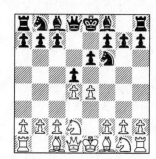

3...♘f6: Early Deviations from the Main Line

1 e4 e6 2 d4 d5 3 ♘d2 ♘f6

Thus far we have studied the most popular and important variations of the 3...♘f6 Tarrasch; the main lines that arise after 4 e5 ♘fd7 5 ♗d3 c5 6 c3 ♘c6 7 ♘e2 cxd4 8 cxd4 f6 9 exf6 ♘xf6 10 ♘f3 ♗d6 11 0-0. In this chapter we will be looking at a number of attractive options for both White and Black, before the main position is reached. In Games 21 and 22 we consider 9...♕xf6, which only came to prominence on the early 1990s. Adherents such as Knaak and Gleizerov have injected some important new ideas into Black's play, which has elevated the line from the assessment 'a bit dodgy' to 'quite playable'. Conversely 9 ♘f4 (Game 23) was an extremely important line during the mid-eighties but it is hardly ever seen now, since White has not found a way to obtain any advantage. In Games 24-26 we consider some other deviations by Black from the main line, namely 8...♘b6, 7...♕b6 (which usually transposes to Games 16-20 from Chapter 2

after 8 ♘f3 cxd4 9 cxd4 f6 10 exf6 ♘xf6 11 0-0 ♗d6) and 6...b6. Games 27 and 28 deal with 7 ♘gf3, which can lead to a pawn sacrifice, although Black also has other respectable ways to play the position. 5 ♘gf3 c5 6 c4?! cannot be recommended, as we see in Game 29. Finally, 4...♘e4 doesn't have a good reputation, but are things really so clear? We take a close look at this underrated move in Games 30 and 31.

Game 21
Korneev-Knaak
Bad Wörishofen Open 1992

---

1 e4 e6 2 d4 d5 3 ♘d2 ♘f6 4 e5 ♘fd7 5 ♗d3 c5 6 c3 ♘c6 7 ♘e2 cxd4 8 cxd4 f6 9 exf6 ♕xf6 10 ♘f3

see following diagram

10...♗d6

10...♗b4+, offering the exchange of bishops, is the old continuation. After 11 ♗d2 ♗xd2+ 12 ♕xd2 0-0 13 0-0 e5 14 dxe5 ♘dxe5 15 ♘xe5 ♕xe5 we reach a position similar to the one discussed in Chapter 2. Theoretically White maintains an infinitesimal edge and Black's position is solid, but slightly depressing. Note that if Black wishes to play with ...♗d6, then 10...h6 is the most accurate move order, preventing White's option in the next note.

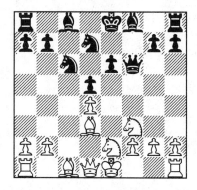

11 0-0

Here 11 ♗g5 ♕f7 12 0-0 0-0 13 ♗h4, threatening ⌀g5 and also intending the positionally desirable ♗g3, gives White a traditional plus. Hence the growing popularity of the move 10...h6.

11...h6 12 ♗c2

The alternative 12 ♗b1 is the subject of Game 22.

12...0-0 13 ♕d3

White's play looks very natural, but in fact it founders on an original defensive manoeuvre.

13...♖d8!

Black's fortifying strategy includes ...⌀f8, covering the weak light squares around the king. This will be followed by ...♗d7-e8-g6! (or h5), after which Black's pieces will co-ordinate perfectly. Simple stuff, but in this game this strategy proves to be mightily effective.

14 a3

14 ♕h7+ ♔f7 is just a waste of time. The queen would soon have to beat a hasty retreat after ...⌀f8.

14...⌀f8 15 b4 ♗d7 16 ♗b2 b5 17 ♗c3 ♗e8 18 ♕e3 ♗g6

The plan has been completed and Black stands well. Now White chooses not to exchange, but this merely leaves Black with two good bishops against two bad ones.

19 ♗b3 ⌀d7 20 ♖ae1 ♖e8 21 ⌀g3 ♗f4 22 ♕e2 a6 23 ⌀e5 ⌀dxe5 24 dxe5 ♕g5 25 ♗b2 ♖ad8

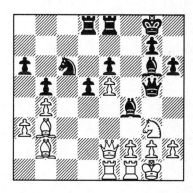

An uncomplicated plan. The d-pawn will roll up the board. White's next move is a sure sign that things are slipping.

26 ⌀h1 ♗h5 27 f3 d4 28 ⌀f2 ♕h4 29 ⌀h3

29 g3 ♗xg3! 30 hxg3 ♕xg3+ 31 ♔h1 ♗xf3+ is the end.

29...♗e3+ 30 ♔h1 ⌀xe5 31 ♕c2 ♗xf3 32 gxf3 ♕xh3 33 ♕e4 ⌀f7 34 f4 ⌀d6 35 ♕e5 ⌀c4 36 ♗xc4 bxc4 37 ♖g1 ♗xg1 38 ♖xg1 ♕f3+ 39 ♖g2 ♕d1+ 40 ♖g1 ♕f3+ 41 ♖g2 ♖e7 42 ♕f6

42...♕xg2+ 0-1

A powerful game by Knaak.

Game 22
Todorovic-Dimitrov
Belgrade 1995

---

1 e4 e6 2 d4 d5 3 ♘d2 ♘f6 4 e5 ♘fd7 5 c3 c5 6 ♗d3 ♘c6 7 ♘e2 cxd4 8 cxd4 f6 9 exf6 ♕xf6 10 0-0

An interesting move order, which eliminates ...♗b4+ options, though after Black's response we arrive at the same position as the previous game. Given that Black's king is a little exposed and he still needs time to develop, grabbing the pawn on d4 is too risky. After 10...♘xd4 11 ♘xd4 ♕xd4 12 ♘f3 ♕f6 13 ♗g5 ♕f7 14 ♕c2! White has a very strong initiative. For example, 14...g6 15 ♖ac1 ♕g7 16 ♖fe1 ♔f7 17 ♕e2 ♘c5 18 b4 1-0 was the brutal finish to Cvachoucek-Iveges, correspondence 1977.

10...♗d6 11 ♘f3 h6 12 ♗b1!?

In Emms-De Francesco, Bad Wörishofen 1996, I tried 12 ♗c2 0-0 13 ♗e3 and after 13...♘e7!? (13...♖d8 is more consistent, when I was planning 14 ♕d2, in order to exchange bishops

with ♗f4) 14 ♕d3 e5 15 ♘xe5 (15 dxe5 ♘xe5 16 ♘xe5 ♗f5!) 15...♘xe5 16 dxe5 ♗xe5 17 ♘g3! I liked my position. My opponent now slid rapidly downhill and after 15...♘f5? 18 ♕xd5+ ♗e6 19 ♕e4 ♗xb2? (19...♖ac8 20 ♘xf5 ♗xf5 21 ♕xf5 ♕xf5 22 ♗xf5 ♖xf5 23 ♖ac1 ♖xc1 24 ♖xc1 is clearly better for White) 20 ♖ab1 ♗e5 21 ♘h5 he was forced to resign.

12...0-0 13 ♕d3

A similar idea to the previous game, except with the bishop on b1. Because of this White need not worry so much about the move ...♘b4.

13...♖d8 14 g3 ♘f8?!

This actually proves to be too slow here. The disadvantage of 12 ♗b1 is that it disconnects the white rooks. Black needs to exploit this by violent means, so I suggest that 14...e5 may be the answer to Black's problems. Indeed, in Baron Rodriguez-Shaked, Cala Galdana 1996, Black equalised after 15 dxe5 ♘dxe5 16 ♘xe5 ♗xe5 17 ♘f4 ♘d4 18 ♕h7+ ♔f7 19 ♕g6+ (19 ♗g6+ ♔e7 20 ♗d3 ♗xf4 21 ♗xf4 ♘e2+! 22 ♗xe2 ♗f5! traps the queen) 19...♕xg6 20 ♗xg6+ ♔f6 21 ♗d3 ♗f5.

15 ♗f4

15...e5 16 dxe5 ♗xe5 17 ♘xe5 ♘xe5 18 ♗xe5 ♕xe5 19 ♗c2 ♗e6 20 ♘f4 ♗f7 21 ♖fe1 ♕xb2?

This runs into an irresistible attack. 21...♕d6 would have restricted White's plus.

22 ♖ab1 ♕xa2 23 ♖e7! ♖ab8?!

23...♖e8 also loses after 24 ♖xf7! ♔xf7 25 ♗b3 ♕a5 26 ♗xd5+. The last chance to continue the game was 23...♖ac8 24 ♖bxb7 ♕xc2 25 ♕xc2 ♖xc2 26 ♖xf7, which still looks very good for White.

24 ♕f5 d4

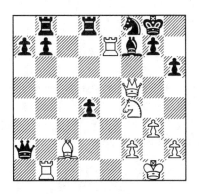

25 ♖xf7! 1-0

Both 25...♕xf7 26 ♗b3 and 25...d3 26 ♖xg7+! ♔xg7 27 ♘h5+ ♔g8 28 ♕g4+ ♔f7 29 ♗b3+ are winning for White.

Game 23
Pirrot-Hertneck
German Bundesliga 1990

---

1 e4 e6 2 d4 d5 3 ♘d2 ♘f6 4 e5 ♘fd7 5 ♗d3 c5 6 c3 ♘c6 7 ♘e2 cxd4 8 cxd4 f6 9 ♘f4!?

see following diagram

9...♘xd4 10 ♕h5+ ♔e7 11 exf6+

This is more accurate than 11 ♘g6+ hxg6 12 exf6+ ♔xf6! (12...♗xf6 transposes to the main game) 13 ♕xh8 ♔f7 14 0-0 ♘c5! and Black is better, e.g. 15 ♕h3 e5 16 ♕e3 ♘xd3 17 ♘f3 ♘xf3+ 18 ♕xf3+ ♗f5 19 g4 e4 20 ♕g2 ♗e6 21 ♗e3 ♘e5 22 f4 ♘f3+ 23 ♖xf3 exf3 24 ♕xf3 ♔g8 25 ♗d4 ♖c8 0-1 Comben-Short, Brighton Zonal 1984.

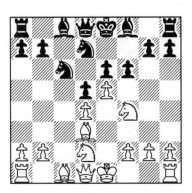

11...♘xf6 12 ♘g6+ hxg6 13 ♕xh8 ♔f7 14 0-0

14 f4, attempting to halt Black's surge in the centre, has been tried in a bid to inject some new life into this variation. Nevertheless, with direct play Black can still drum up an initiative. The game Radlovacki-Rasidovic, Yugoslavian Championship 1991, continued 14...♘c6 15 ♕h4 e5 16 0-0 e4 17 ♗e2 ♘d4 18 ♗d1 ♘f5 19 ♕e1 ♗c5+ 20 ♔h1 ♕h8 21 ♘b3 ♗b6 22 g4 ♘h6 23 g5 ♘hg4 24 ♕g3

see following diagram

24...♘xh2!! 25 ♕xh2 ♗h3 26 ♖g1 ♕h4 27 ♖g3 (or 27 gxf6 ♖h8 with the decisive threat of 28...♗g2+ 29 ♖xg2 ♕e1+) 27...♖h8 28 ♕xh3 ♕xg3! 0-1.

A well-worn alternative line is 14 ♕h4, where no real improvements have been found for White on the stem game Van der Wiel-Timman, Brussels 1986, which continued 14...e5 15 ②f3 ②xf3+ 16 gxf3 ③f5 17 ③xf5 gxf5 18 ③g5 ④a5+ 19 ③f1 g6! (with the idea of ...③g7 and ...④h8) 20 ③xf6 ④a6+ 21 ⑤g2 ④xf6 22 ④xf6+ ⑤xf6 23 ③ac1 ③d6. Here Black is doing well and Timman went on to win the game.

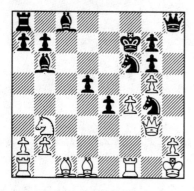

14...e5 15 ②f3 ②xf3+ 16 gxf3 ②h5 17 ③xg6+

Drastic measures are required, otherwise Black will consolidate with ...④f6.

17...⑤xg6 18 ⑤h1 ④h4!

Black does best to give back the piece. 18...②f6 allows 19 ③g1+ ⑤f7 20 ③xg7+ ⑤e6 21 ③g5 ③e7 22 ③xe7+! ④xe7 23 ③c1!

19 ④xf8 ⑤h7?!

It is better to play 19...④h3 20 ③g1+ ⑤h7 21 ④a3 ③f5 22 ③g2 d4, when Black had good compensation in Doric-D'Amore, Formia 1995. After the text move, 19...⑤h7, White should play 20 ④f7!

20 ③g1?! ④xf2 21 ④f7??

One move too late. This allows a very pleasing finish.

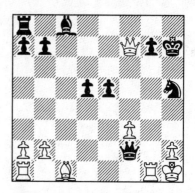

21...③g4!! 0-1

After 22 ③xg4 Black mates with 22...④f1+ 23 ③g1 ②g3+! 24 hxg3 ④h3.

┌─────────────────────────────┐
│ *Game 24*   │
│ **Lputian-Agzamov**   │
│ *USSR Championship 1985*   │
└─────────────────────────────┘

1 d4 e6 2 e4 d5 3 ②d2 ②f6 4 e5 ②fd7 5 ③d3 c5 6 c3 ②c6 7 ②e2 cxd4 8 cxd4 ②b6

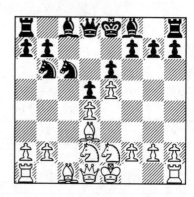

9 0-0

Here White can also take immediate steps on the queenside with 9 a3 a5 10 b3. At first sight these moves seem a little strange, but White is taking prophylactic measures. Black's...a5-a4 will now be answered by b3-b4, establishing a fair share of space. I've had numerous experiences with this line:

a) 10...♗d7 11 0-0 ♗e7 12 f4 f5 13 exf6 ♗xf6 14 ♘f3 a4 15 ♘e5 (the logical 15 b4 is also good for White) 15...axb3 16 ♕xb3 0-0 17 ♗e3 with a clear plus for White in Emms-Hvenkilde, Copenhagen 1992.

b) 10...a4 11 b4 ♗d7 12 0-0 ♗e7 13 f4 g6! (this is stronger than 13...f5) 14 ♗b2 (14 g4!? is critical, although after 14...h5 15 f5 exf5 16 gxf5 ♗xf5 17 ♗xf5 gxf5 18 ♖xf5 ♕d7, White's exposed king offers Black definite counter-chances) 14...h5 15 ♔h1 ♔f8 16 ♖c1 ♔g7 17 ♖f3 ♕e8 and Black had equalised in Emms-Knott, British Championship 1996.

9...♗d7 10 f4 h5 11 ♘f3 ♖c8 12 a3 a5 13 ♘c3 ♘a7 14 h3 ♘c4

Once more 14...g6 looks like the most solid defence. Now White exercises a thematic break.

15 f5! ♕b6 16 ♔h1 ♗e7

Grabbing the b-pawn with 16...♘xb2 allows 17 ♗xb2 ♕xb2 18 ♘a4 ♗xa4 19 ♕xa4+ ♘c6 20 fxe6 fxe6 21 ♗g6+ ♔d7 22 ♖fb1, when White's initiative is becoming menacing.

17 ♕e1!?

Naturally White can defend the b-pawn, but Lputian has something much more enticing in mind.

17...♘xb2 18 ♗xb2 ♕xb2 19 ♘xd5! exd5 20 e6 ♗c6

Or 20...fxe6 21 fxe6 ♗c6 22 ♗g6+ when 22...♔f8 23 ♘h4+ ♔g8 24 ♗f7+ ♔h7 25 ♕e5! and 22...♔d8 23 ♕xa5+ are winning for White.

21 exf7+ ♔f8 22 ♘e5 ♖h6 23 ♕e3 ♕b6 24 ♖ae1 ♗f6 25 ♘g6+ ♖xg6

Naturally not 25...♔xf7, as 26 ♕e6

is mate.

26 fxg6 ♕xd4 27 ♕e2 ♗d7

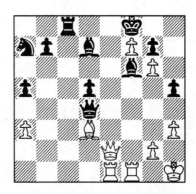

Now 28 ♕xh5 ♕h4 allows Black to hang on. Instead Lputian produced an inspired queen sacrifice which completely ties up his opponent.

28 ♗f5! ♗b5 29 ♗xc8!! ♗xe2 30 ♖xe2 ♗e5 31 ♗d7 ♘c6 32 ♗xc6 bxc6 33 ♖fe1 ♕d3 34 ♖xe5

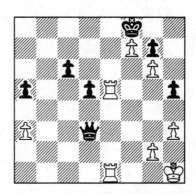

34...♕xg6 35 ♖e8+ ♔xf7 36 ♖1e7+ ♔f6 37 ♖e6+ ♔f5 38 ♖xg6 ♔xg6 39 ♖e6+ 1-0

Game 25
Menke-Wilde
Correspondence 1957

1 e4 e6 2 d4 d5 3 ♘d2 ♘f6 4 e5

♘fd7 5 ♗d3 c5 6 c3 ♘c6 7 ♘e2 ♕b6 8 ♘f3 cxd4 9 cxd4 f6

Usual and best here is 10 exf6 ♘xf6 11 0-0 ♗d6, transposing to the 11...♕b6 lines from the previous chapter.

10 ♘f4?!

After 10 0-0 Black should just go ahead and grab the pawn. Pirrot-Kindermann, Bad Wörishofen 1992, went 10...fxe5 11 dxe5 ♘dxe5 12 ♘xe5 ♘xe5 13 ♘f4 ♘xd3 14 ♘xd3 ♗d6 15 ♕h5+ g6 16 ♕h6 ♕d4 17 ♗f4 ♗f8 18 ♕h3 e5! (18...♗g7 19 ♖ac1 0-0 20 ♖c7 gives White a dangerous attack) 19 ♗xe5 ♕xe5 20 ♕xc8+ ♖xc8 21 ♘xe5 ♗g7 22 ♘d3 ♔d7 23 ♖fc1 ♖c4 24 b3 ♖c6 and Black's bishop and better king ensured an edge in the endgame.

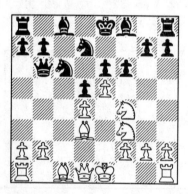

10...fxe5 11 dxe5

Or 11 ♘xe6 e4 12 ♗f4 ♘de5! 13 dxe5 ♗xe6 14 ♘g5 ♗f5 15 ♗e2 ♗b4+ with a clear advantage to Black.

11...♗b4+ 12 ♔f1 ♘dxe5 13 ♘xe5 ♘xe5 14 ♕h5+ ♘f7 15 ♗xh7 ♕d4 16 ♗e3 ♕xb2 17 ♖c1 ♕e5 18 ♕d1 ♖xh7 19 ♕a4+ ♗d7 20 ♕xb4 ♖c8 21 ♖xc8+ ♗xc8 22 ♘g6 ♕f6 23 ♕b1?

After this move Black rapidly takes

over. The only chance is 23 ♕f8+! ♔d7 24 ♕xf7+ ♕xf7 25 ♘e5+ ♔e8 26 ♘xf7 ♔xf7 27 ♗xa7 ♖h4, when Black is still better but White has good drawing chances.

23...♘d6 24 ♘f4 ♘e4 25 g3 g5

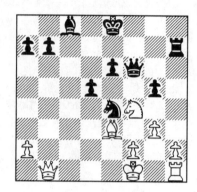

26 ♘xd5

Neither 26 ♘g2 ♘xg3+ nor 26 ♘e2 ♕f3 27 ♖g1 ♖xh2 hit the mark.

26...exd5 27 ♕b5+ ♗d7 28 ♕xd5 ♕a1+ 29 ♔e2 ♗g4+ 30 ♔d3 ♕c3+ 31 ♔xe4 ♖e7+ 32 ♕e5 ♖xe5 0-1

> ### Game 26
> ### Emms-Sträter
> *Hastings 1996*

1 e4 e6 2 d4 d5 3 ♘d2 ♘f6 4 ♗d3 c5 5 e5 ♘fd7 6 c3 b6

This move is an old favourite of Nigel Short's. Before completing his development Black seeks to exchange the light-squared bishops.

7 ♘e2

White can also play to retain bishops with 7 f4 ♗a6 8 ♗b1, e.g. 8...♘c6 9 ♘df3 cxd4 10 cxd4 ♖c8 11 ♘e2 and now:

a) 11...♗b4+ should be answered with 12 ♗d2, as 12 ♘c3? runs into

12...♘cxe5! 13 fxe5 ♖xc3.

b) 11...f5 12 0-0 ♗e7 13 ♖f2 0-0 14 h3 with the usual space plus.

7...♗a6 8 ♗xa6 ♘xa6 9 0-0 ♗e7

9...♘c7, adding further protection to the e6 and d5 squares, is a serious alternative. Emms-Conquest, Norton (rapidplay) 1997, continued 10 ♘f4 ♕c8 11 c4 ♕b7 12 cxd5 ♘xd5 13 ♘f3 h6 14 ♕e2 ♗e7 15 ♘xd5 ♕xd5 16 dxc5 bxc5 17 ♖d1 ♕b7 18 ♗e3, when I felt that I was a little better, although the game was eventually drawn.

10 ♘f4 b5 11 ♕g4 g6

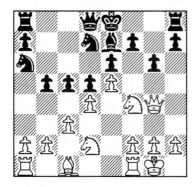

12 h4!

This was introduced by the Greek grandmaster Kotronias against Short. White wants to probe with h4-h5.

12...cxd4

12...♗xh4? allows 13 ♘xe6! fxe6 14 ♕xe6+, when the knight on a6 hangs.

13 cxd4 h5 14 ♕e2

Perhaps 14 ♕h3!? is stronger, preventing 14...♗xh4 on account of 15 ♘xe6. White can then think about ideas involving ♘f3, ♕g3, ♘h3 and ♗g5, infiltrating the weak dark squares on the kingside.

14...♗xh4 15 a4 ♗e7

Varying from Kotronias-Short,

Novi Sad Olympiad 1990, which went 15...♕b6 16 axb5 ♘c7 17 ♘f3 ♗d8?! (17...♗e7 is stronger) 18 ♘h3 ♘xb5 19 ♖d1 ♘b8 20 ♗g5 ♘c6 21 ♕d2 ♗xg5 22 ♕xg5 and White was in the driving seat.

16 axb5 ♘c7 17 ♘b3 ♕b8 18 ♘a5 ♕xb5 19 ♕c2

Naturally White keeps the queens on. During the game I felt that I should have a clear advantage, but it is now apparent that Black has many defensive resources.

19...♕b6 20 ♘c6 ♗c5!

21 ♘xg6! ♖g8!

After 21...fxg6 22 ♕xg6+ ♔f8 23 ♗h6+ ♖xh6 24 ♕xh6+ ♔g8 White has the amazing 25 ♘d8!! (needless to say, found by Fritz) as 25...♖xd8 26 ♕g5+ picks up the black rook. After the game move Black can regain his pawn advantage.

22 ♘f4 ♕xc6 23 b4 ♘b5 24 ♗e3 ♖g4! 25 bxc5 ♘xd4 26 ♗xd4 ♖xf4 27 ♖fd1 ♖f5 28 ♖a5!? ♘xe5 29 ♖e1 ♕c7 30 ♖a6 ♔f8?

Finally going astray in the complications. After 30...♖g5 White should bail out with 31 ♕a4+ ♔f8 32 ♖xe5 ♖xe5 33 ♗xe5 ♕xe5 34 ♖xa7 ♖xa7 35

♕xa7. Black is still a pawn up, but the passed pawn on c5 should ensure a draw.

31 ♕xf5!! exf5 32 ♗xe5 ♕d7 33 ♖h6 f6 34 ♗xf6 ♕a4 35 ♖e7 1-0

Black can only prevent mate with the ludicrous 35...♕a1+ 36 ♗xa1 ♔xe7, after which White is too much material up.

> *Game 27*
> ## Kolev-Herraiz
> *Linares Open 1996*

1 e4 e6 2 d4 d5 3 ♘d2 ♘f6 4 e5 ♘fd7 5 ♗d3 c5 6 c3 ♘c6 7 ♘gf3

Introduced by Viktor Korchnoi in the 1960s, and later advocated by John Nunn, this leads to a speculative offer of a pawn.

7...♕b6 8 0-0 cxd4

8...g6 is discussed in Game 28.

9 cxd4 ♘xd4 10 ♘xd4 ♕xd4 11 ♘f3 ♕b6 12 ♕a4 ♕b4

White's idea was to swing the queen to the kingside with, for example, 12...♗e7 13 ♕g4. 12...♕b4 prevents this.

13 ♕c2

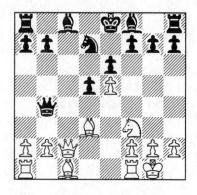

13...♕c5

The most popular move, although White has tended to score well against this. Major alternatives include (in decreasing order of importance):

a) 13...♘c5!? 14 ♗d2 ♕a4 15 b3 ♕d7 16 ♗e2 ♗e7 17 ♗e3 b6 18 b4 ♕a4 19 ♕b2 ♘e4 20 a3 ♗a6 21 b5 ♗b7 22 ♖fc1 ♖c8 23 ♘d4 0-0 24 f3 ♖xc1+ 25 ♖xc1 ♗xa3 26 ♕a2 ♕b4 with great complications in Hellers-Ludvigsen, Nordic Team Championship 1985.

b) 13...♗e7 14 ♗d2 ♕g4 15 ♖ac1 0-0 16 ♗xh7+ ♔h8 17 ♗d3 ♘c5 18 h3 ♕h5 19 ♗g5 with a distinct advantage for White in Emms-Tibensky, Douai Open 1990.

c) 13...h6?! 14 ♗d2 ♕b6 15 ♖ac1 ♗e7 16 ♕a4! is given as clearly better for White by *ECO*, as 16...0-0 allows 17 ♖xc8 ♖axc8 18 ♕xd7.

14 ♕e2 ♗e7 15 ♗e3 ♕a5 16 ♖ac1 0-0 17 ♖c3 ♖e8

Th alternative 17...f5 18 exf6 ♘xf6 19 ♗d4 offers White chances of a direct attack. Emms-Giddins, Gausdal 1993, concluded 19...♗d7 20 ♘g5 h6 21 ♘xe6 ♖fe8 22 ♗f5 ♕a6 (or 22...♗b5 23 ♕d2 ♗xf1 24 ♘xg7! ♔xg7

25 ♖g3+) 23 ♕xa6 bxa6 24 ♘xg7 ♗xf5 25 ♘xf5 ♘e4 26 ♖c6 1-0. After 17...♖e8 Black doesn't weaken the kingside, but does allow an effective version of the Greek gift.

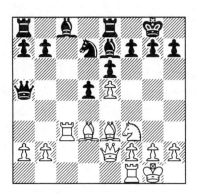

18 ♗xh7+! ♔xh7 19 ♘g5+ ♗xg5

19...♔g8 20 ♕h5 ♗xg5 21 ♗xg5 leads to the game, while 19...♔g6 comes to a sticky end after 20 ♕c2+ f5 21 exf6+ ♔xf6 22 ♗d4+ ♔xg5 23 f4+ ♔h4 24 ♕h7+ ♔g4 25 ♖g3 mate.

20 ♕h5+ ♔g8

20...♗h6 21 ♗xh6 g6 22 ♕h4 ♖h8 White can play 23 ♗d2+ ♔g8 24 ♕xh8+ ♔xh8 25 ♖h3+, but even stronger is 23 ♖fc1!, which leaves Black in helpless state, e.g. 23...♕b6 24 ♗g5+ ♔g8 25 ♖xc8+ ♘f8 26 ♖xa8! ♖xh4 27 ♖xf8+ ♔xf8 28 ♖c8+ ♔g7 29 ♗f6+ ♔h6 30 ♖h8 mate.

21 ♗xg5

---

see following diagram

21...♕xc3

This seems rather extreme, but after 21...♖f8 22 ♗f6!! Black is forced to sacrifice anyway, when 22...♕xc3 (22...♘xf6 23 exf6 doesn't improve matters) 23 bxc3 gxf6 24 exf6 ♘xf6 25 ♕g5+ ♔h7 26 ♕xf6 is winning for

White. Note that 21...♘xe5 allows mate after 22 ♖h3 ♘g6 23 ♕h7+ ♔f8 24 ♕h8+ ♘xh8 25 ♖xh8.

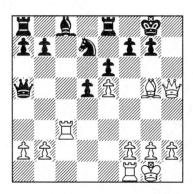

22 bxc3 ♘xe5 23 f4 1-0

Black's situation is hopeless, e.g. 23...♘c4 24 ♖f3 ♘d6 25 ♖h3 f6 26 ♗xf6. A powerfully played game by White.

Game 28
Maksimovic-Farago
Copenhagen Open 1989

---

1 d4 e6 2 e4 d5 3 ♘d2 ♘f6 4 e5 ♘fd7 5 c3 c5 6 ♗d3 ♘c6 7 ♘gf3 ♕b6

In Emms-S.Brown, Surrey Open 1995, my opponent tried an immediate 7...g6, but here I made use of the fact that I hadn't castled. The game continued 8 h4!? ♗g7 9 h5 0-0 10 hxg6 fxg6 (10...hxg6!?) 11 ♕e2! and the semi-open h-file gave White a small edge.

8 0-0 g6!?

This has become a popular alternative to grabbing the pawn.

9 dxc5 ♕c7 10 ♘b3 ♘dxe5

10...♗g7 11 ♘fd4! ♕xe5 12 f4 is a crucial continuation:

a) 12...♕b8 13 f5 e5 14 ♗g5! exd4 15 cxd4 ♘xd4 16 f6 ♗xf6 17 ♗xf6 ♘xf6 18 ♖xf6 and White was better in Korneev-Gleizerov, Katowice 1992.

b) 12...♕f6 13 f5!? gxf5 14 ♗xf5 ♘xd4 15 ♘xd4 exf5 16 ♘xf5 ♘xc5 17 ♕xd5 ♗xf5 18 ♕xc5 ♕e5 19 ♕xe5+ ♗xe5 20 ♖xf5 and White was a clear pawn up in Sutovsky-Yudasin, Israeli Championship 1994, although he actually lost the game in the end. It is difficult to suggest improvements for Black in these lines.

11 ♗f4 ♗g7 12 ♘xe5 ♘xe5

Natural enough, although I don't see much wrong with 12...♗xe5 either.

13 ♗b5+?!

After this move Black's central pawn mass becomes the most important factor. 13 ♖e1 is more testing, when after 13...0-0 14 c4! f6 15 ♖c1 ♕f7 16 cxd5 exd5 17 ♘d4 White had a small plus in Tkachiev-Komarov, France 1996.

13...♗d7 14 ♗xd7+ ♕xd7 15 ♖e1 ♘c4 16 ♖b1 0-0 17 ♘d2 ♕b5 18 ♘xc4 ♕xc4

The opening battle has been well and truly won by Black. The rest of the game is a model demonstration of how to exploit a 2-0 central pawn majority.

19 ♗d6 ♖fc8 20 ♕b3 ♕a6 21 a4 b6 22 cxb6 axb6 23 ♗e5 ♗xe5 24 ♖xe5 ♕xa4 25 ♕xa4 ♖xa4 26 ♔f1 b5 27 ♖e3 b4 28 b3 ♖a7 29 cxb4 ♖b8 30 b5 ♖xb5 31 b4 ♖a4 32 ♖eb3 ♔f8 33 ♔e2 ♔e7 34 ♔d2 e5 35 ♔c3 ♔e6 36 ♖1b2 ♖a7 37 ♔d3 ♖c7 38 ♖c3 e4+ 39 ♔d4 ♖xc3 40 ♔xc3 ♔e5 41 ♖b1 f5 42 ♖b2 f4 43 ♖b1 d4+ 44 ♔c4 ♖b8 45 b5 ♖c8+ 46 ♔b3 d3 47 b6 ♔d4 48 ♔b2 e3 49 b7 ♖b8 50 fxe3+ fxe3 51 ♔c1 ♔c3 52 ♖b6

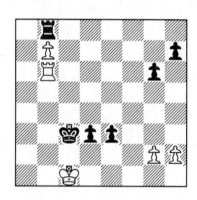

52...d2+ 0-1

53 ♔d1 e2+ 54 ♔xe2 ♖e8+ and the pawn promotes.

Game 29
Emms-S.Clarke
British Championship 1991

---

1 e4 e6 2 d4 d5 3 ♘d2 ♘f6 4 e5 ♘fd7 5 ♘gf3 c5 6 c4?!

An interesting possibility, but not one to cause Black any great deal of concern. I tried this line out a few times, but this game was my last experience with it.

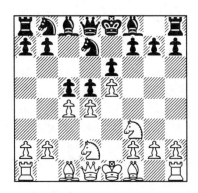

6...♘c6 7 cxd5 exd5 8 ♗d3 cxd4 9 0-0 ♘c5 10 ♘b3 ♗g4 11 ♘xc5 ♗xc5 12 a3 ♗b6 13 ♖e1 0-0 14 ♗c2 ♗h5!

Planning ....♗g6. Apart from the fact that it is doubled, White has no real compensation for the pawn.

15 ♗f4 ♖e8 16 ♕d3 ♗g6 17 ♕d2 ♖c8 18 ♗xg6 hxg6 19 ♖ad1 ♕d7 20 h3 a5 21 g4 a4 22 ♕d3 ♖a8 23 ♖e2 ♖a5 24 ♖de1

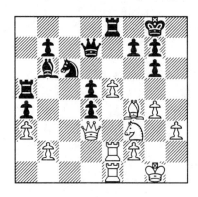

24...♘d8!

Returning the extra pawn in exchange for a 'good knight versus bad bishop' scenario. White also has to worry about Black's other d-pawn.

25 ♘xd4 ♗xd4 26 ♕xd4 ♘e6 27 ♕d2 ♖b5 28 ♗g3 d4 29 f4 ♖b3 30

♖g2 ♘c5 31 f5 ♕d5

31...gxf5 32 gxf5 ♕xf5 is strong.

32 e6 fxe6 33 fxg6 ♘d3?!

33...♘e4 34 ♕f4 ♘g5 would have been very nasty.

34 ♖b1 e5? 35 ♕g5 ♖f8 36 ♕h5 ♖f3

37 ♗h4!

Turning the tables. White threatens 38 ♕h7+ ♔f8 39 ♕h8+ ♕g8 40 ♗e7+.

37...♖f6 38 ♕h7+ ♔f8 39 ♗xf6 1-0

Game 30
Seul-Zach
Biel 1997

---

1 e4 e6 2 d4 d5 3 ♘c3 ♘f6 4 e5 ♘e4 5 ♘xe4 dxe4

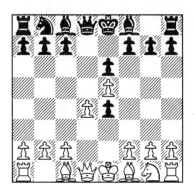

6 ♗e3

Note that although White played 3 ♘c3 in this game, Tarrasch players would reach the same position with 3 ♘d2. The other main alternative here is 6 ♗c4, intending to ignore rather than surround the e4-pawn. However, the pawn does have some nuisance value. After 6...a6 7 a4 b6 8 ♘h3 ♗b7 9 ♘f4 ♘c6 10 ♗e3 ♘e7 11 0-0 g6 12 ♕e2 ♘f5 13 ♖fd1 ♗h6! Black retained counter-chances in Aseev-Lputian, Russia 1984. Indeed Black was able to seize the advantage after 14 a5 0-0 15 axb6 cxb6 16 ♗xa6?! ♗xf4! 17 ♗xb7 ♘xd4 18 ♕c4 ♖xa1 19 ♖xa1 ♗xe5 20 ♗xe4 ♕h4. After 6 ♗e3 Black has to play very actively, else the e-pawn will simply disappear for nothing.

6...c5 7 dxc5 ♘d7 8 ♕g4 ♘xc5 9 ♗b5+ ♘d7 10 ♘e2 ♕a5+ 11 ♘c3 a6 12 ♗xd7+ ♗xd7

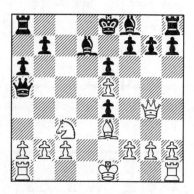

13 ♗d4!

13 ♕xe4 is recommended in *ECO*, assigning White a clear plus. However, 13...♗c6 14 ♕g4 ♗a3! is very embarrassing for the first player.

13...♗c6 14 0-0-0 0-0-0 15 ♕f4!?

15 ♔b1 threatens ♘xe4, but Black can play an unclear exchange sacrifice: 15...♖xd4! 16 ♖xd4 ♕xe5, when the

two bishops and kingside pawn phalanx offer reasonable compensation.

15...♗a3?

Black just loses valuable time with this move. Perhaps he should try 15...♖d7 16 ♔b1 ♗b4 17 ♘xe4 ♖hd8 18 c3 ♗d5 19 a3 ♗e7, with some possible play on the light squares around the white king. As the game goes, Black gets no compensation for the pawn.

16 ♕e3 ♗e7 17 ♔b1 ♖d7 18 ♘xe4 ♖hd8 19 ♖d3 ♔b8 20 ♖hd1

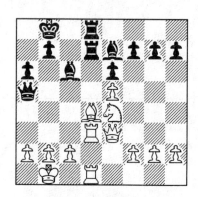

White has consolidated successfully and is now simply a pawn up.

20...♔a8 21 b3 ♖c8 22 ♗c3 ♖xd3 23 ♖xd3 ♕c7 24 ♘d6 ♖d8 25 ♗d4 ♖f8 26 ♘c4 ♗xg2 27 ♗b6 ♕c6 28 f3 ♗f1 29 ♘a5 ♕b5 30 a4 ♕b4 31 ♖d7 ♖c8 32 ♖xb7 ♗c5 33 ♗xc5 ♕xc5 34 ♕e4 ♗d3 35 ♖c7+ 1-0

Game 31
Balashov-Borngässer
Wisla 1992

1 e4 e6 2 d4 d5 3 ♘d2 ♘f6 4 e5 ♘e4 5 ♗d3 ♘xd2 6 ♗xd2 c5 7 dxc5 ♘d7!

Preparing to capture on c5 with the

knight, when the knight will hassle the bishop on d3. After 7...♘c6 8 ♘f3 ♗xc5 9 0-0 ♗d7 10 c3 h6 11 b4 ♗b6 12 a4 a6 13 b5 axb5 14 axb5 ♖xa1 15 ♕xa1 ♘a5 16 ♕a4! ♗c5 17 ♖a1 b6 18 ♕g4 White had a strong initiative in Akopian-Naumkin, Vilnius 1988.

8 ♘f3 ♘xc5 9 0-0 ♗e7

On this or the next move Black should probably capture on d3. One recent example of such play was G.Mohr-Sulava, Croatian Cup 1997, which continued 9...♘xd3 10 cxd3 ♗d7 11 ♗g5 ♕a5 12 a3 ♖c8 13 ♖c1 ♖xc1 14 ♕xc1 h6 15 b4 ♕a6 16 ♗e3 ♗e7 17 ♕c7 ♗d8 18 ♕c5 b6 19 ♕d6 ♗e7 20 ♕b8+ ♗d8 21 ♕d6 ♗e7 and the players agreed a draw.

10 ♖e1 0-0

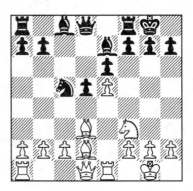

11 ♗f1!

No more chances! Now White's pawn wedge on e5 guarantees a nice space advantage.

11...♕b6 12 ♗c3 ♗d7 13 ♗d4 ♕c7 14 ♖e3 a5 15 ♖c1 b6 16 c3 a4 17 g3 ♗c6 18 h4 ♖ae8 19 ♗h3 ♘e4 20 ♘d2 f5 21 exf6 ♗xf6 22 ♗xf6 ♖xf6 23 ♘xe4 dxe4 24 ♕e1

Black has eliminated the e5-pawn, but is left saddled with a chronically weak pawn. As soon as this is rounded up, Black sees no reason to continue the game.

24...b5 25 ♖d1 ♗d5 26 a3 ♖ef8 27 ♖d2 ♖f3 28 ♗g2 ♖xe3 29 ♕xe3 ♕e5 30 ♖d4 1-0

Summary

The 3...♘f6 Tarrasch offers plenty of offbeat variations for both sides that are worth an outing. Of course, due preparation is advisable before venturing out with a new line.

1 e4 e6 2 d4 d5 3 ♘d2 ♘f6 4 e5

4...♘fd7

    4...♘e4

        5 ♘xe4 – *Game 30*; 5 ♗d3 – *Game 31*

5 ♗d3

    5 ♘gf3 c5

        6 c3 ♘c6 7 ♗d3 – see Games 27 and 28 (by transposition)

        6 c4 – *Game 29*

5...c5 6 c3 ♘c6

    6...b6 – *Game 26*

7 ♘e2

    7 ♘gf3 ♕b6 8 0-0 *(D)*

        8...cxd4 – *Game 27*

        8...g6 – *Game 28*

7...cxd4

    7...♕b6 8 ♘f3 cxd4 9 cxd4 f6 *(D)*

        10 exf6 ♘xf6 11 0-0 ♗d6 – *Games 16-20*

        10 ♘f4 – *Game 25*

8 cxd4 f6 *(D)*

    8...♘b6 – *Game 24*

9 exf6

    9 ♘f4 – *Game 23*

9...♕xf6 10 ♘f3 h6 11 0-0 ♗d6 12 ♗c2

    12 ♗b1 – *Game 22*

12...0-0 – *Game 21*

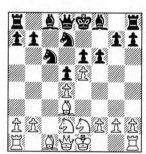

          8 0-0   *9...f6*   *8...f6*

CHAPTER FOUR

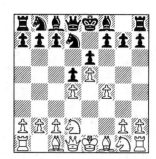

3...♘f6: The Big Pawn Front with 5 f4

1 e4 e6 2 d4 d5 3 ♘d2 ♘f6 4 e5 ♘fd7 5 f4

In many ways 5 f4 introduces White's most ambitious plan against 3...♘f6. He bolsters the e5-pawn and plans to develop his pieces behind an impressive centre, before slowly squashing Black on the kingside. That's the theory, and it happens quite a lot in practice too, but of course Black does have some moves too. The downside to 5 f4 (compared to 5 ♗d3) is that it doesn't contribute towards White's development. Consequently, Black can obtain quicker and more dangerous counterplay against the d4-pawn. Another facet of this line is that White is often forced to go on a little walk with his king, which is not to everyone's taste. Normally it would be completely safe behind that huge phalanx of pawns, but Games 32-34 show that Black does have some ingenious ways of causing a few problems. Game 35 sees a relatively new concept for White, the lavish 8 h4, which puts paid to any ...g7-g5 breaks.

In this line Black does better to play more quietly and try his luck on the queenside. Finally, Game 36 discusses the rare 7...♕a5, planning immediate queenside play with ...b7-b5-b4.

Game 32
Emms-Kosten
British Championship 1985

1 e4 e6 2 d4 d5 3 ♘d2 ♘f6 4 e5 ♘fd7 5 f4 c5 6 c3 ♘c6 7 ♘df3 cxd4 8 cxd4 ♕b6 9 g3 ♗b4+ 10 ♔f2 g5!?

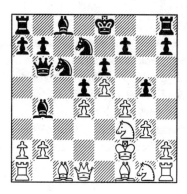

This move turned a few heads when it was first unleashed on the tournament circuit. White can capture in two ways, but neither move wins a pawn.

The more conventional 9...f6 is discussed in Game 34.

11 ♗e3

Dealing with the incidental threat of ...g5-g4. The main alternative 11 fxg5 is the subject of Game 33, while 11 h3 should be met by 11...gxf4. Vasiukov-M.Gurevich, Moscow 1987, continued 12 gxf4 f6 13 ♗e3 ♗e7!, when the combined ideas of ...♘f8-g6, ...♗d7 and ...0-0-0 ensure that Black has enough counterplay against the white centre.

11...f6

11...g4 is possible anyway, and may be even more reliable than 11...f6. Certainly Black seems to be doing okay after 12 ♘d2 f6 or 12 ♘h4 ♗e7.

12 ♗h3 0-0

This move is often preceded by the capture on e5. After 12...fxe5 13 fxe5 0-0 we have:

a) 14 ♗g4, which transposes to the main game.

b) 14 ♗xe6+ ♔h8 15 ♔g2 g4! and now:

b1) 16 ♗xg4 ♘dxe5 17 dxe5 (17 ♗xc8 ♘c4!) 17...♕xe3 18 ♗xc8 ♖axc8, when Black is extremely active.

b2) 16 ♘g5 ♘dxe5 17 ♕c2 ♘g6 18 h3 ♗e7! 19 ♘f7+ ♔g8! 20 ♘h6+ ♔g7 with a very unclear position in Eisen-Chapman, correspondence 1989.

c) 14 ♔e2!? (another king move, but one that does have its points) 14...♗e7 15 b3 ♘db8 16 ♗g4 ♗d7 17 ♘h3 h6 18 ♕b1, when White has avoided any catastrophes and therefore stands slightly better, as in Read-Wikman, correspondence 1993

d) 14 ♖c1!? ♔h8 15 ♗g4 ♗e7 16 ♕d2 and here Black should probably play 16...♗b4.

13 ♗g4

13 ♗xe6+ ♔h8 14 ♗xd5 would be a brave (some would say foolish) attempt at refuting Black's opening play. However, it is clear that after 14...fxe5 15 dxe5 ♗c5 16 ♕b3 gxf4 17 gxf4 ♘b4 Black develops some menacing play for the pawns.

13...fxe5 14 fxe5

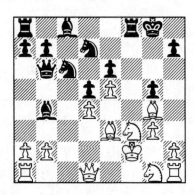

14...♗c5!!

This incredible idea was a suggestion of George Botterill, and was judged as one of the top theoretical novelties of the year by the prestigious *Chess Informant*. Since Botterill's suggestion had already been published in the *British Chess Magazine*, I was quite aware of it and had even dismissed it as good for White. Obviously I hadn't seen far enough.

15 ♗xe6+ ♔h8 16 dxc5 ♕xb2+ 17 ♗d2

see following diagram

17...g4!

This was the real shock. I had been

expecting 17...♘dxe5 18 ♗xc8 ♖axc8 19 ♔g2, when I don't think that Black has enough for the piece. Instead I was rudely awoken, and didn't react well to the new circumstances.

18 ♗xd5?

There are two other ways for White to continue the fight:

a) 18 ♗xg4 ♕d4+ 19 ♔g2 ♕xg4 20 ♗c3 ♘xc5 21 e6+ ♔g8 22 ♕xd5 ♘xe6 is given by Kosten as slightly better for Black.

b) 18 ♖b1! looks best. I can't find anything special for Black after 18...♕d4+ 19 ♗e3!, so perhaps 18...♕xe5 19 ♗xd7 ♕d4+ is stronger. Then 20 ♔g2 gxf3+ 21 ♘xf3 ♖xf3! 22 ♔xf3 ♗xd7 gives Black a strong attack. A safer path is 20 ♗e3 ♕xd1 21 ♖xd1 ♗xd7 22 ♖xd5 ♗e6, with a roughly equal endgame.

18...♘dxe5 19 ♗xc6

Giving up all the light squares, but 19 ♔g2 gxf3+ 20 ♘xf3 ♘xf3 21 ♗xf3 ♖d8 is just winning for Black. The rest of the game was not my greatest chess experience.

19...bxc6 20 ♖b1 ♕d4+ 21 ♗e3 ♘d3+ 22 ♔e2 gxf3+ 23 ♘xf3 ♕e4 24 ♕xd3

24...♗a6! 25 ♕xa6 ♕xf3+ 26 ♔d2 ♖fd8+ 27 ♔c2 ♕e4+ 28 ♔b2 ♖ab8+ 29 ♔a3 ♕xe3+ 30 ♖b3 ♕xc5+ 31 ♔b2 ♖d2+ 32 ♔b1 ♖xb3+ 0-1

After going so far, perhaps I should have allowed mate after 33 axb3 ♕c2+ 34 ♔a1 ♕b2.

Some openings just do not suit certain players. After this game I decided that I don't like wandering around with my king after just ten moves!

Game 33
Slobodjan-De la Villa Garcia
Pamplona 1996

---

1 e4 e6 2 d4 d5 3 ♘d2 ♘f6 4 e5 ♘fd7 5 f4 c5 6 c3 ♘c6 7 ♘df3 ♕b6 8 g3 cxd4 9 cxd4 ♗b4+ 10 ♔f2 g5 11 fxg5

The safest and hence the most popular way of dealing with 10...g5.

11...♘dxe5 12 ♘xe5 ♘xe5

---
see following diagram

---

13 ♗e3

Black can also answer 13 ♔g2 with 13...♘c4, e.g. 14 ♘f3 ♗d7 15 b3 ♘d6 16 ♗f4 ♘e4 17 ♖c1 ♗d6 with equality in Yakovich-Gleizerov, Russia 1987.

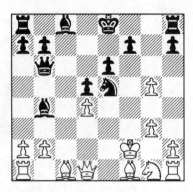

13...♘c4!

Naturally 13...♘c6 is also possible, but this seems to be the most reliable way of equalising. After the exchange on c4 Black can lay claim to many important light squares.

14 ♗xc4 dxc4 15 ♘f3 ♗d6 16 ♕c2 ♕c6 17 ♖he1 0-0

There also seems nothing wrong with the immediate 17...b5, planning 18...♗b7.

18 ♗f4 b5 19 ♗xd6 ♗b7! 20 ♕e4 ♕xe4 21 ♖xe4 ♗xe4 ½-½

After 21...♗xe4 22 ♗xf8 ♔xf8 it is about equal, although there is still plenty of fight left in the position.

Game 34
Mohrlok-Schrancz
Correspondence 1989

---

1 e4 e6 2 d4 d5 3 ♘d2 ♘f6 4 e5 ♘fd7 5 c3 c5 6 f4 ♘c6 7 ♘df3 cxd4 8 cxd4 ♕b6 9 g3 f6

Before the discovery of 10...g5, this was Black's most risky and challenging try against 5 f4. Black is prepared to sacrifice a piece in order to destroy White's central pawn cover. Note that the move order is quite interchange-able. For example, Black often goes 7...♕b6 8 g3 f6 9 ♗h3 cxd4 10 cxd4, reaching the same position.

10 ♗h3 fxe5 11 fxe5 ♗b4+ 12 ♔f1 0-0 13 ♔g2 ♘dxe5!?

Black strikes before his opponent can consolidate his position.

14 dxe5 ♘xe5

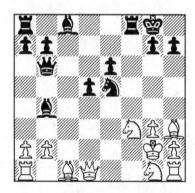

15 ♕e2!

This has been shown to be the only real major test of Black's sacrifice. Against other lines Black seems to be holding his own at least.

a) 15 ♕b3 ♗c5 16 ♕xb6 ♗xb6 17 ♗f4 ♘d3 18 ♗d6 19 ♖f1 e5! 20 ♗xe5 (20 ♘xe5?? ♘e1+! 21 ♖xe1 ♖f2 is mate) 20...♗xh3+ 21 ♘xh3 ♖e8! 22 ♖e1 ♖fe7! and Black regained the piece in Smagin-Rosjak, Skopje 1987.

b) 15 ♗f4 ♘g6 16 ♖c1? (16 ♘e2 looks stronger) 16...♖xf4! 17 gxf4 ♘xf4+ 18 ♔f1 ♗d7 19 a4 ♖f8 and White didn't last very long in Yasseen-Moran, Dubai Olympiad 1986.

15...♘xf3

15...♘c4 16 b3 ♗c3 17 ♖b1 seems to favour White, e.g. 17...♗f6 18 ♕c2 ♘d6 (or 18...♘e3+ 19 ♗xe3 ♕xe3 20 ♖e1 with a clear edge) 19 ♗a3 ♖d8 20 ♗xd6 ♖xd6 21 ♖e1 ♗d7 22 ♘e5! ♗xe5 23 ♖xe5 ♖c8 24 ♕d2 ♖dc6 25 ♖e2 and White had consolidated his extra piece in Eisen-Onoda, correspondence 1990.

16 ♘xf3 e5 17 ♗xc8 ♖axc8 18 ♘xe5 ♕e6 19 ♗f4 ♖f5 20 ♖ac1

20...♖cf8

Following a suggestion of Knaak's. 20...♖e8 21 ♕b5! was also good for White in Ermenkov-Knaak, Bulgaria-East Germany 1983. Instead, damage limitation can be achieved with 20...♖xc1 21 ♖xc1 g5 22 ♖c7! (22 ♕g4 ♖xe5 23 ♖c8+ ♗f8! 24 ♕xe6+ ♖xe6 25 ♗xg5 ♔f7 is equal) 22...♗d6 23 ♖xb7 ♗xe5 24 ♗d2!, which Mohrlok assesses as only slightly better for White.

21 ♕e3!

This is stronger than Knaak's 21 h4, and puts a big question mark over the merit of Black's previous move.

21...g5 22 ♘g4 ♕g6 23 ♗e5 h5 24 ♖c7! hxg4 25 ♖g7+ ♕xg7 26 ♗xg7 ♖f2+

26...♔xg7 is stronger, but the simple pawn snatch 27 ♕xa7 still gives White a clear plus. The rest is easy.

27 ♕xf2 ♖xf2+ 28 ♔xf2 ♗c5+ 29 ♔e2 ♔xg7 30 ♖d1 d4 31 ♖c1 b6 32 a3 a5 33 ♔d3 1-0

Game 35
Beliavsky-Kindermann
Munich 1991

---

1 e4 e6 2 d4 d5 3 ♘d2 ♘f6 4 e5 ♘fd7 5 f4 c5 6 c3 ♘c6 7 ♘df3 ♕b6 8 h4!? cxd4 9 cxd4 ♗b4+ 10 ♔f2 f6

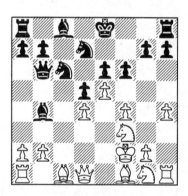

11 ♗e3! ♗e7 12 ♕d2!

This is more accurate than 12 ♖b1, e.g. 12...a5 13 ♘e2 0-0 14 ♘g3 fxe5 15 fxe5 and now Black can try the typical sacrifice 15...♘dxe5! 16 dxe5 d4 17 ♗d2 ♘xe5.

12...0-0 13 ♖d1 a5!

Brutal attempts do not work here. After 13...fxe5 14 fxe5 ♘dxe5 15 dxe5 d4 White holds on to the e5-pawn

with 16 ♗f4! ♗b4 17 ♕c1. 13...a5! is
an excellent long-term move. Black
sees the queenside as the area of counterplay, and so he starts to claim some
space on that side. It just remains to
block the kingside at the most desirable moment.

14 ♔g3 a4 15 ♗d3 ♕d8 16 ♘e2 f5

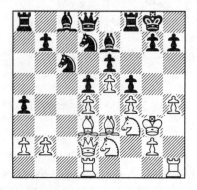

We now enter a heavy manoeuvring
stage of the game, where Black's
chances are not worse.

**17 h5 ♘b6 18 ♔f2 ♘b4 19 ♗b1
♘c4 20 ♕c3 ♗d7 21 a3 ♘c6 22
♖dg1 b5 23 g4 b4 24 axb4 a3! 25
gxf5 exf5 26 ♗a2 ♗e6 27 ♘g5 ♕d7
28 ♘xe6 ♕xe6 29 ♗xc4 ♗xb4 30
♕c2 dxc4 31 bxa3 ♗xa3 32 ♗d2
♖fd8 33 ♗c3 ♗e7 34 ♕d2 ♕d5 35
♖h3 ♖a3 36 ♕c2 ♕e6 37 ♖h2 ♖da8
38 ♖b1 ♖b3 39 ♖d1 ♕d5 40 ♕xf5
♖a2 41 ♕h3 ♘b4 42 ♔g1 ♘d3 43
♕c8+ ♗f8 44 e6 ♖a8?**

44...♖xe2! would have capped off an
excellent positional performance from
the German grandmaster. After 45
♖xe2 ♘xf4 46 e7 ♘xe2+ 47 ♔f2 ♕f7+
Black is winning, e.g. 48 ♔xe2 ♕xe7+
49 ♔d2 ♕g5+ 50 ♔c2 ♕g2+ 51 ♖d2
♕e4+ 52 ♔d1 ♖b1 mate. 44...♖a8 allows White to scrape half a point.

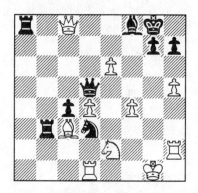

**45 ♕d7 ♕xd7 46 exd7 ♖b7 47 h6
♖xd7 48 hxg7 ♖xg7+ 49 ♖g2 ♖a2
50 ♖d2 ♖xd2 51 ♗xd2 ♔f7 52
♖xg7+ ♗xg7 53 ♔g2 ♔e6 ½-½**

**1 e4 e6 2 d4 d5 3 ♘d2 ♘f6 4 e5
♘fd7 5 c3 c5 6 f4 ♘c6 7 ♘df3 ♕a5**

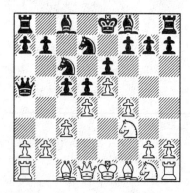

Adding pressure to the centre by
pinning the c-pawn. This move was
popular in the seventies, but is hardly
ever seen nowadays. Another quieter
move is the blocking 7...f5. Ye Jiang-
chuan-Short, Lucerne 1989, continued
8 ♗d3 cxd4 9 cxd4 ♗e7 10 ♘e2 ♘b6

11 h3 0-0 12 g4 (Ye recommends 12 a3! a5 13 b3, planning to meet 13...a4 with 14 b4) 12...a5 13 a4 ♘b4 14 ♗b1 ♗d7, and Black's queenside counterplay was well under way.

8 ♗e3 b5 9 dxc5 b4

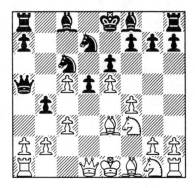

10 ♘d4

This move, a big novelty at the time, has put the whole line to rest. Previously 10 a3 had been the main move, but Black gets sufficient play with the pawn sacrifice 10...b3! 11 ♕xb3 ♗xc5.

10...♕xc5

Or 10...♗b7 11 a3! bxc3 12 b4 ♕d8 13 ♘gf3, when the c3-pawn will soon die and Black will be swamped by the mass of queenside pawns.

11 ♕a4 bxc3

11...♗b7 is powerfully met by 12 ♗b5, so Black is forced into a ropey piece sacrifice.

12 ♕xc6 cxb2 13 ♖b1 ♕a3 14 ♔f2 ♖b8 15 f5 ♗b7 16 ♕c7 ♗a6 17 ♕xa7 ♕xa2 18 ♘gf3 ♗c4

18...♕xb1 loses to 19 ♗b5!

19 ♕xa2 ♗xa2 20 ♗b5 ♗a3 21 fxe6 fxe6 22 ♘xe6 ♗xb1 23 ♖xb1 ♔e7 24 ♘ed4

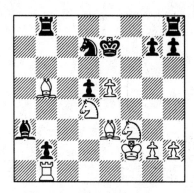

Black has managed to regain some of his lost material, but now the four White minor pieces run rampant, creating deadly threats around the black king.

24...♖hc8 25 ♘c6+ ♖xc6 26 ♗xc6 ♖c8 27 ♗g5+ ♔e6 28 ♘d4+ ♔xe5 29 ♗xd7 ♖c1 30 ♘f3+ ♔d6 31 ♗f5 ♗c5+ 1-0

Summary

It seems that Black has several ways of creating enough confusion against White's impressive looking centre. As of yet, no real answer has been found to 10...g5, and this is probably the single biggest reason for the decline in popularity of 5 f4.

1 e4 e6 2 d4 d5 3 ♘d2 ♘f6 4 e5 ♘fd7 5 f4 c5 6 c3 ♘c6 7 ♘df3

7...♕b6 *(D)*
> 7...♕a5 – *Game 36*

8 g3
> 8 h4 – *Game 35*

8...cxd4 9 cxd4 ♗b4+ *(D)*
> 9...f6 – *Game 34*

10 ♔f2 g5 11 ♗e3 *(D)*
> 11 fxg5 – *Game 33*

11...f6 – *Game 32*

7...♕b6

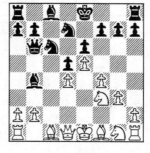

9...♗b4+

11 ♗e3

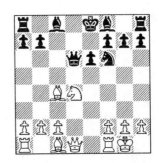

CHAPTER FIVE

3...c5 4 exd5 ♕xd5:
Main Line with 10 ♘xd4

1 e4 e6 2 d4 d5 3 ♘d2 c5 4 exd5 ♕xd5 5 ♘gf3 cxd4 6 ♗c4 ♕d6 7 0-0 ♘f6 8 ♘b3 ♘c6 9 ♘bxd4 ♘xd4 10 ♘xd4

This is one of the most important positions in the whole of the French Tarrasch. White has a clear development advantage and he will attempt to utilise this in order to build up a large initiative, while Black's main trump card is his pawn structure, including the 4-3 majority on the kingside. Often White's attempts at a direct attack crash disastrously against this solid defensive wall of pawns. Black also tries to gain time by developing with tempo (e.g. ...♕c7, attacking c4, and ...♗d6, hitting the h2-pawn). From humble beginnings this variation is now firmly established as a favourite defence of some of the world's leading players.

From the starting position of the main line Black has two main options, 10...a6 and 10...♗d7. Both moves prepare a later ...♕c7 and ....♗d6, but 10...a6 (Games 37-42) has generally been the choice of most of the top players, as it eliminates any ♘b5 ideas for White. Play can then become extremely sharp, as illustrated by the number of crazy games in this section. The theory in certain positions has even spiralled out of all proportions. For example, in Games 37 and 38 powerful novelties late on have dramatically altered the assessments of whole variations.

10...♗d7 (Games 43-45) usually leads to quieter positions where Black has less chance of being rolled over, but White often secures the long-term advantage of the bishop pair. That said, there is also plenty of scope here for both sides to liven up the proceedings.

Game 37
Bowden-Levitt
England 1997

1 e4 e6 2 d4 d5 3 ♘d2 c5 4 ♘gf3 cxd4 5 exd5 ♕xd5 6 ♗c4 ♕d6 7 0-0 ♘f6 8 ♘b3 ♘c6 9 ♘bxd4 ♘xd4 10

♘xd4 a6 11 ♖e1

White's main alternatives here, 11 ♗b3 and 11 b3, are considered in Games 41 and 42 respectively.

11...♕c7

The slower 11...♗d7 is the subject of Game 40.

12 ♗b3 ♗d6 13 ♘f5!?

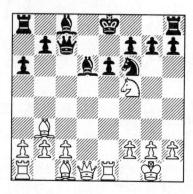

This concept is well known here. White readily sacrifices material for an attack against the black king. Despite the fact that it has been tested in numerous grandmaster games, no firm conclusions have yet been reached.

The quiet 13 h3 causes Black fewer problems, as we shall see in Game 39.

13...♗xh2+ 14 ♔h1 0-0 15 ♘xg7! ♖d8!

Apparently this defensive resource was Kasparov's discovery. Earlier this whole line had been deemed dubious for Black on account of 15...♔xg7 16 ♕d4 (planning ♕h4 and ♗h6+) 16...e5 17 ♕h4 ♘g4 18 f3 ♕d8 19 ♗g5 f6 20 ♗c1! and Black is in trouble. Emms-W.Lowe, Halifax Open 1991, continued 20...♕d4 21 fxg4 ♗f4 22 c3 ♕c5 23 ♗xf4 exf4 24 ♖ad1 and White had a winning advantage.

16 ♕f3 ♔xg7 17 ♗h6+ ♔g6

Not 17...♔xh6 18 ♕xf6+ ♔h5 19 ♖e3, when Black can safely resign.

18 c3 ♘h5

Clearing the way for the f-pawn. We shall look at the other major defence (18...♘d5) in the next game.

19 ♗c1

Following Michael Adams's recipe (see below). This move, threatening ♕g4+, has the advantage of not blocking the e-file, which can be vital in many variations. However, Jonathan Levitt had prepared an extremely significant novelty. The other critical line is 19 ♗e3, as played by Sergei Rublevsky (Rublevsky has worked with Kasparov, so on that evidence alone we must take this move seriously!):

a) Levitt's 19...♗f4 is still possible, but not quite so effective, as after 20 g4 ♘g3+ 21 fxg3 ♗xe3 22 ♕xe3 White's pieces are better co-ordinated than in the main game. In particular, the white queen patrols the dark squares around the black king. Nevertheless, Black still seems to be just about okay. For example, 22...h6 23 ♗c2+ ♔g7 24 g5 h5 25 ♖ad1 b6 26 ♕f4 ♗b7+ 27 ♔h2 ♕xf4 28 gxf4 ♗f3 29 ♖d3 ♗g4 30 ♔g3 f6 31 ♖ee3 ½-½ was the conclusion of Forster-Levitt, Hastings 1997.

b) 19...f5 20 g4 ♘f6 21 gxf5+ exf5 22 ♕g2+ ♘g4 23 f3 ♗d7 (23...b6!? should be considered, as developing the bishop on b7 prevents ♖e6xc6 ideas) 24 ♗d4 ♕g3 25 fxg4 ♗c6 26 ♖e6+ ♔g5 27 ♖xc6 bxc6 28 ♕xh2 ♕xh2+ 29 ♔xh2 fxg4 30 ♖f1 ♖f8 31 ♗f7! (setting up a mating net) 31...♖ab8 32 ♔g3 ♖xf7 33 ♖xf7 and White won easily in Rublevsky-S.Ivanov, Elista 1997. No doubt the last word hasn't been spoken here yet.

19...♗f4!

In Adams-McDonald, England 4NCL 1997, Black played 19...f5 20 g4 b5?!, but after 21 gxh5+ ♔g7 22 ♕g2+ ♔f7 23 ♕h3 Adams won comfortably. Of course 20...♘f6 is more challenging, but White can win brilliantly with 21 ♗xe6 ♗xe6 22 ♖xe6 ♔f7 23 ♗g5!! ♔xe6 24 ♕xf5+ ♔d6 25 ♕xf6+ ♔c5 26 b4+ ♔b5 27 a4+ ♔c4 28 ♕e6+ ♔d3 (or 28...♖d5 29 ♕e4+) 29 ♕e3+ ♔c4 30 ♕e2+ ♖d3 (30...♔b3 31 ♕a2+ ♔xc3 32 ♖c1+ and 30...♔d5 31 ♖d1+ ♔c6 32 ♕c4+ ♔b6 33 ♗e3+ also wins for White) 31 ♖a3! and Black must give up the rook to prevent ♕a2 mate.

20 g4

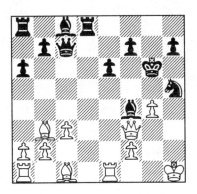

20...♘g3+!

This inventive move changes the entire complexion of the position. Black gives back the extra piece, but in return he receives relative king safety and time to complete development. Added to this, White's own king also suffers from too much air. If anything, I prefer Black.

21 fxg3 ♗xc1 22 ♖axc1 b6 23 ♗c2+ ♔g7 24 ♗e4 ♖b8 25 ♖f1 ♕e7 26 g5 ♗b7 27 ♖ce1 ♖d2 28 ♕f6+ ♕xf6 29 gxf6+ ♔h6

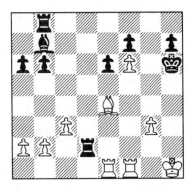

The weakness on f6, coupled with Black's active rook on d2, add up to a decisive advantage for Black.

30 ♖f4 ♗xe4+ 31 ♖exe4 ♖bd8 32 ♖b4 b5 33 ♔g1 ♔g6 34 ♖f1 ♖8d5 35 ♖f2 ♖xf2 36 ♔xf2 a5 37 ♖g4+ ♔xf6 38 ♔e3 h5 39 ♖f4+ ♖f5 40 ♖h4 ♖g5 41 ♔f3 ♖f5+ 42 ♔e3 ♔g5 43 b4 ♖e5+ 44 ♔d3 ♖d5+ 45 ♔e3 axb4 46 ♖xb4 f5 47 a3 e5 48 c4 bxc4 49 ♖xc4 e4 50 ♖c8 ♖d3+ 51 ♔f2 ♖xa3 52 ♖g8+ ♔f6 53 ♖h8 ♖a2+ 54 ♔g1 ♔e5 55 ♖xh5 e3 56 ♖h8 ♔e4 57 ♖f8 ♖a1+ 58 ♔g2 e2 59 ♖e8+ ♔d3 0-1

A well played game and an important theoretical battle.

Game 38
Adams-Dreev
Wijk aan Zee 1996

1 e4 e6 2 d4 d5 3 ♘d2 c5 4 exd5
♕xd5 5 ♘gf3 cxd4 6 ♗c4 ♕d6 7 0-0
♘f6 8 ♘b3 ♘c6 9 ♘bxd4 ♘xd4 10
♘xd4 a6 11 ♖e1 ♕c7 12 ♗b3 ♗d6
13 ♘f5!? ♗xh2+ 14 ♔h1 0-0 15
♘xg7! ♖d8! 16 ♕f3 ♔xg7 17 ♗h6+
♔g6 18 c3 ♘d5 19 ♖ad1!

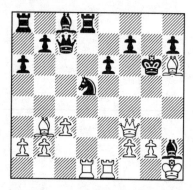

A fantastic suggestion from Jon
Speelman which completely changed
the theoretical opinion of 18...♘d5.

The point is that 19...♔xh6 is impossible due to 20 ♖xd5! and now:

a) 20...exd5 21 ♕f6+ ♔h5 22 ♗d1+
♗g4 23 ♗xg4+ ♔xg4 24 f3+ ♔g3 25
♕g5+ ♔f2 26 ♕e3+ ♔g3 27 f4+ ♔g4
28 ♕h3+ ♔xf4 29 ♕xh2+ and 30
♕xc7.

b) 20...♖xd5 21 ♕f6+ ♔h5 22 ♖e3
and Black can resign.

Also losing is 19...♗e5 20 ♗c1
(another point of 19 ♖ad1 – the bishop
can return to c1 without disconnecting the rooks) 20...f5 21 c4 ♘b4 22
♖xd8 ♕xd8 23 ♖xe5 ♘d3 24 ♕g3+.
19...f5 20 ♗c1 ♗d6 21 ♗xd5 exd5

22 ♖xd5

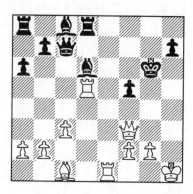

White is already winning. Basically
Black cannot cope with the direct
threats of ♖d1 and ♕h3.
22...♗d7 23 ♕h3 ♗f8

No defence works, e.g. 23...f4 24
♖e6+ ♗xe6 25 ♕xe6+ ♔g7 26 ♖g5+
mates, while 23...h5 24 ♕h4 and
23...♗f4 24 ♖e7 h5 25 ♖exd7 are also
terminal.
24 ♖e3 ♔g7 25 ♖g3+ ♔h8 26 ♕h4!

26...♗e6 27 ♗f4 ♗e7 28 ♗xc7 1-0

Game 39
Jansa-Brunner
Bad Wörishofen 1989

1 e4 e6 2 d4 d5 3 ♘d2 c5 4 ♘gf3

cxd4 5 exd5 ♕xd5 6 ♗c4 ♕d6 7 0-0
♘f6 8 ♘b3 ♘c6 9 ♖e1 a6 10 ♘bxd4
♘xd4 11 ♘xd4 ♕c7 12 ♗b3 ♗d6 13
h3 0-0 14 ♗g5 b5!

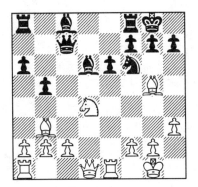

A popular idea. Black readily accepts a weakened pawn structure on
the kingside, knowing that the bishop
pair and the half-open g-file will pres-
ent him with more than enough compensation. Naturally White has no
need to capture on f6, but then Black
would simply continue ...♗b7, reaching a comfortable position.
15 ♗xf6 gxf6 16 ♕h5 ♗b7 17 c3
♔h8 18 ♕h6 ♖g8! 19 ♕xf6+ ♖g7

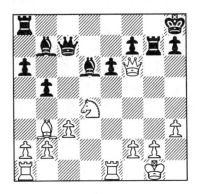

Black's dangerous initiative is worth
at least a pawn. Note that White's earlier h2-h3 has presented fresh prob-

lems, as 20 g3 can be simply answered
by 20...♗xg3 with a mating attack.
20 f3 ♖ag8 21 g4 ♕c5 22 ♔g2 ♗c7
23 ♖e2 ♕d6 24 ♖h1 a5!

Black temporarily concentrates on
the queenside, with the aim of de-
stroying the support for the knight on
d4. Now 25 ♘xb5 runs into 25...♕g3+
26 ♔f1 ♗d8!, trapping the queen.
25 ♗c2 b4 26 ♗d3 a4 27 h4

Understandably White is desperate
for counterplay, but this move seriously weakens the pawn on g4.
27...♗d8 28 ♕e5 ♕xe5 29 ♖xe5
♖xg4+ 30 ♔f1 ♖f4

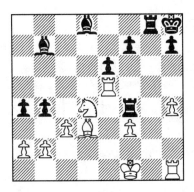

Black's strategy has been a complete
success. The rest of the game is not
significant.
31 ♖h5 f5 32 ♔e2 ♗b6 33 ♖f1
♗xd4 34 cxd4 ♖xd4 35 ♖h6? ♖xd3
36 ♔xd3 ♗a6+ 37 ♔e3 ♗xf1 38
♖xe6 ♖g2 39 ♖e8+ ♔g7 40 ♖a8 a3
41 bxa3 ♖xa2 42 ♖a7+ ♔g6 43 h5+
♔xh5 0-1

Game 40
Adams-Speelman
England 1991

---

1 e4 e6 2 d4 d5 3 ♘d2 c5 4 exd5

♕xd5 5 ♘gf3 cxd4 6 ♗c4 ♕d6 7 0-0
♘f6 8 ♘b3 ♘c6 9 ♘bxd4 ♘xd4 10
♘xd4 a6 11 ♖e1 ♗d7 12 c3 ♕c7

13 ♗b3

13 ♕e2 is less flexible, but nevertheless quite playable. The game Emms-
Danielian, Cappelle la Grande 1994,
continued 13...♗d6 14 ♗g5 (14 h3 is
obviously also possible) 14...0-0-0! (this
strong and natural move was new at
the time. As soon as I saw it could be
played, I knew my opponent would
oblige. Previously 14...0-0 had been
tried, but note that 14...♗xh2+ is too
risky: 15 ♔h1 ♗f4 16 ♗xf6 gxf6 17
♗xe6! fxe6 18 ♘xe6 ♗xe6 19 ♕xe6+
♔f8 20 ♕xf6+ ♔g8 21 ♖e7 is winning
for White) 15 ♘f3 h6 16 ♗h4 ♗c6 17
♘e5 ♗xe5 18 ♕xe5 ♕xe5 19 ♖xe5 g5
20 ♗g3 ♘e4! and I was frantically try-
ing to equalise.

13...0-0-0

A different option is to castle kingside after 13...♗d6 14 h3 0-0. Then a
surprising sequence can arise with 15
♗g5, e.g. 15...♗f4 16 ♗xf6 gxf6 17
♕h5 ♔h8 18 ♗c2 f5 19 ♘xf5! exf5 20
♖e7 ♕c6 21 ♖xd7 ♖g8! 22 g4! ♕xd7 23
♗xf5 ♗h2+! 24 ♔xh2 ♕d6+ 25 ♔g1
♖g7

when the bishop and two pawns
cancel out the rook. After 26 ♗c2
♕b6 27 ♗b3 ♕g6 the chances were
roughly equal in Hünerkopf-Luther,
Munich 1992.

14 ♕e2 ♗d6 15 h3 ♔b8?!

Given that Black soon runs into
trouble, perhaps he should consider
beginning kingside operations immediately with 15...h6 or 15...♖hg8.

16 a4 h6 17 ♗e3 ♖he8 18 ♘f3!

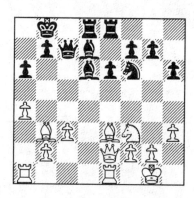

With the idea of a4-a5, when White
threatens ♗b6. It is now clear that
White's attack will come first.

**18...♗c6 19 a5 ♘d7 20 ♘d4 ♗e4
21 ♗a4 e5 22 ♘c2 ♗c6 23 ♗xc6
♕xc6 24 ♘b4! ♗xb4 25 cxb4 ♘f6
26 ♖ac1 ♕a4**

The last chance was 26...♕b5.
27 ♕c4 ♘d5 28 ♗b6 ♘xb6 29 ♕c7+ ♔a8 30 axb6

Black's back-rank weaknesses are absolutely fatal.

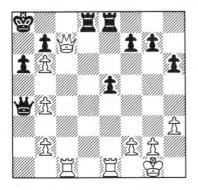

30...♕d7 31 ♖xe5 ♖f8 32 b5 1-0

After 32...♕xc7 33 bxc7 ♖c8 34 b6 and White can win at leisure.

Game 41
Svidler-Glek
Haifa 1996

---

1 e4 e6 2 d4 d5 3 ♘d2 c5 4 ♘gf3 cxd4 5 exd5 ♕xd5 6 ♗c4 ♕d6 7 0-0 ♘f6 8 ♘b3 ♘c6 9 ♘bxd4 ♘xd4 10 ♘xd4 a6 11 ♗b3 ♗d7

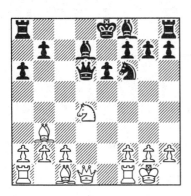

Keeping the pressure on d4.

11...♕c7 can transpose to the main lines after 12 ♖e1. White also has the independent try 12 ♕f3, but after 12...♗d6 13 h3 0-0 14 ♗g5 ♘d7 15 c3 b5 16 ♖ad1 ♘c5! 17 ♗c2 ♗b7 18 ♕h5 ♗e4 Black exchanged the dangerous bishop and had no problems in Hellers-Hübner, Wijk aan Zee 1986.

12 c3 ♕c7

Also possible is 12...0-0-0 13 ♖e1 ♕c7 14 ♕e2 ♗d6 15 h3, transposing to the previous game.

13 ♗g5 h5!?

Black has three alternatives here:

a) 13...♘e4 14 ♗h4 ♕f4 15 g3 ♕h6 16 ♕e2 ♘d6 and now Glek gives 17 ♕e5, intending 17...f6? 18 ♘xe6!! fxe5 19 ♘c7 mate.

b) 13...♗d6 14 ♗xf6 gxf6 15 ♕h5 ♕c5 16 ♕f3 ♕e5 17 g3 0-0-0 18 ♖fe1 ♕g5 19 ♗c4!, with the idea ♗f1-g2, when White had an edge in Kudrin-Remlinger, Philadelphia 1992.

c) 13...0-0-0 14 ♗xf6 gxf6 15 ♕h5 ♗e8 with a small plus for White.

14 ♕f3 ♗d6 15 h3 ♗h2+ 16 ♔h1 ♗e5 17 ♖fe1 0-0-0 18 ♖ad1 ♖dg8?!

This looks a little peculiar. Given that Black never really gets going with his attack, the rook remains largely redundant here.

19 ♕e3!

A very powerful move. White's queen eyes the dark squares on the queenside and may be able to jump to a7 at some point.

19...♗d6 20 ♘f3 ♗c5 21 ♕d2 ♘g4 22 ♗f4!

The strongest move of the game. White sacrifices a pawn, but calculates that the forthcoming attack will prove decisive.

22...♘xf2+ 23 ♔h2 ♕d8 24 ♖e5 ♗b6 25 ♕d6

Threatening ♕b8 mate.

25...♘xd1

25...♗c7 leads to an amazing position after 26 ♖c5 ♗c6 27 ♖xc6!! bxc6 28 ♕xc6 ♘xd1 29 ♘d4!! (Har-Zvi).

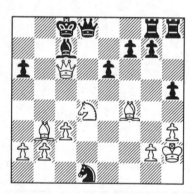

Despite his material advantage of two rooks for a bishop, Black is completely helpless against White's variety of threats.

26 ♖c5+ ♗c6

Or 26...♗xc5 27 ♕b8 mate.

27 ♖xc6+ bxc6 28 ♕xc6+ ♕c7

28...♕c7 looks good, until one realises that after 29 ♘d4 we have transposed to the note to 25...♘xd1.

29 ♗xc7 ♗xc7+ 30 ♔g1 ♖d8 31

♕xa6+ ♔b8 32 ♘d4!

The game as a contest is over. The black king is just too open.

32...♖d6 33 ♘c6+ ♖xc6 34 ♕xc6 ♖d8 35 ♗c2 ♖d6 36 ♕e8+ ♖d8 37 ♕b5+ ♔c8 38 ♕a6+ 1-0

An irresistible attacking display from Svidler. It seems that Black was lost after the casual 18...♖dg8.

Game 42
G.Timoshenko-Danielian
Cappelle la Grande 1994

---

1 e4 e6 2 d4 d5 3 ♘d2 c5 4 exd5 ♕xd5 5 ♘gf3 cxd4 6 ♗c4 ♕d6 7 0-0 ♘f6 8 ♘b3 ♘c6 9 ♘bxd4 ♘xd4 10 ♘xd4 a6 11 b3 ♕c7 12 ♗b2 ♗d6 13 ♘f3 b6!?

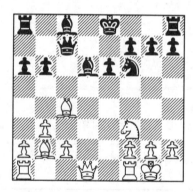

I like this move. Previously 13...b5 had been the choice, when after 14 ♗d3 ♗b7 15 ♖e1 0-0 16 ♘e5 ♖ad8 17 ♕e2 ♘d5! 18 ♕g4 f5 19 ♕h4 ♘b4 20 ♖e2 ♘xd3 21 ♘xd3 ♗e4 22 ♖ae1 ♖fe8 Black was equal in Tiviakov-Psakhis, Rostov na Donu 1993. 13...b6 is more enterprising, as with White's bishops pointing menacingly towards the kingside, it seems logical for Black to castle on the other side of the board.

13...b6 permits this without allowing White to open up the position with a2-a4.

14 ♖e1 ♗b7 15 ♗d3

15 ♗xe6 fxe6 16 ♖xe6+ looks enticing, but after the simple 16...♔d7 I can't find a decent way to continue the attack.

15...♘d5!

Offering a long-term pawn sacrifice, since after 16 ♗xg7 ♖g8 17 ♗b2 ♘f4 18 g3 ♘xd3 19 ♕xd3 0-0-0 Black has play down the half-open g-file and a dominating bishop on the long diagonal. All in all, this amounts to excellent compensation for the pawn.

16 a4 0-0-0 17 g3 ♔b8 18 ♗xg7?

White's position was already nothing to write home about, so I imagine Timoshenko's philosophy was that he may as well have a pawn for his troubles. Unfortunately, this runs into some real danger.

18...♖hg8 19 ♗e5 ♗xe5 20 ♘xe5 f6 21 ♘c4 ♘c3 22 ♕h5 ♕c6

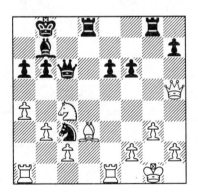

The diagram says it all. White can hardly hope to survive this position.

23 f3 ♖g5 24 ♕h3 ♖xd3 25 cxd3 ♕xf3 26 ♘d6 ♖h5 27 ♕f1 ♕h1+ 28 ♔f2 ♕f3+ 29 ♔g1 ♕h1+ 30 ♔f2

♕xh2+ 31 ♔e3 ♖e5+ 32 ♘e4 ♘d5+ **0-1**

33 ♔d4 ♕b2+ 34 ♔c4 ♖xe4+ 35 dxe4 ♕c3 is mate.

A pleasing game from the Armenian; 13...b6 looks like a very useful move.

Game 43
Emms-Bibby
British Championship 1990

---

1 e4 e6 2 d4 d5 3 ♘d2 c5 4 ♘gf3 cxd4 5 exd5 ♕xd5 6 ♗c4 ♕d6 7 0-0 ♘f6 8 ♘b3 ♘c6 9 ♘bxd4 ♘xd4 10 ♘xd4 ♗d7

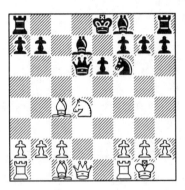

This is slightly more solid looking than 10...a6.

11 c3

The normal move here. 11 b3 is considered in Game 45.

11...♕c7 12 ♕e2 0-0-0

The quieter 12...♗d6 is the subject of the next game.

13 a4!

The most direct and the best move. White simply wants to play ♘b5, which would encourage a favourable exchange and open the a-file for his queen's rook.

13...h5

Black has two other attacking possibilities here:

a) 13...♗d6 14 g3! (after the exchange on b5, White will have ample control of the light squares, so this move doesn't really weaken the kingside; and in any case Black seems to be okay after 14 h3 ♗h2+ 15 ♔h1 ♗f4) 14...h5 15 ♘b5 ♗xb5 16 axb5 b6 17 ♖a4! (the rook usefully patrols the fourth rank, for both attack and defence) 17...♔b8? (17...h4 is better, although White still maintains an edge with 18 ♕f3) 18 ♗g5! and White was better in Adams-Djurhuus, Oakham 1992.

b) 13...♘g4 14 g3 h5 15 ♗g5! ♖e8 16 ♘b5 ♕c5 17 ♗f4 ♗xb5 18 ♗xb5 ♖d8 19 b4 1-0 was the sharp finish to Rachels-Rahman, Los Angeles 1991.

14 h3

The immediate 14 ♘b5 ♗xb5 15 axb5 also gives White a plus, e.g.

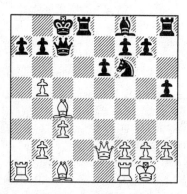

a) 15...♗c5 16 ♖a4! ♔b8 (16...♘g4 17 g3! – Djurhuus) 17 g3 e5 18 ♗e3 h4 19 ♖fa1 hxg3 20 hxg3 ♖h3 21 ♗xc5 ♕xc5 22 b4 ♕d6 23 ♖xa7 e4 24 ♕e3 was winning for White in S.Pedersen-Djurhuus, Oslo 1992.

b) 15...♘g4 16 g3 ♗c5 17 ♔g2 (17 ♖a4 is also good, transposing to the last note) 17...♔b8 18 ♖a4 ♖he8?! (the more direct 18...e5, intending ...f7-f5 and ...h5-h4, suggests itself as an improvement) 19 h3 ♘f6 20 ♗g5 ♖d7 21 ♖fa1 ♘d5 22 ♗xd5! ♖xd5 23 ♗f4 e5 24 b4 ♕d7 25 ♗g5 ♗b6 26 c4 ♖d3 27 c5 ♕xb5 28 ♔h2! ♗c7 29 ♖xa7 ♔c8 30 ♖a8+ ♗b8 31 ♖d1 and Black resigned in Adams-Lautier, Biel 1991, as 31...e4 allows 32 ♗f4.

14...♗d6

Or 14...♗c5 15 b4 ♗xd4 16 cxd4 ♔b8 17 b5 ♖c8 18 ♗d3 ♘d5 19 ♕f3 f5 20 a5 with a readymade attack in Kosashvili-Djurhuus, Santiago 1990.

15 ♘b5 ♗xb5 16 axb5 ♗c5 17 ♕f3 ♘g4?

This runs into trouble. A stronger alternative is 17...♕e5. For example, 18 ♗f4 ♕e4 19 ♕xe4 ♘xe4 20 ♗e3!? ♗xe3 (20...♔b8!?) 21 fxe3 ♘d2 22 ♖xf7 ♘xc4 23 ♖xa7 ♘d6?? (23...♘b6 24 ♖axb7 ♖d7 25 ♖bxd7 ♘xd7 26 ♖xg7 is unclear) 24 ♖a8 mate, Emms-Gunter, London (rapidplay) 1997.

18 ♗f4 e5 19 ♗g3 ♘xf2 20 ♗xf2

This is adequate for an advantage, but 20 ♕f5+! would have been even stronger, e.g. 20...♔b8 (or 20...♖d7 21 ♗xf2 ♗xf2+ 22 ♖xf2 ♕xc4 23 ♖xa7) 21 ♗xf2 ♗xf2+ 22 ♖xf2 ♕xc4 23 ♕xe5+ ♕c7 24 ♕xc7+ ♔xc7 25 ♖xf7+ and White is a clear pawn up.

20...♗xf2+ 21 ♕xf2 ♕xc4 22 ♕xa7 ♖h6

The material balance is still level, but Black's shaky king position gave me confidence. His defence is extremely tricky, if possible at all. All the same, I didn't have to work as hard as I first thought.

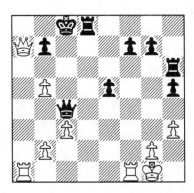

23 b3 ♕e6 24 ♕c5+ ♔b8 25 ♕a7+
♔c8 26 ♖a4 ♕b6+ 27 ♕xb6 ♖xb6
28 ♖xf7 ♖xb5 29 ♖a8 mate

1 e4 e6 2 d4 d5 3 ♘d2 c5 4 exd5
♕xd5 5 ♘gf3 cxd4 6 ♗c4 ♕d6 7 0-0
♘f6 8 ♘b3 ♘c6 9 ♘bxd4 ♘xd4 10
♘xd4 ♗d7 11 c3 ♕c7 12 ♕e2 ♗d6

This is a less ambitious line than
12...0-0-0. Black accepts a slight disadvantage consistent with giving up the
bishop pair in an open position.

13 ♘b5 ♗xb5 14 ♗xb5+ ♔e7 15 g3

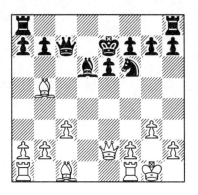

15...h5?!

This seems very natural, but in fact
it only helps White, as the g5-square is
weakened. Black has two better ideas:

a) 15...a6 16 ♗a4 ♖hd8 17 ♕f3 h6 18
♗e3!? ♖ac8 19 ♗d4 e5?! (Djurhuus
suggests 19...b5 and gives 20 ♗b3 ♗c5
21 ♗xc5+ ♕xc5 22 a4 ♖d2 as equal) 20
♗e3 e4 21 ♕e2 ♔f8 22 ♖ad1 ♗e5 23
♗b3! and White had increased the traditional bishop pair advantage in
Rozentalis-Djurhuus, Oslo 1992.

b) 15...♖hd8 16 ♖e1 ♖ac8 17 ♕f3! a6
18 ♗f1 ♕c6 19 ♕xc6 ♖xc6 20 ♗g2,
when White's light-squared bishop
had arrived on its best diagonal in
A.Sokolov-Andersson, Clermont-
Ferrand 1989. Sokolov went on to win
a long endgame.

**16 h4 ♘g4 17 ♔g2 a6 18 ♗a4 ♖hc8
19 ♗g5+! ♔f8**

Psakhis gives 19...f6?! 20 ♖ae1! fxg5?
21 ♕xe6+ ♔f8 22 ♗b3 ♘f6 23 hxg5 as
winning for White.

**20 ♖ad1 b5 21 ♗c2 b4 22 ♗e4
♖ab8 23 cxb4 ♖xb4 24 ♖c1**

Of course White can also simply
grab a pawn with 24 ♕xa6. Psakhis
plays for more.

**24...♗c5 25 b3 ♕d7 26 ♗f3 f6 27
♖fd1 ♖d4 28 ♗d2 e5**

28...♖d8 29 ♖xc5 ♖xd2 30 ♖xd2
♕xd2 31 ♖xh5 wins.

29 ♖xc5! ♖xc5 30 ♗b4 ♕d6

The triple pin along the diagonal is
decisive. Neither 30...♕c7 31 ♖xd4
exd4 32 ♗xg4 hxg4 33 ♕c4 nor
30...♖xd1 31 ♗xc5+ ♖d6 32 ♕xa6 save
Black.

31 ♗xg4 1-0

31...hxg4 32 ♖xd4 exd4 33 ♕c4
wins.

Game 45
Kopilov-Kahn
Correspondence 1991

1 e4 e6 2 d4 d5 3 ♘d2 c5 4 ♘gf3 cxd4 5 exd5 ♕xd5 6 ♗c4 ♕d6 7 0-0 ♘f6 8 ♘b3 ♘c6 9 ♘bxd4 ♘xd4 10 ♘xd4 ♗d7 11 b3

Given that this move leads to immense complications that are not unfavourable for Black, it is surprising how often 11 b3 has been played, especially when White has a safe and good alternative in 11 c3. Many of the critical variations are very similar, with small nuances such as the position of White's rooks as the only difference.

11...0-0-0 12 ♗b2 ♕c7 13 ♕e2 h5 14 ♘f3

After 14 h3 ♘g4! White has nothing better than to returning to the main game with 15 ♘f3, as the greedy 15 hxg4 fails to 15...hxg4 16 g3 ♗c5 17 ♖fd1 ♗c6!, and White can resign.

14...♘g4

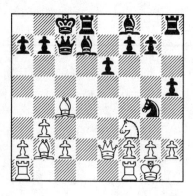

15 h3

The other main try is 15 ♖ad1. After 15...♗d6 16 h3 ♗c6 17 ♖fe1 ♗c5

18 ♖xd8+ ♕xd8 19 ♗xe6+ fxe6 20 ♕xe6+ ♔b8 (20...♗d7 21 ♕c4 ♕b6 22 ♗d4 wins for White) 21 hxg4 hxg4 22 ♗e5+ ♔a8 23 ♕xg4 ♗xf3 Glek assesses the position as unclear. Looking a little further, we can discount 24 ♕xf3 on account of 24...♖f8! 25 ♗f4 g5 26 ♗xg5 ♖xf3 27 ♗xd8 ♗xf2+ 28 ♔f1 ♖f8 29 ♗e7 ♖f7 and the bishop is lost. That leaves 24 gxf3 ♕d2 25 ♖f1 ♗xf2+! 26 ♖xf2 ♕e1+ 27 ♔g2 ♕h1+ 28 ♔g3 ♕g1+ 29 ♖g2 ♕e1+ with a perpetual check.

15...♗c6 16 ♖fd1 ♗c5 17 hxg4

An attempt to improve upon 17 ♖xd8+, when 17...♕xd8 18 hxg4 hxg4 19 ♗xe6+ fxe6 20 ♕xe6+ ♗d7 21 ♕c4 gxf3 22 ♕xc5+ ♗c6 gave Black sufficient compensation in Lanka-Glek, USSR 1989.

17...hxg4 18 ♗e5! ♖xd1+ 19 ♕xd1 ♕e7 20 ♘h2 ♕g5! 21 ♗g3

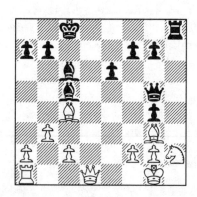

21...♖xh2! 22 ♗xh2

22 ♔xh2 ♕h6+ 23 ♔g1 ♗xg2! wins beautifully after 24 ♔xg2 ♕h3+ 25 ♔g1 ♕xg3+ 26 ♔h1 ♕h3+ 27 ♔g1 g3. Now White bails out for a draw.

22...g3 23 ♗xg3 ♕xg3 24 ♕f1 ♕f4 25 ♖d1 ♗d6 26 ♖xd6 ½-½

The position is completely level.

Summary

I don't believe for a moment that we've heard the last of the 11 ♖e1 ♕c7 12 ♗b3 ♗d6 13 ♘f5!? argument, the assessment of which seems to change from day to day. One thing is clear: both players have to know their stuff well before entering into the labyrinth of complications. White seems able to keep a nagging edge against 10...♗d7 with the simple 11 c3 and 12 ♕e2.

1 e4 e6 2 d4 d5 3 ♘d2 c5 4 exd5 ♕xd5 5 ♘gf3 cxd4 6 ♗c4 ♕d6 7 0-0 ♘f6 8 ♘b3 ♘c6 9 ♘bxd4 ♘xd4 10 ♘xd4

10...a6
> 10...♗d7 *(D)*
>> 11 c3 ♕c7 12 ♕e2
>>> 12...0-0-0 – *Game 43*
>>> 12...♗d6 – *Game 44*
>> 11 b3 – *Game 45*

11 ♖e1
> 11 ♗b3 – *Game 41*
> 11 b3 – *Game 42*

11...♕c7
> 11...♗d7 – *Game 40*

12 ♗b3 ♗d6 13 ♘f5 *(D)*
> 13 h3 – *Game 39*

13...♗xh2+ 14 ♔h1 0-0 15 ♘xg7 ♖d8 16 ♕f3 ♔xg7 17 ♗h6+ ♔g6 18 c3 ♘h5 *(D)*
> 18...♘d5 – *Game 38*

19 ♗c1 – *Game 37*

10...♗d7

13 ♘f5

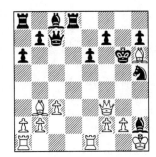

18...♘h5

CHAPTER SIX

3...c5 4 exd5 ♕xd5: Early Deviations from the Main Line

1 e4 e6 2 d4 d5 3 ♘d2 c5 4 exd5 ♕xd5

Given the density of the theoretical material in the last chapter, it is perhaps not surprising that some White players, with less study time on their hands, have preferred to play one of the more sedate variations that we shall study here. In particular, 10 ♕xd4 (Games 46-48) is still very common. In the very early days of this variation the queen exchange was supposed to give White an easy edge. In those days, however, the strength of the queenside pawn majority tended to be grossly overestimated. It is now common knowledge that, with a little care, Black can equalise after 10 ♕xd4, so nowadays the queen recapture is basically used by two sets of players: those who have immense belief in their ability to extract something from nothing in the endgame; and those who are intent on killing the position for a quick draw. Black players must respect the first category and look to punish the second! One more thing

about 10 ♕xd4: Don't be fooled by the cross-section of results in the three games given here. In real life there is a far higher percentage of draws.

Moving on to more stimulating material, it is worth taking a good look at Zapata's 9 ♕e2 (Game 49) and Ljubojevic's 9 ♖e1 (Game 50), as there may well be some hidden ideas for both sides in these lines. Sergei Smagin's 7 ♕e2 (Game 52) is also very interesting, and can be especially dangerous against the unprepared player. We could also see a resurgence of the little known 5 dxc5, which naturally received a bad press after Kasparov's lost with it against Anand. However, more recently young Russian players such as Svidler and Rublevsky have not been afraid to repeat the line, as we see in Game 55.

From Black's point of view, the most important sideline is 6...♕d8, in conjunction with 7...a6, which has been used by strong grandmasters with a varying degree of success (see Game 54). This line does have the advantage of flexibility, as the king's knight can decide between e7 and f6. On the flip side, Black has to be very careful not to wind up too far behind in development. Finally, two other sidelines for Black are also considered: 6...♛d6 7 0-0 ♘c6 (Game 51) and 6...♛d8 7 0-0 ♘e7 (Game 53).

Game 46
Wessman-Wiedenkeller
Swedish Championship 1989

---

1 e4 e6 2 d4 d5 3 ♘d2 c5 4 exd5 ♛xd5 5 ♘gf3 cxd4 6 ♗c4 ♛d6 7 0-0 ♘f6 8 ♘b3 ♘c6 9 ♘bxd4 ♘xd4 10 ♛xd4

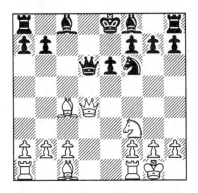

10...a6

10...♛xd4 and 10...♗d7 are considered in Games 47 and 48 respectively.

11 ♗f4 ♛xd4 12 ♘xd4 b5 13 ♗e2 ♗b7 14 ♘b3

The immediate 14 c4 led to speedy equality in Renner-Levitt, Augsburg 1989, after 14...bxc4 15 ♗xc4 ♗e7 16 ♖ac1 ♘d5 17 ♗e5 0-0 18 ♘b3 a5 19 ♖fd1 ♖fc8 20 ♗b5 a4 21 ♖xc8+ ♖xc8 22 ♗xa4 ♖a8 23 ♗b5 ♖xa2. With the text move White plans to harass the black bishop with ♘a5.

14...♗d5!

14...♗e7 does nothing to halt White's plan. After 15 c4 bxc4 16 ♘a5 ♗d5 17 ♘xc4 ♗c5 18 ♖ac1 0-0 19 a3 a5 20 ♘xa5 ♖xa5 21 ♗c7 ♗xa3 22 ♗xa5 ♗xb2 White had some winning chances in Hübner-Klinger, Biel 1986.

15 a4 b4 16 a5

Fixing the pawn on a6, but it has to be said that the c2-pawn is just as weak. White's next few moves are hardly the best options, but in any case Black is already a little better, as he has a simple plan of attack.

16...♗e7 17 ♘d2 0-0 18 ♘c4 ♖ac8 19 ♘b6? ♖xc2 20 ♗xa6 ♖xb2 21 ♗b5 b3 22 a6 ♖a2 23 ♖xa2 bxa2 24 ♖a1 ♗c5 25 ♘c4 ♘e4 26 ♖xa2 g5!

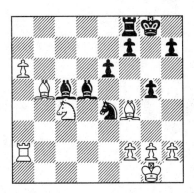

27 ♗e3?

This just loses material. The last chance was 27 ♗g3, although White's uncoordinated pieces ensure that Black retains the advantage after 27...♘c3 28 ♖b2 ♖a8.

27...♗xe3 28 fxe3 ♘c3 29 e4 ♗xc4 0-1

After 30 ♗xc4 ♘xa2 31 ♗xa2 Black can even round up the a6-pawn with 31...♖c8, intending ...♖c6. Some might say that the result was an apt punishment for White's insipid opening play, but see the next game...

Game 47
Tiviakov-Chernin
Podolsk 1993

1 e4 e6 2 d4 d5 3 ♘d2 c5 4 exd5 ♛xd5 5 ♘gf3 cxd4 6 ♗c4 ♛d6 7 0-0 ♘f6 8 ♘b3 ♘c6 9 ♘bxd4 ♘xd4 10 ♛xd4 ♛xd4 11 ♘xd4 ♗d7 12 ♗e2!

Tiviakov shows an excellent understanding of this endgame. Without any provocation, the bishop retreats to e2, from where it can reach the h1-a8 diagonal. This is undoubtedly the best place for this bishop in this line.

12...♗c5 13 ♘b3 ♗b6 14 a4 a6 15 ♗f3 0-0-0 16 ♗d2 ♗c6

Black feels obliged to contest the long diagonal. This is indeed the correct decision, but the resulting split pawns will give White a tiny edge.

17 ♗xc6 bxc6 18 ♗c3 ♖hg8 19 ♖fe1! ♖d5 20 ♘d2 ♘g4 21 ♖e2 ♖gd8 22 ♖f1 ♗d4 23 ♘c4 ♖c5 24 ♗xd4 ♖xd4 25 b3

Despite the apparent activity of the black pieces, it is still White who has the superior structure and the winning

chances. In particular, the white knight has found an impressive outpost on c4. Black should be able to hold on with passive defence, but in the heat of a tournament situation, this is often easier said than done. Instead Chernin makes a practical decision to sacrifice an exchange for a pawn, eliminating the knight in the process. Tiviakov's endgame technique, however, cannot be questioned.

25...♖cxc4!? 26 bxc4 ♖xc4 27 ♖a1 ♘f6 28 ♖a3 ♔c7 29 g3 h6 30 ♔f1 a5 31 ♔e1 ♘e4 32 ♖ee3 g5 33 f3 ♘d6 34 ♔d1 ♖c5 35 ♔c1 h5 36 ♖ac3 ♖f5 37 ♖ed3 ♘c8 38 g4! hxg4 39 fxg4 ♖e5 40 ♖d4 ♘b6 41 ♖h3 c5 42 ♖d1 ♖e4 43 ♖f3 ♖xg4 44 ♖xf7+ ♔c6 45 ♖f6 ♘xa4 46 ♖xe6+ ♔b5 47 ♖d3! ♖f4 48 ♖g3 g4 49 ♖e1 c4 50 ♖eg1 ♖f2 51 ♖3g2 ♖f3 52 ♖xg4 ♘c3 53 ♖h1! a4? 54 h4 a3 55 h5 ♖f2 56 ♖gh4!

White still could have blown it. The careless 56 h6 allows 56...♘a2+ 57 ♔b1 ♘c3+ with a perpetual, as 58 ♔a1 runs into 58...♖xc2 and ♖a2 mate. Now 56...♘a2+ 57 ♔b1 ♘c3+ 58 ♔a1 ♖xc2 can be answered by 59 ♖4h2! The rest is easy, as the h-pawn, supported by the two rooks, marches relentlessly up the board.

56...♖f7 57 h6 ♖h7 58 ♖g4 ♔c5 59 ♖g7 ♖h8 60 h7 a2 61 ♔b2 1-0

After 61...♖b8+ 62 ♔xc3 ♖b1 White finishes off with 63 ♖g5+ ♔b6 64 ♖h6+ ♔a7 65 ♖g7+. An impressive exhibition by Tiviakov, but not all of us have his endgame powers.

Game 48
Slobodjan-Luther
Lippstadt 1997

---

1 e4 e6 2 d4 d5 3 ♘d2 c5 4 exd5 ♕xd5 5 ♘gf3 cxd4 6 ♗c4 ♕d6 7 0-0 ♘c6 8 ♘b3 ♘f6 9 ♘bxd4 ♘xd4 10 ♕xd4 ♗d7

A perfectly playable alternative to 10...a6 and 10...♕xd4, although as you would expect, there are many direct transpositions.

11 ♗e3 ♕xd4 12 ♗xd4 ♖c8 13 ♘e5 ♗c5 14 ♖ad1

---
see following diagram

14...♗xd4

14...♔e7 is also possible. After 15 ♘xd7 ♗xd4 16 ♖xd4 Brodsky recommends the nuance 16...♖hd8! 17

♖fd1 ♖xd7 18 ♖xd7+ ♘xd7, which he assesses as equal. If instead 16...♘xd7 17 ♖fd1 ♖hd8 18 f4 White may be a shade better.

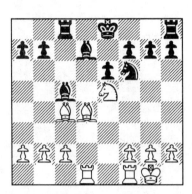

15 ♖xd4 ♔e7 16 ♖fd1 ♖hd8 17 f3

17 ♘xd7 ♖xd7 18 ♖xd7+ ♘xd7 would transpose to the previous note. After 17 f3 Black can retain the bishop, although the position remains 'dishwater dull', as well as totally equal. The rest of the moves see both sides displaying ample technique to obtain a draw.

♗e8 18 ♖xd8 ♖xd8 19 ♖xd8 ♔xd8 20 ♔f2 ♘d7 21 ♘xd7 ♗xd7 22 f4 ♔e7 23 ♔e3 ♔d6 24 ♔d4 f6 25 ♗d3 h6 26 h4 b6 27 g3 ♗c6 28 a3 ♗e8 29 ♗e4 ♗f7 30 ♗d3 ♗e8 31 b4 ♗f7 32 c3 ♗e8 33 c4 e5+ 34 fxe5+ fxe5+ 35 ♔e3 ♗f7 36 ♗e2 ♗g6 37 ♗d3 ♗f7 38 ♗e2 ½-½

This is an appropriate juncture to end our discussion on 10 ♕xd4 lines. The final position is utterly lifeless.

Game 49
Zapata-Dolmatov
Tilburg 1993

---

1 e4 e6 2 d4 d5 3 ♘d2 c5 4 ♘gf3

cxd4 5 exd5 ♕xd5 6 ♗c4 ♕d6 7 0-0
♘f6 8 ♘b3 ♘c6 9 ♕e2!?

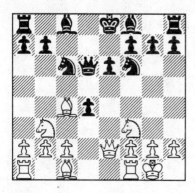

9...♗e7

Also critical is 9...a6, after which
White has two options:

a) 10 a4 (in my opinion the inser-
tion of a2-a4 and ...a7-a6 has helped
Black, who now doesn't have to
worry about possibilities of ♗b5 or
♘b5) 10...♗e7 11 g3 (11 ♗g5 e5 12
♖fe1 ♗g4 13 h3 ♗xf3 14 ♕xf3 0-0 15
♗h4 e4 was clearly better for Black in
Siklosi-Brinck Claussen, Copenhagen
1988) 11...e5 12 ♘g5 0-0 13 f4 and here
Black should play 13...♗g4! 14 ♘xf7
♗xe2 15 ♘xd6+ ♗xc4 16 ♘xc4 e4
with an awesome looking centre.

b) 10 ♖d1! looks more testing, e.g.
10...b5 11 ♗d3 ♕c7 12 a4 b4 13 ♗c4
♗b7 14 ♘bxd4 ♘xd4 15 ♖xd4 ♗c5 16
♖h4 h5 17 h3 ♘d5 18 ♗g5 ♗e7 19
♖d1 a5 20 ♗b5+ ♔f8 21 ♖c4 and
Black's king is awkwardly placed on
f8. Geller-Dolmatov, Moscow 1992,
continued 21...♕d8 22 ♗xe7+ ♕xe7
23 ♘e5 ♔g8 24 ♘c6 ♕f6 25 ♖xd5
exd5 26 ♘e7+ ♔f8 27 ♖c7 ♖b8.

Here Geller played 28 ♘c8? g6!, and

eventually lost. Instead White can win
with the brilliant 28 ♖xb7!! ♖xb7 29
♘g6+ ♔g8 30 ♕e8+ ♔h7 31 ♕xh8+
♔xg6 32 ♗d3+ ♔g5 33 h4+ ♔xh4 34
♕c8!, threatening the rook and also
mate with 35 g3+ ♔g5 36 f4+ ♔h6 37
♕h8.

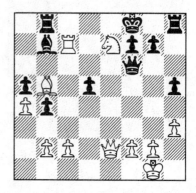

10 ♗g5 0-0 11 ♖fe1 a6 12 ♖ad1 b5
13 ♗d3 ♗b7 14 c3 ♖fe8 15 ♗b1
♕c7 16 ♘bxd4 ♘xd4 17 ♘xd4 ♖ad8

So finally White has recaptured the
d4-pawn and a typical middlegame
position has arisen: White's active
pieces against Black's super-solid pawn
structure.

18 ♕d3 g6 19 ♕h3 ♘h5!?

20 ♗h6?!

In this type of position White often

only gets 'one bite of the cherry'. A chance of a sacrifice presents itself with 20 ♘xe6!, when after 20...fxe6 (20...♖xd1 21 ♖xd1 fxe6 22 ♕xe6+ ♔f8 23 ♖d7 wins) 21 ♕xe6+ Black has to be extremely careful, e.g.

a) 21...♔f8? 22 ♖xd8 ♕xd8 23 ♗h6+ ♘g7 24 ♗xg6!! hxg6 25 ♕xg6 ♗f6 26 ♖xe8+ ♕xe8 27 ♕xf6+ ♕f7 28 ♗xg7+ with a winning position.

b) 21...♔g7! 22 ♖xd8 ♗xd8 23 ♗h6+ ♔xh6 24 ♕xe8 with an unclear imbalance of rook and two pawns against bishop and knight. This may still be slightly better for White.

20...♗f6 21 ♕g4 e5 22 ♘f5 ♖xd1 23 ♖xd1 ♖d8 24 ♗e3 ♘f4 25 ♗xf4 exf4 26 ♘d4 b4

White's kingside demonstration has got absolutely nowhere, and Black is just about to take over operations. In particular, the pair of bishops will make White suffer painfully in this open position.

27 ♕e2 bxc3 28 bxc3 ♕xc3 29 ♘b3 ♖xd1+ 30 ♕xd1

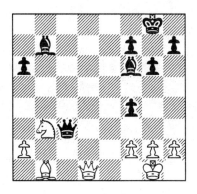

A pawn up, with a dominating position, one would normally expect Dolmatov to convert to the full point with ease. Strangely, however, the game drifts towards a draw.

30...f3?!

Looks strong, but this pawn is picked up in the endgame.

31 g3 a5 32 ♕d2 ♕xd2 33 ♘xd2 ♗d5 34 a4 ♗g5

After 34...♗c6 35 ♗c2 ♗c3 36 ♘e4 ♗b4 Black's can still play for the win with the bishop pair. Perhaps a draw was all the Russian technician needed.

35 ♗e4 ♗xd2 36 ♗xd5 ♔g7 37 ♗xf3 g5 38 ♔f1 f6 39 ♔e2 ♗b4 40 ♗e4 h6 41 ♔f3 ♗c3 42 ♔g4 ♗b4 43 ♔f5 ♗e1 44 f4 gxf4 45 ♔xf4 ♗b4 46 ♔f5 ♗c3 47 ♗d5 ♗b4 48 ♗b3 ♗c3 49 ♗d1 ♗b4 50 ♗h5 ♗c3 51 ♔e6 ♗b4 52 ♔d5 ½-½

Game 50
Winsnes-Lein
Gausdal 1990

---

1 e4 e6 2 d4 d5 3 ♘d2 c5 4 exd5 ♕xd5 5 ♘gf3 cxd4 6 ♗c4 ♕d6 7 0-0 ♘f6 8 ♘b3 ♘c6 9 ♖e1

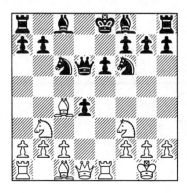

Ljubojevic's idea, which has never really caught on. White struggles just to regain the pawn and this gives Black the chance to co-ordinate fully and reach a comfortable middlegame.

9...♗d7 10 g3 ♗e7 11 ♗f4 ♕b4 12 ♕d3 0-0 13 ♗c7?!

This is probably too ambitious, although it is quite surprising how quickly White's position deteriorates. I prefer 13 a3 ♕b6 14 ♘fxd4 ♘xd4 15 ♕xd4 with a level position.

13...♗d8 14 a3 ♕e7 15 ♗f4 ♗b6 16 ♘fxd4 ♘xd4 17 ♘xd4 ♕c5! 18 ♖ad1 ♖ac8 19 ♗b3 ♕h5 20 ♕e2 ♘g4 21 f3

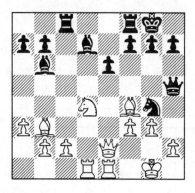

21...e5! 22 ♗xe5 ♖ce8 23 f4 ♔h8! 0-1

White has no defence to ...f7-f6.

Game 51
M. del Campo-Escobedo Tinajero
Mexico 1991

---

1 e4 e6 2 d4 d5 3 ♘d2 c5 4 ♘gf3 cxd4 5 exd5 ♕xd5 6 ♗c4 ♕d6 7 0-0 ♘c6

see following diagram

8 ♘e4!

When I first encountered 7...♘c6 I thought that Black's move order was irrelevant, so I bashed out 8 ♘b3, expecting to transpose to normal lines after 8...♘f6 9 ♘bxd4. I then remem-ber being slightly surprised and a little annoyed when my opponent didn't co-operate. Instead there came 8...e5 9 ♕e2 ♗e7?! (after 9...♗e6! it is not clear how White can justify his pawn deficit) 10 ♖d1 ♕c7 11 ♗d5 ♗g4 12 ♕c4 ♔f8 13 ♖e1 ♗f6 14 c3! and White went on to win in Emms-I.Andersen, Cappelle la Grande 1992. 8 ♘e4 was suggested to me by the American GM Ilya Gurevich, and it does seem a logical way to exploit the omission of ...♘f6.

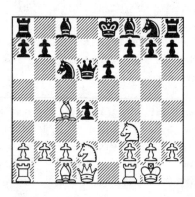

8...♕d8 9 ♕e2 ♗e7 10 ♖d1 ♘f6 11 c3!

Recovering the pawn and entering a favourable IQP position.

11...♘xe4 12 ♕xe4 0-0 13 cxd4 ♘b4 14 ♖e1 ♗f6 15 ♗f4 ♘d5 16 ♗e5 ♗xe5 17 dxe5 b6 18 ♗xd5! ♕xd5 19 ♕xd5 exd5 20 ♖ac1 ♗e6 21 ♘d4

The opening has been a complete success for White. He has cleverly converted his advantages and is now left with a 'good knight versus bad bishop' situation. Added to this Black has a weak d-pawn, while White can advance the kingside pawn majority without any difficulty. White probably already holds a decisive advantage.

**21...♖fc8 22 ♖xc8+ ♖xc8 23 f4 g6
24 ♔f2 ♔f8 25 h3 h5 26 ♔f3 ♗f5
27 g4 hxg4+ 28 hxg4 ♗e4+ 29 ♔e3
♔e7 30 f5 a6 31 f6+ ♔d7 32 ♔f4
♖e8 33 e6+!**

This sacrifice gives the white king a decisive entry square, where it can support the f6-pawn. Black's battle against this monster of a passed pawn is doomed to failure.

**33...fxe6 34 ♔e5 g5 35 f7 ♖f8 36
♔f6 ♖h8 37 ♘xe6 ♖h6+ 38 ♔xg5
♖g6+ 39 ♔h5 ♖xe6 40 f8♕ ♗g6+
41 ♔g5 ♖xe1 42 ♕g7+ ♖e7 43
♕xg6 ♖e6 44 ♕d3 b5 45 ♕xd5+
♖d6 46 ♕xd6+ 1-0**

> ## Game 52
> ## Anka-I.Almasi
> *Hungary 1997*

**1 e4 e6 2 d4 d5 3 ♘d2 c5 4 exd5
♕xd5 5 ♘gf3 cxd4 6 ♗c4 ♕d6 7
♕e2!? ♘f6 8 ♘b3 ♘c6 9 ♗g5**

---

see following diagram

9...a6

Black has no real route to comfortable equality by giving the pawn back,

so it is best to hold on to it as long as possible, even just for nuisance value. Other moves include:

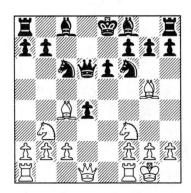

a) **9...♗d7 10 0-0-0 0-0-0 11 ♘bxd4
♘xd4 12 ♖xd4 ♕b6 13 ♕e5 ♕c5 14
♖hd1** with an edge to White in Palac-Touzane, Nice 1994.

b) **9...♕b4+ 10 ♗d2 ♕b6 11 0-0-0
♗d7 12 ♗g5 0-0-0 13 ♘fxd4 ♘b4 14
a3 ♘bd5 15 ♗xd5 exd5 16 f3 ♗d6 17
g3** and again White was slightly better in Rozentalis-Glek, Antwerp 1993.

10 0-0-0 b5 11 ♗d3 ♗e7!

This is safer than 11...♗b7. Smagin-Levitt, Amantea 1993, continued 12 ♘bxd4 ♘xd4 13 ♘xd4 0-0-0 ('castling into it' has never been more apt)

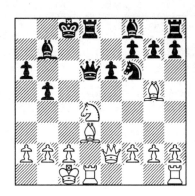

14 **♗xb5!! axb5 15 ♘xb5 ♕b4 16**

Xxd8+! &xd8 17 Xd1+ &c8 18 Xd4
Wa5 19 Wc4+ and Black resigned on
account of 19...&b8 20 &f4+ &a8 21
Xd8+! Wxd8 22 Wa4+.

12 &b1

Naturally White would like to re-
claim the pawn with 12 ∆bxd4 ∆xd4
13 ∆xd4, but then 13...Wd5! hits a2
and g5. After 14 &xf6 &xf6 15 &b1
Wc5! 16 &e4 Xa7 Black's two bishops
gave him an edge in V.Ivanov-
Zakharov, Russia 1994. Note that 17
&c6+ doesn't help White. After
17...&e7 18 We4 Xc7 the black king is
quite safe, while the bishop on c6 is a
liability. Now, however, Black can
hold onto the extra pawn.

12...e5 13 h3 &e6

After 13...∆d5 14 &xe7 ∆dxe7 15
Xhe1 f6 White can break open the
centre to his advantage with 16 c3!

14 Xhe1 ∆d7?

After this Black's position collapses.
14...Xc8! is a greater test for White.
The game Smagin-Marjanovic, Yugoslavia 1994, continued 15 g4 (15 ∆xe5?
fails to 15...Wxe5 16 Wxe5 ∆xe5 17
Xxe5 ∆d7) 15...∆d7 and White didn't
have enough compensation for the
pawn. In his notes Smagin suggests 15
&h4 as the best try for White, intending 15...∆d7 16 &g3, when the pressure persists. This line needs practical
tests.

**15 &xe7 &xe7 16 &e4 Xhc8 17
&xc6 Wxc6**

see following diagram

**18 ∆xe5 ∆xe5 19 ∆xd4! Wxg2 20
Wxe5 Wg6 21 ∆f5+ 1-0**

21...&e8 22 ∆d6+ &e7 23 ∆xc8+
Xxc8 24 Wd6+ is terminal.

Game 53
Yandimerov-R.Nikitin
Russia 1997

**1 e4 e6 2 d4 d5 3 ∆d2 c5 4 exd5
Wxd5 5 ∆gf3 cxd4 6 &c4 Wd8 7 0-0
∆e7 8 ∆b3 Wc7 9 We2 ∆g6 10
∆bxd4!**

10 ∆fxd4, intending f2-f4-f5, was
shown to be artificial in the game Adams-Dreev, Dortmund 1994, which
went 10...a6 11 f4 &e7 12 f5?! exf5 13
∆xf5 &xf5 0-0 15 ∆d4 ∆d7!16 &e3
∆f6 17 &h1 Xae8 and Adams's lunge
had only served to weaken his king.

10...a6

Against 10...&e7 White could try 11

♘b5 ♕b6 12 ♗e3 ♗c5 13 ♗xc5 ♕xc5
14 ♕e3! ♕xe3 15 fxe3 with an edge.

11 ♗b3

11 ♗xe6!? fxe6 12 ♘xe6 ♗xe6 13
♕xe6+ is a dangerous piece sacrifice
which worked well for White in For-
ster-Vaganian, Biel 1994. After
13...♕e7? 14 ♕c8+ ♕d8 15 ♕xb7
Black's king didn't survive too long.
13...♗e7 would have been more stub-
born.

**11...♗e7 12 ♖e1 0-0 13 ♗g5 ♗d6
14 ♕d3 h6?**

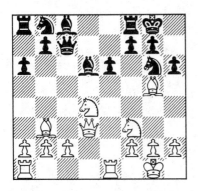

Black's development disadvantage
has reached serious proportions.
However, his position would still be
playable but for this move, which allows a powerful sacrifice.

**15 ♘xe6!! ♗xe6 16 ♖xe6 fxe6 17
♕xg6 ♘c6 18 ♖d1 ♘e5 19 ♕xe6+
♔h8 20 ♖xd6 ♘xf3+ 21 gxf3 ♖ae8
22 ♕g6 ♕a5 23 ♗xh6 1-0**

Game 54
Emms-L.B.Hansen
Bronshoj Jubilee 1995

**1 e4 e6 2 d4 d5 3 ♘d2 c5 4 ♘gf3
cxd4 5 exd5 ♕xd5 6 ♗c4 ♕d6**

In fact, the most common move or-

der to reach the diagram position below is 6...♕d8 7 0-0 a6 8 ♘b3 ♕c7,
which avoids 8 ♘e4.

7 0-0 a6 8 ♘b3

8 ♘e4!? may be a way for White to
exploit Black's move order, e.g.
8...♕c7 9 ♗b3 ♗e7 10 ♘xd4 ♘f6 11
♖e1 with an edge for White.

8...♕c7

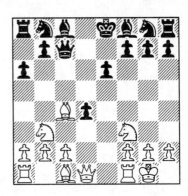

9 ♕e2

The major alternative is 9 ♕xd4!?
Practical play suggests that White can
secure an advantage, e.g. 9...♘c6 10
♕h4 ♗d6 11 ♗d2 ♘ge7 (11...♘f6 12
♗h6!) 12 ♗d3 ♗d7 (12...♘e5 may be
stronger) and now:

a) 13 ♖ad1 0-0-0 14 ♘g5! ♘g6 15
♕h3 ♘ge5 16 ♗e2 and White was better, although he later lost, in Akopian-
Dreev, Linares 1995.

b) 13 ♗c3 f6 14 ♕h5+ ♔f8 15 ♘c5
♘d5 16 ♘xd7+ ♕xd7 17 ♗d2 and on
this occasion White converted his advantage in Nisipeanu-Priehoda, Budapest 1996.

9...♗d6 10 ♘bxd4 ♘e7

The main nuance in this line. This
knight develops at e7 rather than f6.

11 ♖d1

11 ♖e1 is a critical alternative, e.g.

11...0-0 (11...♘bc6! looks safer) 12 ♘g5 h6 13 ♘xf7!! ♔xf7 14 ♘xe6 ♗xe6 15 ♕xe6+ ♔e8 16 ♗xh6 ♖f6 17 ♕g8+ ♔d7 18 ♖xe7+ ♗xe7 19 ♖d1+ ♔c6 20 ♕d5+ ♔b6 21 ♗e3+ ♗c5

22 b4 ♔a7 23 ♗xc5+ b6 24 ♗d4 ♖d6 25 ♕e5 ♘d7 26 ♕xg7 ♕c6 27 ♗f1 ♖c8 28 c3 ♖c7 29 ♕g3 ♔b7 30 ♗e2 ♘f6 31 ♗f3 ♘d5 32 c4 ♖e7 33 ♗xd5 ♖xd5 34 cxd5 ♕a4 35 ♕c3 and Black resigned in Slobodjan-Kaminski, Halle 1995. A brilliant attacking display from the soon-to-be World Junior Champion.

11...♘bc6

Black has to be a little careful, e.g. 11...0-0? 12 ♗xe6! fxe6 13 ♘xe6 ♕b6 14 ♘xf8 ♔xf8 15 ♕d3 is very strong for White. Nevertheless 11...♘bc6 is perfectly satisfactory for Black.

12 ♘xc6 ♘xc6 13 ♗d3 ♗d7

13...0-0 once again 'castles into it': 14 ♗xh7+ ♔xh7 15 ♘g5+ gives White a strong attack. Here I was most concerned over the simplifying move 13...♘e5!, when after 14 ♘xe5 ♗xe5 15 h3 0-0 White has no advantage whatsoever.

14 b3 0-0-0

Now I was ready to answer

14...♘e5 with the continuation 15 ♗b2! ♘xf3+ 16 ♕xf3 ♗xh2+ 17 ♔h1 ♗e5 18 ♗xe5 ♕xe5 19 ♕xb7, when White is better.

15 ♗b2 e5 16 c4 f6 17 a3 ♖he8 18 ♗e4?

This is far too casual. After 18 ♕c2, clamping down on the light squares, I still prefer White.

18...f5! 19 ♗xc6 ♗xc6 20 c5 ♗xc5 21 ♘xe5

21 ♖xd8+ ♕xd8 22 ♘xe5 ♕d5 is the end for White, so a pawn goes down the drain. The rest of the game proves to be a highly successful grovel.

21...♖xd1+ 22 ♖xd1

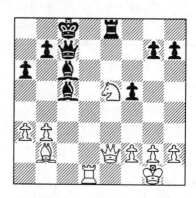

22...♗xa3! 23 f4 ♗xb2 24 ♕xb2 ♕b6+ 25 ♔h1 ♖d8 26 ♖xd8+ ♕xd8 27 h3 ♕d5?

27...♗e4 keeps Black firmly in control. After the game move White is able to create enough counterplay for a draw.

28 ♔h2 ♕e4 29 ♘xc6 bxc6 30 ♕xg7 ♕xf4+ 31 ♔h1 h6 32 ♕e7 ♔b8 33 b4 ♕g5 34 ♕d6+ ♔b7 35 ♕d7+ ♔b6 36 ♕d4+ ♔c7 37 ♕a7+ ♔d6 38 ♕c5+ ♔d7 39 ♕a7+ ♔e6 40 ♕xa6 ♕c1+ 41 ♔h2 ♕f4+ 42 ♔h1 ♕e4 43 ♕c8+ ♔d5 44 ♕f8 ♕e1+ 45

♔h2 ♕e5+ 46 ♔h1 ♕e1+ ½-½

Game 55
Rublevsky-Beliavsky
Novosibirsk 1995

1 e4 e6 2 d4 d5 3 ♘d2 c5 4 exd5 ♕xd5 5 dxc5 ♗xc5 6 ♘gf3 ♘f6 7 ♗d3 0-0 8 ♕e2 ♘bd7!

Played by Anand against Kasparov. The knight is most useful here, as it adds extra protection to the kingside and will not obstruct the black bishop when it fianchettoes on b7.

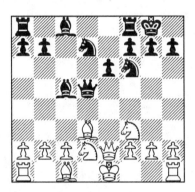

9 b3

Kasparov-Anand, Reggio Emilia 1991, continued 9 ♘e4 b6! 10 ♘xc5 ♕xc5 (10...♘xc5 is also okay for Black) 11 ♗e3 ♕c7 12 ♗d4 ♗b7 13 0-0-0 ♘c5! 14 ♗e5 ♘xd3+ 15 ♖xd3 ♕c4 and Black was fine. Indeed, the game ended in a rare Kasparov defeat with the white pieces.

9...a5!?

Discouraging White from castling queenside, although in this game White will not be deterred. Also feasi-

ble is 9...♘g4 10 0-0 ♘de5. Now 11 ♘xe5 ♕xe5! is equal, while Svidler-Savchenko, Kazan 1995, ended in a quick draw after 11 ♗e4 ♘xf3+ 12 ♘xf3 ♕h5 13 h3 ♘f6 14 ♗b2 ♘xe4 15 ♕xe4 f6 16 ♖ad1 ½-½. Note that 13 ♗b2 would have been met by 13...♘xh2!

10 ♗b2 b6 11 0-0-0 ♗b7 12 ♖he1?!

This turns out to be too pedestrian. Beliavsky recommends the direct 12 g4, intending g4-g5, when 12...♘xg4 fails simply to 13 ♗e4, winning material. Now Black gets in first.

12...a4 13 ♘e4 ♕h5 14 ♘fg5 ♕h6 15 ♔b1 axb3 16 axb3 ♗a3 17 ♘xf6+?

The start of a hallucination, based on a horrendous oversight. 17 ♗d4! was stronger, after which Beliavsky planned 17...♘d5!? 18 ♘xh7 ♖fc8 with good compensation for the pawn.

17...♘xf6

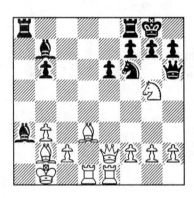

18 ♗xf6? ♕xf6 19 ♗xh7+ ♔h8 20 ♕h5

Threatening mate in two, but...

20...♕b2 mate!

Summary

Of White's alternatives in this chapter, perhaps the most dangerous are the early ♕e2 ideas and the neglected 5 dxc5. It seems that further games are still required before an accurate assessment can be made on the 6...♕d8 and 7...a6 line.

1 e4 e6 2 d4 d5 3 ♘d2 c5 4 exd5 ♕xd5

5 ♘gf3
>   5 dxc5 – *Game 55*

5...cxd4 6 ♗c4 ♕d6
>   6...♕d8 7 0-0 *(D)*
>>   7...♘e7 – *Game 53*
>>   7...a6 8 ♘b3 ♕c7 – *Game 54* (by transposition)

7 0-0
>   7 ♕e2 – *Game 52*

7...♘f6
>   7...♘c6 – *Game 51*
>   7...a6 – *Game 54*

8 ♘b3 ♘c6 *(D)* **9 ♘bxd4**
>   9 ♕e2 – *Game 49*
>   9 ♖e1 – *Game 50*

9...♘xd4 10 ♕xd4 *(D)* **a6**
>   10...♕xd4 – *Game 47*
>   10...♗d7 – *Game 48*

11 ♗f4 – *Game 46*

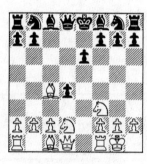

7 0-0   8...♘c6   10 ♕xd4

CHAPTER SEVEN

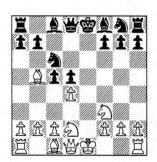

3...c5 4 exd5 exd5:
Main Line with 6 ♗b5

1 e4 e6 2 d4 d5 3 ♘d2 c5 4 exd5 exd5 5 ♘gf3 ♘c6 6 ♗b5

All the rage in the seventies and early eighties, interest has slowly waned in this line, as Black players have searched for more dynamic ways to combat the Tarrasch, including the ...♕xd5 variation and ...e6xd5 in conjunction with an early ...a7-a6 or ...♘f6. The general consensus in the old 5...♘c6 line is that White can play for a risk-free plus by concentrating his efforts against the isolated queen's pawn (IQP). On the other hand, it must be said that Black has no problems with piece activity and this line has appealed to IQP specialists such as Vaganian, Dolmatov, Lputian, Uhlmann, and of course Korchnoi, all of whom have scored notable successes.

In Games 56-58 we study the popular 11 ♗d3, a slightly paradoxical idea, given that White's main plan is to pile up on the d5-pawn. In many positions White even goes for a kingside attack with c2-c3, ♗c2 and ♕d3. This is actually quite a dangerous plan and

Black players really need to know their stuff here. In contrast 11 ♗g5 (Game 59) heads for a quieter position more typical of the IQP Tarrasch. The same can also be said of 10 ♘bd4 (Game 60), although this is thought to be less threatening for Black.

In Games 61-62 we see the less popular 9...♗b6, a perfectly natural looking move. The only problem with it is that White has the even more natural idea of 10 ♖e1 and 11 ♗e3, which seems to secure an advantage. Finally, 6...cxd4 is considered in Game 63.

Game 56
M.Read-Goncalves
Correspondence 1989

---

1 e4 e6 2 d4 d5 3 ♘d2 c5 4 exd5 exd5 5 ♘gf3 ♘c6 6 ♗b5 ♗d6 7 dxc5

This is a more exact move order than 7 0-0, which allows Black the idea of 7...cxd4. After 8 ♘b3 ♘ge7 9 ♘bxd4, White has been forced into the ♘b3-d4 lines, a tempo less for each side (see Game 60).

7...♗xc5

7...♕e7+ crops up from time to time, but it doesn't really cause White any problems. For example, 8 ♕e2 ♕xe2+ 9 ♔xe2 ♗xc5 10 ♘b3 ♗b6 11 ♗e3 ♗g4 12 h3 ♗h5 13 ♗xb6 axb6 14 ♘bd4 and Black's wrecked structure gave White a definite plus in Tal-Korchnoi, Moscow 1973.

8 0-0 ♘ge7 9 ♘b3 ♗d6

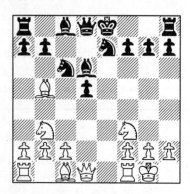

10 ♖e1 0-0 11 ♗d3 h6

Of course Black would like to continue with 11...♗g4, but this falls for 12 ♗xh7+! ♔xh7 13 ♘g5+, regaining the piece with a winning position. Indeed, this is one of the points behind 11 ♗d3, since after 11...h6 White has time to avoid the annoying pin.

12 h3 ♘f5

Paving the way for the black queen to reach f6, where it can support the advance of the d-pawn and allow a rook to go to d8.

13 c3 ♕f6

The other main alternative here, 13...♗c7, is the subject of Game 58.

14 ♗c2 ♗e6

Bolstering the d5-pawn, although

Black can also play 14...♖d8, which may be stronger (see the next game).

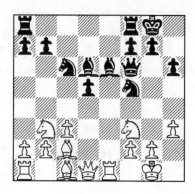

15 ♕d3 ♖fe8 16 ♗d2!?

White simply wants to double the rooks on the e-file, when the pressure on e6 may become surprisingly annoying. The direct 16 g4 is also playable, when after 16...♘h4 17 ♘xh4 ♕xh4 18 ♕h7+ ♔f8 19 ♔g2 ♕f6 20 ♗e3, Uhlmann assesses White's chances as slightly better.

16...g6 17 ♖e2

A change of plan with 17 ♕b5?! is inadvisable. Ernst-Vaganian, Copenhagen 1988, continued 17...♘h4 18 ♘xh4 ♕xh4 19 ♕xb7? ♗xh3! and here White should have bailed out with 20 ♕xc6, which leads to a draw after 20...♗h2+ 21 ♔f1 ♗xg2+ 22 ♔xg2 ♕g4+ 23 ♔h1 ♕f3+ 24 ♔xh2 ♕xf2+ 25 ♔h3 ♕f3+.

17...♖ac8

17...♗f8 was played in Wolff-Benjamin, San Francisco 1991, but after 18 ♖ae1 ♘d6 19 ♘bd4 ♘e4 20 ♘xe6 ♖xe6 21 ♗b3 ♘xd2 22 ♕xd2 the isolated d-pawn was doomed. At first I thought that 17...♖ad8 might be an improvement for Black. Nevertheless, this causes brand-new problems with 18 ♖ae1 ♗f8 19 g4 ♘d6 20 g5! (exploiting the fact that a rook is on d8; 20...hxg5 21 ♗xg5 picks up an exchange) 20...♕h8 21 ♖xe6 fxe6 22 ♕xg6+ ♕g7 23 gxh6 ♕xg6+ 24 ♗xg6 and White is clearly better.

18 ♖ae1 ♗f8 19 g4! ♘d6

19...♘h4 20 ♘xh4 ♕xh4 21 ♖xe6! is a recurrent theme which runs throughout this game: 21...fxe6 (21...♖xe6 22 ♖xe6 fxe6 23 ♕xg6+ ♗g7 24 ♕xe6+) 22 ♕xg6+ ♗g7 23 ♖xe6 ♖f8 24 ♕h7+ ♔f7 25 ♖xh6 is the end for Black.

20 ♘c5 ♘e5 21 ♖xe5 ♖xc5

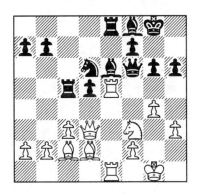

22 ♗e3! ♘c4 23 ♗d4 ♘xe5

Read gives two other tries which lose quickly:

a) 23...♘xb2 24 ♕e2 ♕e7 25 ♗xg6 fxg6 26 ♗xc5 ♕xc5 27 ♖xe6.

b) 23...♕e7 24 ♖xe6 fxe6 25 ♕xg6+ ♗g7 26 ♗xc5.

24 ♘xe5 ♗c8

24...♕h4 once again allows 25 ♘xg6!, e.g. 25...♗f5 26 ♖xe8! ♗xd3 27 ♖xf8+ ♔h7 28 ♖xf7+ ♔g8 29 ♖g7 mate. After 24...♗d7 White can play 25 ♖e3!, as 25...♗b5 allows 26 ♘d7! ♕d6 27 ♖xe8 ♗xd3 28 ♘xf8 f6 29 ♗xc5 and White has far too much ma-

terial for the queen.

25 ♖e3 ♖xe5

Giving back the exchange, but other moves are no better:

a) 25...♕h4 26 ♘xg6 ♖xe3 27 ♘e7+.

b) 25...♕g5 26 ♘xg6 ♕xg6 (26...fxg6 27 ♗xc5 and 26...♖xe3 27 ♘e7+ ♗xe7 28 ♕h7+ ♔f8 29 ♕h8+ ♕g8 30 ♗g7+ both win for White) 27 ♖xe8 ♖c6 (27...♕xd3 28 ♖xf8+!) 28 ♕xg6+ fxg6 29 ♗a4 ♖c7 (or 29...♖c4 30 ♗b5 ♖c7 31 ♗e5) 30 ♗e5 ♖c4 31 ♗b5 ♖c5 32 ♗d6 and White wins (Read).

26 ♖xe5 ♕f4 27 ♖e8! 1-0

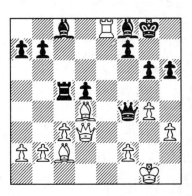

At first sight this seems like an early resignation, but in fact Black is completely lost here. 27...♖c6 runs into 28 ♗e3 and 29 ♗xh6, while 27...♕c1+ 28 ♔g2 ♖c7 29 ♗e3 ♕e1 30 ♕xd5 is also winning. A model game in which Read cleverly mixed a kingside attack with the usual play against the IQP.

Game 57
Asrian-Lputian
Yerevan 1995

---

1 e4 e6 2 d4 d5 3 ♘d2 c5 4 exd5 exd5 5 ♗b5+ ♘c6 6 ♘gf3 ♗d6 7 dxc5 ♗xc5 8 0-0 ♘ge7 9 ♘b3 ♗d6

10 ♖e1 0-0 11 ♗d3 h6 12 h3 ♘f5 13 c3 ♕f6 14 ♗c2 ♖d8 15 ♕d3 g6

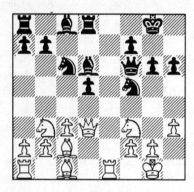

16 ♕d2!?

This very unusual concept of blocking the c1-bishop with the queen has in fact been witnessed before in this variation (see Game 58 for the same idea in a slightly different position). In contrast the idea of ♗d2, followed by doubling on the e-file is not so effective here, e.g. 16 ♗d2 a5! 17 a4 b6! (cutting across White's plan as 18 ♖e2 is hit by 18...♗a6) 18 ♕e2 ♗a6 19 ♗d3 ♗xd3 20 ♕xd3 ♘e5 21 ♘xe5 (21 ♕xd5? falls for 21...♘d3! 22 ♕xd3 ♗h2+) 21...♗xe5 22 ♖ad1 d4 23 cxd4 ♘xd4 24 ♗c3 ♘c6 25 ♗xe5 ♘xe5 26 ♕c3 ♖xd1 27 ♖xd1 ♖d8 28 ♖xd8+ ♕xd8 and here the players agreed a draw in I.Gurevich-Lputian, Philadelphia World Open 1994, as after 29 ♕xe5 Black regains the piece with 29...♕d1+ 30 ♔h2 ♕xb3.

16...♗f8 17 ♕f4

After 17 ♘h2 ♕g7! (prophylaxis against ♘g4) 18 ♘g4 h5 19 ♘e3 (19 ♗xf5 ♗xf5 20 ♘h6+ ♕xh6 21 ♕xh6 ♗xh6 22 ♗xh6 d4 is equal according to V.Ivanov) 19...♘fe7 20 ♕e2 ♕f6 Black had no real problems in

V.Ivanov-Lastin, Russia 1994. He will follow up with ...♗g7, ...♗e6 and ...d5-d4.

17...♗g7 18 ♕c7??

This move is simply too ambitious. White should have simply played 18 ♗d2, or perhaps the visual 18 ♕h2!?, intending ♗f4, keeping absolute control over the important h2-b8 diagonal.

18...♘d6!

The simplest ideas are usually the best! Black just threatens to trap the queen with ...♖d7. To avoid this White has to give up a vital pawn.

19 ♘c5 ♗xh3! 20 gxh3

20 ♘xb7 loses to 20...♖ac8, as indeed it does on move 21.

20...♕xf3 21 ♖e3 ♕h5

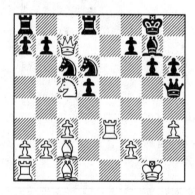

I doubt whether this was the position that White had envisaged before playing 18 ♕c7. White is a pawn down, his king has no shelter and his queen has nothing to show for her 'walkabout'. Someone of Lputian's undoubted class had no difficulty putting this one away.

22 ♘d7 ♘f5 23 ♗xf5 ♕xf5 24 ♘c5 d4! 25 cxd4 ♘xd4 26 ♘e4 ♘f3+ 27 ♔g2 ♘h4+ 28 ♔f1

Or 28 ♔h1 ♖d1+ 29 ♔h2 ♗e5+.
28...♕b5+ 0-1

It is checkmate in all lines. 29 ♔g1 ♖d1+ 30 ♔h2 ♖h1+ 31 ♔xh1 ♕f1+ 32 ♔h2 ♕g2 is one possible finish.

Game 58
Smagin-B.Lalic
Sochi 1987

---

1 e4 e6 2 d4 d5 3 ♘d2 c5 4 ♘gf3 ♘c6 5 exd5 exd5 6 ♗b5 ♗d6 7 dxc5 ♗xc5 8 0-0 ♘ge7 9 ♘b3 ♗b6 10 ♖e1 0-0 11 ♗d3 h6 12 h3 ♘f5 13 c3 ♗c7

The other main approach. Black mimics his opponent by piling up on the b8-h2 diagonal. It is White, however, who creates the initial threats.

14 ♗c2 ♕d6 15 ♕d3 g6 16 ♕d2!?

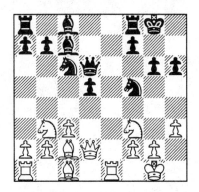

Once more we see this queen move. On first impression the alternative 16 g4 looks decisive, as if the knight retreats then White simply gobbles the h6-pawn. However, Black has the surprising response 16...♗b6! (threatening ...♕g3+) 17 ♔g2 ♗xf2! 18 ♔xf2 ♕g3+ 19 ♔e2 ♘d6! 20 ♗xh6 ♖e8+ 21 ♔d1 ♕xh3 with extreme complications.

16...h5 17 ♗xf5 ♗xf5 18 ♕h6 ♖fe8

18...♗e4 19 ♘bd2 f5 was suggested as an improvement on Black's play but it now appears that there is a major flaw in this move. Here are two practical examples:

a) 20 g3? ♖f6 21 ♘xe4 fxe4 22 ♘h4 ♘e5 23 ♗f4 ♕e6 24 ♗xe5 ♗xe5 25 ♕g5 ♗c7 26 ♖e2 ♖af8 27 ♘g2 ♕f7 28 ♕d2 ♗b6 29 ♘f4 h4 and Black went on to win in Tolnai-Schmittdiel, Dortmund 1989.

b) 20 ♘xe4 fxe4 21 ♘g5 ♕h2+ 22 ♔f1 ♖xf2+ (this was previously thought to give Black a perpetual check but White has an amazing resource) 23 ♔xf2 ♕g3+ 24 ♔f1! (24 ♔e2 ♕d3+ 25 ♔f2 ♕g3+ was the supposed draw) 24...♖f8+ 25 ♗f4!! ♖xf4+ (25...♕xf4+ 26 ♔e2 ♕f2+ 27 ♔d1 and Black runs out of checks) 26 ♔g1 ♘e5 27 ♕h7+ ♔f8 28 ♘e6+ ♔e8 29 ♘xc7+ ♔d8 30 ♕h8+ ♔d7 31 ♕e8+ 1-0 Holzke-Tondivar, Groningen 1997.

19 ♗e3 ♕f8 20 ♕xf8+ ♔xf8 21 ♖ad1 ♖ad8

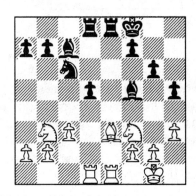

Now White wins a pawn with a small combination. If instead 21...♗e6 22 ♘c5 keeps a small advantage.

22 ♖xd5 ♖xd5 23 ♗h6+ ♔g8 24 ♖xe8+ ♔h7 25 ♗d2 ♗b1?

After 25...♘e5! 26 ♘xe5 ♖xe5 27 ♖xe5 ♗xe5 it would have been very difficult for White to convert the extra pawn, as Black would boast the bishop pair as compensation. After the game move White can favourably give back the extra pawn in order to drum up a direct attack against the black king.

26 c4 ♖f5 27 ♗c3 g5

27...f6 28 ♘bd4 ♘xd4 29 ♖e7+ ♔g8 30 ♘xd4 ♖c5 31 ♘e6 is also an easy win. Black just cannot co-ordinate his pieces for a successful defence.

28 ♘bd2 ♗xa2 29 ♘e4 ♗d8 30 ♘d6 ♖f4 31 ♗d2

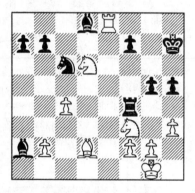

31...♖xf3

31...♖f6 32 ♘xg5+ ♔g6 33 ♖g8+ ♔h6 34 ♘e8! is also hopeless.

32 gxf3 ♗e7 33 ♘xb7 ♗f6 34 ♗c3 ♗xc3 35 bxc3 ♗xc4 36 ♘d8 ♗b5 37 ♘xc6 ♗xc6 38 ♖e7 ♔g6 39 ♖xa7 ♗xf3 40 c4 ♔f6 41 ♖a3 ♗b7 42 ♖e3 h4 43 c5 ♗d5 44 ♔h2 ♔f5 45 ♖e8 ♗b7 46 ♖g8 1-0

Game 59
Agnos-Lputian
Linares 1996

---

1 e4 e6 2 d4 d5 3 ♘d2 c5 4 exd5

exd5 5 ♘gf3 ♘c6 6 ♗b5 ♗d6 7 dxc5 ♗xc5 8 0-0 ♘ge7 9 ♘b3 ♗d6 10 ♖e1 0-0 11 ♗g5

Karpov's positional approach, which he introduced against Korchnoi in their 1974 match. White immediately activates his dark-squared bishop, before it can be blunted with ...h7-h6. In some lines White simply exchanges on e7. The main idea, however, is the manoeuvre ♗h4-g3, swapping the dark-squared bishops. Once again in the Tarrasch, this plan, though quite time-consuming, presents Black with some difficult problems to solve. Active piece play offers the only chance for him to achieve equality.

11...♗g4 12 ♗h4 ♖e8 13 ♗g3 ♗xg3 14 hxg3 ♕b6!

A good move. Once the dark-squared bishops are exchanged, the queen sits very nicely on this square. Often Black follows up with ...a7-a5, planning ...a5-a4, which may loosen White's control over the d4-square.

15 a4 h5!?

15...a6 16 ♗xc6 ♗xf3 17 ♕xf3 bxc6 18 ♕e3 probably keeps an edge for White, who controls many dark squares on the queenside.

16 ♕d3 ♗f5 17 ♕d2 a6

Possibly this was an intended improvement over the earlier move 17...♗e4, which was played in Ivanchuk-Vaganian, Novgorod 1995. That game continued 18 ♘fd4 ♘xd4 19 ♕xd4 ♘c6 20 ♕xb6 axb6 21 ♖e2 ♔f8 22 ♖d1 ♗f5 23 ♖ed2 ♖ed8 24 f3 g6 25 ♔f2 ♔e7 26 c3 ♗e6 27 ♘d4 ♘xd4 28 ♖xd4 ♖dc8 29 ♖b4 ♖c5 30 ♗d3 ♖c6 31 ♗c2 ♖a5 32 ♗b3 and White's edge had persisted. It has to be said that 17...a6 doesn't really alter the general assessment of the position, which is a little better for White.

18 ♗f1 ♖ac8 19 ♘bd4 ♗e4 20 c3 ♔f8!?

This provokes White into some real action. 20...♘xd4 is an alternative, though after 21 ♘xd4 ♘c6 22 ♘xc6 bxc6 23 a5 White fixes the a6-pawn, which becomes a weakness.

21 a5!?

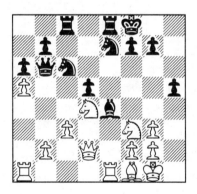

An inventive pawn sacrifice, which is hardly typical of this line. Given that it is difficult to foresee that White's attack will quickly gather momentum, one can hardly blame Lputian for grabbing the pawn. Nevertheless, the super-safe 21...♕c7 should be considered, especially as the a5-pawn will not run away.

21...♘xa5 22 ♘e5 ♔g8 23 ♕f4 f6 24 ♘d7 ♕d8

The greedy 24...♕xb2 runs into a brilliant combination: 25 ♖xa5 ♕xc3 26 ♖xe4 dxe4 27 ♘xf6+ gxf6 28 ♖xh5 ♕xd4

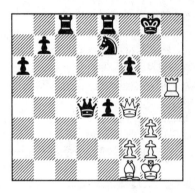

29 ♗c4+!! ♖xc4 30 ♕g4+ ♔f8 31 ♖h8+ ♘g8 (31...♔f7 32 ♖h7+ ♔f8 33 ♕g7 mate) 32 ♕xg8+ ♔e7 33 ♕xe8+ ♔d6 34 ♕b8+ ♔c6 35 ♖d8 ♕a1+ 36 ♔h2 ♔b6 37 ♖d7! and it is unlikely that the black king will survive very long. Even after the sober 24...♕d8 the attack persists.

25 ♘xf6+! gxf6 26 ♖xe4 dxe4 27 ♕xf6 ♘ec6 28 ♕g6+ ♔f8 29 ♘f5

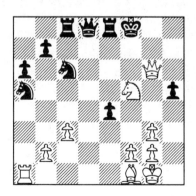

White is a rook down, but the threat of b2-b4 followed by ♗c4 is extremely difficult to meet. The queen and knight once more prove to be an irresistible attacking force. If now 29...♕c7 30 b4 ♘e5 31 ♕f6+ ♔g8 32 ♖xa5 the white rook also enters the attack and Black cannot set up a defence. The move chosen by Lputian also fails to stem the flow.

29...♖c7 30 b4 ♖f7 31 ♕h6+ ♔g8 32 ♕xh5 ♖e6 33 bxa5 ♕f6 34 ♗c4 ♖fe7 35 ♘xe7+ 1-0

A powerful attacking display by Agnos.

Game 60
Emms-Prandstetter
Barcelona 1993

---

1 e4 e6 2 d4 d5 3 ♘d2 c5 4 exd5 exd5 5 ♘gf3 ♘c6 6 ♗b5 ♗d6 7 0-0 ♘ge7 8 dxc5 ♗xc5 9 ♘b3 ♗d6 10 ♘bd4

This position can also arise after 7...cxd4 8 ♘b3 ♘ge7 9 ♘bxd4 (with one tempo less for either side). This variation was given a thorough testing in the 1974 Karpov-Korchnoi match, the general verdict being that White's advantage was just too minute to cause his opponent serious trouble.

10...0-0 11 c3 ♗g4 12 ♕a4 ♕d7

12...♗h5 is a fully playable alternative. Howell-Psakhis, Bled 1995, continued 13 ♗e2 a6 14 ♗e3 ♕c7 15 h3 ♘a5! 16 ♖ad1 ♖ad8 17 ♖fe1 h6 18 ♘h4 ♗xe2 19 ♖xe2 ♘c4 (once the knight reaches this square, Black has often solved his difficulties) 20 ♘df5 b5 21 ♕c2 (21 ♕xa6? ♖a8 22 ♕xb5 ♖fb8 23 ♘xd6 ♖xb5 24 ♘xb5 ♕b7 is

better for Black) 21...♘xf5 22 ♘xf5 ♖fe8 23 ♗d4 ♗f8 24 ♖de1 ♕d7 25 b3 ♘d6 and the players agreed a draw. This is a good example of accurate play by Black. In the final position White has absolutely nothing.

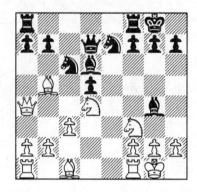

13 ♖e1

13 ♗e3 is probably more precise. Then after 13...a6 14 ♗e2 ♘xd4 15 ♕xd4 ♘c6 the queen can retreat to d2. That said, following 16 ♕d2 ♖fe8 17 ♖ad1 ♖ad8 18 ♗b6 ♗c7 19 ♗xc7 ♕xc7 20 ♖fe1 h6 White had only an infinitesimal edge in Karpov-Korchnoi, Moscow (game 16) 1974.

13...a6 14 ♗e2 ♘xd4! 15 ♕xd4 ♘c6 16 ♕d1 ♖fe8

An exchange of minor pieces often favours the side battling against the isolated pawn, as the weakness of the IQP becomes more pronounced as the endgame approaches. Here, however, Black is perfectly co-ordinated and even has a slight development advantage.

17 ♗e3 ♖ad8 18 ♕c2 h6 19 ♖ad1 ♕c7 20 h3 ♗h5 21 ♔f1?!

A ludicrous attempt to centralise the king for the endgame! Black could have exploited this immediately by

21...♖xe3! 22 fxe3 ♗g3, when White has to start thinking about how to equalise.

21...♗f4 22 ♕f5!? ♗xe3 23 ♕xh5 ♗a7 24 ♗d3

24 ♖xd5 allows 24...♕b6! 25 ♘d4 ♕xb2, when I prefer Black.

24...♕b6?!

This leads to problems. 24...d4! 25 cxd4 ♘xd4 26 ♖xe8+ ♖xe8 27 ♘xd4 ♗xd4 is the simplest way to draw.

25 ♖xe8+ ♖xe8 26 ♖d2 d4 27 cxd4!

Black was hoping for 27 ♘xd4 ♘xd4 28 cxd4 ♕b4. Around this stage I realised that I actually had some real winning chances.

27...♕c7 28 ♖c2 ♕f4 29 ♕g4! ♕xg4 30 hxg4 ♘b4

The best move. 30...♘xd4 31 ♖c7! ♖b8 32 ♗c4 is clearly better for White, while after 30...♗xd4 White doesn't play 31 ♖xc6 bxc6 32 ♘xd4 ♖d8, but instead 31 ♗xa6 ♘b4 32 ♖c4 bxa6 33 ♖xb4.

31 ♖d2?!

As both players were entering into big time-trouble, the inevitable errors creep in. 31 ♖c3 is stronger here, as 31...♘xa2 can then be met by 32 ♖c7. Now 31...♘xa2 should have been

tried.

31...g6?! 32 a3 ♘xd3 33 ♖xd3 ♖e4 34 ♖c3 b5?! 35 d5 b4? 36 ♖c7 ♗b6 37 ♖c6 ♗d4

This drops a piece, but Black's position was already hopeless, e.g. 37...♗d8 38 ♖c8 ♖e8 39 d6 bxa3 40 bxa3 ♔g7 41 d7 ♖h8 42 ♘e5.

38 ♖c4 bxa3 39 bxa3 1-0

A somewhat scrappy game, and a rather fortuitous victory for White.

Game 61
Jansa-Votava
Prague 1993

---

1 e4 e6 2 d4 d5 3 ♘d2 c5 4 ♘gf3 ♘c6 5 exd5 exd5 6 ♗b5 ♗d6 7 dxc5 ♗xc5 8 0-0 ♘ge7 9 ♘b3 ♗b6

A common alternative to the usual 9...♗d6.

10 ♖e1!

The plan involving ♖e1 and ♗e3 is by far the most popular idea for White. If truth be told, most Black players shy away from 9...♗b6 for precisely this reason. Other ideas pale by comparison. For example, 10 ♘bd4 0-0 11 c3 ♗g4 12 ♗e2 ♘xd4 13 ♘xd4 ♗xe2 14 ♘xe2 ♘c6 15 ♘f4 d4 16 cxd4 ♗xd4 gave Black no problems at all in Renet-Korchnoi, Paris (rapidplay) 1990.

10...0-0 11 ♗e3 ♗g4 12 ♗xb6 axb6

The sharper 12...♕xb6 will be examined in the next game. There is nothing really to this position apart from Black's dodgy pawn structure, which gives White a small but obvious advantage.

13 ♗e2 ♕d6 14 c3 ♖fd8 15 ♘fd4 ♗xe2 16 ♖xe2 ♘g6 17 ♘f5 ♕f6 18

♘bd4 ♘ce5 19 g3 ♘c4 20 ♕c2 ♘ge5 21 b3 ♘a3?! 22 ♕d2 ♘c6 23 ♖ae1 ♔h8 24 ♕d3

Black has done his best to create complications, but to no avail. The knight on a3 is out of the game and White has control over the all-important e-file.

24...g6 25 ♘h6 ♘xd4 26 cxd4 ♕g7 27 ♘g4 h5 28 ♘e5 ♖ac8 29 ♘f3 ♕f6 30 ♔g2 ♔g7 31 ♖e7

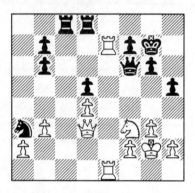

31...♖c2

This leads to a rather abrupt end. 31...♖d6 32 ♖xb7 ♖c2 has been suggested an improvement, but White can also win here with 33 b4 ♖dc6 34 ♖ee7! ♖6c3 35 ♖xf7+ ♕xf7 36 ♖xf7+ ♔xf7 37 ♘e5+.

32 ♖1e6! 1-0

A nice finish. Both 32...♕xe6 33 ♖xe6 fxe6 34 ♘e5 ♔f8 35 ♕xg6 and 32...♕f5 33 ♕xf5 gxf5 34 ♖xb6 ♖xa2 35 ♘h4 are hopeless for Black.

Game 62
Dvoirys-Tondivar
Leeuwarden 1994

---

1 e4 e6 2 d4 d5 3 ♘d2 c5 4 exd5 exd5 5 ♘gf3 ♘c6 6 ♗b5 ♗d6 7

dxc5 ♗xc5 8 ♘b3 ♗b6 9 0-0 ♘ge7 10 ♖e1 0-0 11 ♗e3 ♗g4 12 ♗xb6 ♕xb6

After 12...♕xb6 it is White who winds up with doubled pawns, but Black has to sacrifice one of his own for this privilege.

13 ♗xc6 ♘xc6 14 ♕xd5 ♘b4 15 ♕e4 ♗xf3 16 gxf3

Black hopes that his opponent's wrecked kingside pawn structure will be enough compensation for the pawn. However, White's pieces become extremely active over the next few moves, rendering these weaknesses insignificant. This line has very few takers at master level.

16...♖ad8 17 ♖ad1

This temporary sacrifice of the a-pawn is probably stronger than 17 ♖e2 ♖d6!? 18 c3 ♖e6 19 ♕c4 ♖g6+ 20 ♔h1 ♕f6 21 f4 ♕h4 22 ♘d2, which occurred in Ivanchuk-Dokhoian, Yerevan 1989. In this position 22...♕h3! has been suggested as a way to keep things going for Black, e.g. 23 f3 ♘c6 24 ♖g1 ♖d8 and White is certainly not in complete control.

17...♖xd1 18 ♖xd1 ♘xa2 19 ♖d7 ♕f6 20 ♘d4

Tondivar was actually repeating one of his previous games, which had gone 20 ♖xb7 ♕xb2 21 ♖xa7 h5 22 ♔g2 ♘c1 23 ♘d4 ♕c3 24 ♕f4 ♕e1 25 ♕e3 ♖e8 26 ♕xe1 ♖xe1 27 ♖a1 1-0 Jansa-Tondivar, Ostend 1993. No doubt he had some improvement lined up, although I can't see anything special. In any case, Dvoirys got his new move in first.

20...♕g5+ 21 ♔f1 ♕c1+ 22 ♔g2 ♕xb2

Now that the king is more strongly placed on g2, White would have answered 22...♕g5+ with 23 ♕g4.

23 ♖xb7 ♕c3 24 ♖xa7 ♘b4 25 ♖a4!

White has kept the extra pawn, and now initiates a surprising attack which is immediately decisive.

25...♕c5 26 ♘f5

26...♖b8

Other moves also lose:

a) 26...♘c6 27 ♖c4.

b) 26...♘d5 27 ♕xd5 ♕xd5 28 ♘e7+.

c) 26...♘xc2 allows the prettiest finish, as 27 ♘e7+ ♔h8 28 ♕xh7+! ♔xh7 29 ♖h4+ leads to mate.

27 c3!

27 ♖a8 allows the defence 27...♕f8, so White deflects the queen. Black has

no choice as the knight has no useful retreat square.

27...♕xc3 28 ♖a8 1-0

Since 28...♕c7 runs into 29 ♕e8+. A powerful performance from Dvoirys. The onus is on Black to come up with a substantial improvement here.

Game 63
T.Ravi-Dolmatov
Calcutta 1996

---

1 e4 e6 2 d4 d5 3 ♘d2 c5 4 ♘gf3 ♘c6 5 exd5 exd5 6 ♗b5 cxd4

This is a clever attempt to steer the game into ♘bd4 lines, which would arise after 7 0-0 ♗d6 8 ♘b3 ♘ge7 9 ♘bxd4. At the moment it is not immediately obvious how White should best avoid this transposition.

7 ♕e2+

After 7 ♘xd4 ♗d7 8 ♕e2+ ♕e7 9 ♘2b3 ♕xe2+ 10 ♘xe2 ♘f6 11 ♗e3 a6 12 ♗xc6 ♗xc6 13 0-0-0 0-0-0 14 ♗d4 ♘d7 15 ♘g3 ♖g8 16 f3 g6 17 ♘e2 ♗d6 the position was equal in Brodsky-Dolmatov, Novgorod 1995. The d-pawn is difficult to attack in the absence of a light-squared bishop.

7...♕e7

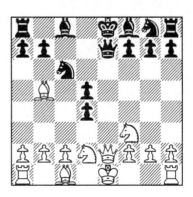

8 ♘xd4

8 ♘e5!? leads to some crazy chess after 8...♗d7 9 ♗xc6 bxc6 10 0-0 ♚d8!? (preparing ...f7-f6) 11 ♘b3 f6 12 ♗g5!? fxg5 13 ♘a5 ♕e8! The first time this bizarre position occurred was in the game Ivanchuk-Dolmatov, Manila Interzonal 1990, where the players called it off here and agreed a draw! Five years later Dolmatov was brave enough to play on with his extra piece and was rewarded after 14 ♖fe1 ♚c7!? 15 ♕f3 ♗b4 16 ♕g3 ♗d6 17 c4 ♘f6! 18 ♘axc6?! (18 c5 is the only chance) 18...♘e4! 19 ♖xe4 dxe4 20 c5 ♗xe5 21 ♘xe5 ♚c8! 22 ♘c4 ♕e7 23 ♘d6+ ♚d8 24 ♕b3 ♗c6 25 ♕c4 ♕f6 0-1 Svidler-Dolmatov, Haifa 1995. White needs something new here, otherwise the piece sacrifice looks rather dubious.

8...♕xe2+ 9 ♚xe2 ♗d7 10 ♘2f3 ♗c5 11 ♗e3 ♘xd4+ 12 ♘xd4 ♗xd4 13 ♗xd7+ ♚xd7 14 ♗xd4 f6 15 ♖hd1 ♘e7 16 c4

16 ♗c5 ♖ac8 17 ♗xe7 ♚xe7 18 c3 ♖c5 is dead level, so White tries to change the character of the position.

16...♚e6 17 cxd5+ ♘xd5

The minimal advantage of the bishop against the knight in an open position means that White can play on. Indeed White keeps a small edge all the way to the final position, but Ravi decided not to test Dolmatov's undoubted technique.

18 ♖d2 ♖hd8 19 ♚f3 ♘b4 20 a3 ♘c6 21 ♖e1+ ♚f7 22 ♖ed1 ♖ac8 23 ♗c3 ♖xd2 24 ♖xd2 ♚e6 25 ♚e4 h5 26 f4 ♘e7 27 g3 ♘f5 28 ♚f3 ♖c7 29 h3 ♘d6 ½-½

Summary

In the main line with 9...♗d6 it seems that White has reasonable chances for an advantage with either 11 ♗d3 or the older 11 ♗g5. 9...♗b6 still has a poor reputation and this line needs some major surgery before it becomes playable. If Black really has to capture with 12...axb6 (as in Game 61) then I suspect we won't see much of this line in future. The variation with 6...cxd4 (Game 63) certainly merits further investigation, but even here Black players may have to accept that White can always make an easy draw.

1 e4 e6 2 d4 d5 3 ♘d2 c5 4 exd5 exd5 5 ♘gf3 ♘c6 6 ♗b5 ♗d6
     6...cxd4 – *Game 63*

7 dxc5
     7 0-0 cxd4 8 ♘b3 0-0 9 ♘bxd4 – *Game 60* (by transposition)

7...♗xc5 8 0-0 ♘ge7 9 ♘b3 ♗d6
     9...♗b6 10 ♖e1 0-0 11 ♗e3 ♗g4 12 ♗xb6 *(D)*
          12...axb6 – *Game 61*
          12...♛xb6 – *Game 62*

10 ♖e1
     10 ♘bd4 – *Game 60*

10...0-0 11 ♗d3 *(D)*
     11 ♗g5 – *Game 59*

11...h6 12 h3 ♘f5 13 c3 ♛f6
     13...♗c7 – *Game 58*

14 ♗c2 ♗e6 *(D)*
     14...♖d8 – *Game 57*

15 ♛d3 – *Game 56*

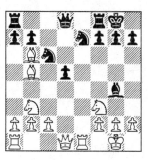

12 ♗xb6   *11 ♗d3*   *14...♗e6*

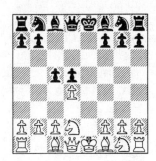

CHAPTER EIGHT

3...c5 4 exd5 exd5: Fifth Move Alternatives

1 e4 e6 2 d4 d5 3 ♘d2 c5 4 exd5 exd5

In the last decade 5 ♘gf3 ♘c6 has gradually been overtaken in the popularity stakes by the even more reliable 5...♘f6. Old references had discarded this natural move (for no particular reason), but top players such as the super-solid Russian GMs Evgeny Bareev and Alexei Dreev have now shown that Black can obtain a fully playable game with this move, with results that reflect their convictions. In Games 64-67 we look at various attempts for White to squeeze out an opening edge against 5...♘f6.

5...a6 (Games 68-70) is a more risky and ambitious attempt for Black, and is ideally suited to those going all or for the win. White can either capture on c5 immediately, or invite Black to clamp on the queenside with ...c5-c4. Note that the position after 5...a6 is often reached via the move order 1 e4 e6 2 d4 d5 3 ♘d2 a6 4 ♘gf3 c5 5 exd5 exd5.

5 ♗b5+ has various transpositional possibilities, but there are also some significant independent lines too, as we shall see in Games 71-73.

Game 64
Tiviakov-Dreev
Wijk aan Zee 1996

1 e4 e6 2 d4 d5 3 ♘d2 c5 4 exd5 exd5 5 ♘gf3 ♘f6

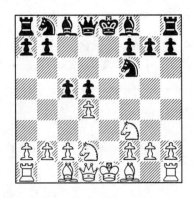

6 ♗b5+

6 ♗e2 is seen from time to time, but the general view is that it gives Black less problems than the main line. One recent example continued 6...♘c6 7

0-0 &e7 8 dxc5 &xc5 9 ♘b3 &b6 10 &g5 0-0 11 c3 ♖e8 12 &h4 h6 13 ♖e1 g5! 14 &g3 ♘e4 15 ♘fd4 f5! 16 &h5 ♖f8 and Black had a very active position in Onischuk-Kramnik, Tilburg 1997.

6...&d7 7 &xd7+ ♘bxd7 8 0-0 &e7 9 dxc5 ♘xc5 10 ♖e1

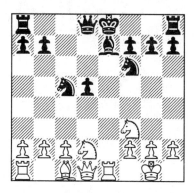

The start of a logical plan which was introduced by the Swiss GM Lucas Brunner. White's idea is quite clear: He plans ♘f1 and &e3-d4, followed by ♘e3 and possibly ♕d3 and ♖ad1. The white pieces would then be very harmoniously placed and the d5-pawn would also come under pressure.

10 ♘d4 and 10 ♘b3 are considered in Games 66 and 67 respectively.

10...0-0 11 ♘f1 ♖e8!

The stem game Brunner-Atalik, Kecskemet 1991, varied with 11...♘ce4?! 12 &e3 ♖c8 13 &d4 &d6 14 ♘e3 &b8 15 ♕d3! ♖e8 16 ♖ad1 ♕d6, and now instead of 17 g3?! White should have just played 17 &xf6! ♘xf6 18 c4 with a big advantage, as the d-pawn drops. It was hardly surprising that the idea beginning with 10 ♖e1 became popular for

White after this game, although Black's play was far from inspiring.

12 &e3 ♘fe4

Apart from the challenging 12...a4, which is the subject of the next game, Black has also tried:

a) 12...b5 13 &d4 ♘e6 14 &e5 ♘g4 15 ♘e3 ♘xe3 16 ♖xe3 ♕d7 17 ♕d2 ♖ad8 18 ♖d1 ♘c5 19 &c3 &f8 20 ♖xe8 ♕xe8 21 &d4 ♘e4 22 ♕a5 and Black's pawns were looking rather vulnerable in Yurtaev-Ulibin, Russia 1997.

b) 12...a6 (too slow) 13 c3 ♖c8 14 ♕c2! ♕c7 15 ♖ad1 b5 16 &d4 and once more White has reached an ideal set-up, as in Kasparov-Short, London (rapidplay) 1993.

13 c3 ♕d6 14 ♘g3 &f8 15 ♕c2 ♕a6 16 ♖ed1 ♖ad8 17 ♘g5! ♘xg5

After 17...♕g6 18 ♘5xe4 dxe4 19 ♖xd8 ♖xd8 20 &xc5 &xc5 White doesn't play 21 ♘xe4? because of 21...♖e8 22 ♖e1 f5 winning a piece, but 21 ♕xe4!, which leaves him a clear pawn up.

18 &xg5 ♖d7 19 &e3 b6 20 ♕f5 g6?!

This concedes a slight weakness on f6, which White is able to utilise. 20...♕b7 would have kept White's plus to a minimum.

21 ♕g4 ♘e6 22 &d4! ♕b5 23 ♘h5 &e7 24 &f6 d4?

24...&f8 would have been a better defence, although after 25 &e5 &e7 26 ♖d2 the weaknesses around the black king still give White a clear advantage. After 24...d4? White reaches a very pleasant endgame.

25 &xe7 ♕xh5 26 ♕xh5 gxh5 27 &f6 d3 28 ♖d2 ♘f4 29 ♔f1 ♖e2 30

罝ad1

For the first 30 moves White's play has been quite exemplary. It might seem that Black is quite active here, but appearances can be a little deceptive. The d3-pawn is in fact a real defect in this position, and should be picked off soon. If you add this to Black's other weak pawns on the kingside, White has virtually a winning position. Tiviakov's technique, however, couldn't cope with Dreev's gritty resistance and his bamboozling knight moves. In fact, in the end he was quite relieved to make a draw!

30...包e6 31 g3 罝xd2 32 罝xd2 罝d5 33 含g2 h6 34 c4!? 罝d6 35 含f3 含h7 36 盒e5?

36 含e3 包c5 37 盒d4 罝e6+ 38 含f3 包e4 39 罝xd3 gets rid of that annoying d-pawn.

36...包g5+! 37 含f4 罝d7 38 h4 包h3+ 39 含f3? 包g1+! 40 含e4 罝e7! 41 罝d1 包h3 42 含f5 包xf2 43 罝d2 包g4 44 盒d4? 包e3+ 45 含f4 包xc4 46 罝xd3 罝d7! 47 b3 包a3 48 罝d2

There is still time for White to blow it completely. 48 含e4?? 包c2, intending ...f7-f5+, wins for Black.

48...包b1 49 罝d3 ½-½

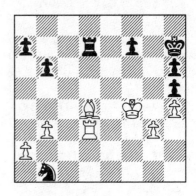

> **Game 65**
> **I.Gurevich-Bareev**
> *Hastings 1992*

1 e4 e6 2 d4 d5 3 包d2 c5 4 exd5 exd5 5 包gf3 包f6 6 盒b5+ 盒d7 7 盒xd7+ 包bxd7 8 0-0 盒e7 9 dxc5 包xc5 10 罝e1 0-0 11 包f1 罝e8 12 盒e3 a5!?

A very deep move indeed. Black is not merely content to centralise his pieces and await events. With 12...a5 he aims to gain space on the queenside and possibly also weaken White's pawn structure.

13 豐e2

After 13 盒d4 包e6 14 盒e5 盒c5! 15

♖e2 ♘e4 16 ♘e3 ♘6g5 White has to play with care just to equalise, e.g. 17 ♘xg5 (17 ♕xd5?! ♗xe3 18 ♕xd8 ♗xf2+ 19 ♖xf2 ♖axd8 20 ♖e2 ♘xf3+ 21 gxf3 ♖xe5 22 fxe4 f5 wins a pawn) 17...♕xg5 18 ♗d4 ♘xf2 19 ♖xf2 ♗xd4 20 ♕xd4 ♕xe3 21 ♕xd5 ♖e7 22 ♖d1 h6 and the players shook hands on a draw in Rozentalis-M.Gurevich, Belfort 1997.

13...♕d7 14 ♘d4 a4 15 a3

White feels obliged to prevent the possible ...a4-a3, but now Black obtains a bind on the light squares in the centre and on the queenside.

15...♘ce4 16 ♕b5 ♕c7! 17 ♖ad1 ♘d6 18 ♕d3 ♘c4 19 ♗c1 ♗c5 20 ♘f5 ♘g4 21 ♘5e3 ♗xe3 22 fxe3 ♘f6

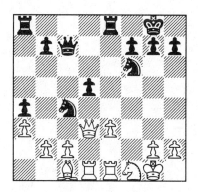

Without making any obvious blunders, White has managed to reach quite a hideous position. Both c4 and e4 are excellent outposts for the black pieces, while White has been saddled with weak pawns on e3 and b2. Given the way things have gone so far, it is quite a miracle that Gurevich survived this position.

23 ♕d4 ♘d6 24 ♕f4 ♖e4 25 ♕g3 ♖c4 26 c3 ♕b6 27 ♕f3 ♘de4 28

♖d4 ♕c6 29 ♖ed1 ♖e8 30 ♖1d3 ♘g5 31 ♕d1 ♘ge4 32 ♖xc4 dxc4 33 ♖d4 b5 34 ♗d2 ♘c5 35 ♗e1 ♘fe4 36 ♕f3 ♕e6 37 ♘g3 g6 38 ♘xe4 ♘xe4 39 ♗h4 h6 40 h3 ♔g7 41 ♔h1 ♕c6 42 ♗d8 ♖e6 43 ♔g1 ♕e8 44 ♖d5 ♘g5 45 ♕f4

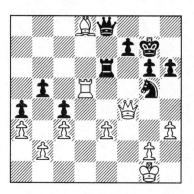

Black has lost control and no longer possesses any real advantage. Now 45...♖xe3 loses to 46 ♗f6+ ♔h7 47 ♖d8, so Black bails out.

45...♘e4 46 ♗c7 ½-½

Game 66
Karpov-Bareev
Linares 1994

---

1 e4 e6 2 d4 d5 3 ♘d2 c5 4 exd5 exd5 5 ♘gf3 ♘f6 6 ♗b5+ ♗d7 7 ♗xd7+ ♘bxd7 8 0-0 ♗e7 9 dxc5 ♘xc5 10 ♘d4 ♕d7!

The queen often finds itself parked on a light square in this line. Here it patrols the sensitive f5-square, which the knight on d4 was eyeing.

11 ♘2f3 0-0 12 ♗f4

The main alternative is 12 ♘e5 ♕c8! and now:

a) 13 ♕f3 ♖e8 14 ♘f5 ♘ce4 15 c3 and here not 15...♗d8?! 16 ♘g4 ♖e6

17 h3 with an edge to White in Van der Wiel-Korchnoi, Wijk aan Zee 1992, but either 15...♗c5 or 15...♗f8, both of which seem perfectly satisfactory for Black.

b) 13 ♘d3 ♘ce4 14 ♗f4 a6 15 ♖e1 ♗d6 16 c3 ♖e8 17 ♗xd6 ♘xd6 18 ♖xe8+ ♕xe8 19 ♕c2 ♕d7 20 ♖e1 ♖e8 with a dull and equal position in Arnason-Dolmatov, Moscow 1990.

12...♖fe8 13 ♖e1

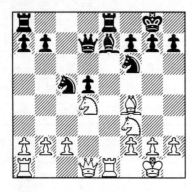

13...♗f8

An early game in this line went 13...♘ce4 14 ♘e5 ♕d8 15 ♘d3! ♖c8 16 c3 ♗f8 17 ♕b3 and the knights were very nicely placed on d3 and d4, ensuring White an edge in Adams-Short, English Championship 1991.

14 ♘e5 ♕a4!?

Naturally Black can also consider 14...♕c8 and 14...♕d8.

15 c3 ♕a6 16 ♕e2 ♕xe2 17 ♖xe2 ♗d6

Allowing a neat trick, although it is not clear that this changes the assessment that much. White has a minuscule plus, which shouldn't really be enough for victory.

18 ♘d7! ♗xf4

18...♖xe2? 19 ♘xf6+ gxf6 20 ♗xd6

saddles Black with further worries on the kingside, after which White would have real winning chances.

19 ♖xe8+ ♖xe8 20 ♘xc5 ♗c7! 21 ♘d3

Karpov suggests 21 ♔f1 ♗b6 22 ♘cb3 as a way of keeping a pull, but once again it is nothing too serious for Black.

21...♗b6 22 ♘b3 ♔f8 23 ♖d1 a5 24 ♔f1 ♖c8 25 ♘d2 a4 26 a3 g5 27 ♘f3 g4 28 ♘h4 d4 29 cxd4 ♗xd4 30 ♘f5 ♗b6 31 ♘b4 ♘e4 32 f3 gxf3 33 gxf3 ♘c5 34 h4 ♖d8

This error is a prelude to a 'blunder of the year' contender. After 34...♗d8! 35 ♘d5 ♘e6 Black is very close to the draw.

35 ♖d5

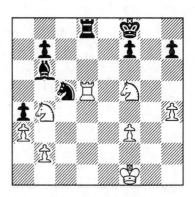

35...♗a7?? 36 ♖xd8 mate

A shocking finish and a reminder that it happens to the best of us! After such a disaster it only seems fair to include an instructive Bareev victory.

Game 67
I.Gurevich-Bareev
Biel 1993

---

1 e4 e6 2 d4 d5 3 ♘d2 c5 4 exd5

exd5 5 ♘gf3 ♘f6 6 ♗b5+ ♗d7 7 ♗xd7+ ♘bxd7 8 0-0 ♗e7 9 dxc5 ♘xc5 10 ♘b3 ♘ce4

It is not a good idea for Black to allow an exchange of these knights:

a) 10...♘xb3?! 11 axb3 and the semi-open a-file can only help White.

b) 10...0-0 11 ♘xc5 ♗xc5 12 ♗g5 ♖c8 13 c3 ♖c6 14 ♘e5 ♖e6 15 ♘g4 ♗e7 16 ♘e3 with a comfortable plus for White in Tal-Benko, Skopje 1972.

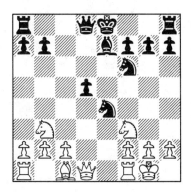

11 ♗f4

Another plan is 11 ♘fd4 ♕d7 12 ♕f3, planning to plonk a piece on the f5-square. White then has two options after 12...0-0:

a) 13 ♕f5 g6! (Black doesn't fear a queen exchange) 14 ♕xd7 ♘xd7 and the d-pawn is quite safe.

b) 13 ♘f5 ♗d8! 14 ♗e3 g6 15 ♘g3 ♖e8! 16 c3 a5 17 ♘d4 ♖a6 18 ♖ad1 ♘g4 19 ♘c2 ♖f6 and Black had a strong initiative in Kotronias-Psakhis, Chalkidiki 1992.

11...0-0 12 ♕d3 ♖e8 13 ♗e5!? ♕d7 14 a4 a6 15 ♖fd1 ♖ac8 16 c3 ♗d8!

Once again we see this clever move. From d8 the bishop may shoot to c7 or b6, where it applies pressure on the central squares. There now follows a long bout of manoeuvring in which nothing much happens, which is quite typical for a position like this.

17 h3 h6 18 a5 ♖c6 19 ♗xf6 ♘xf6 20 ♘fd4 ♖c8 21 ♘c2 ♗c7 22 ♘e3 ♖cd8 23 ♘d4 ♖e4! 24 ♘f3 ♕c6 25 b4 ♖de8 26 ♔f1

26 ♘xd5? ♘xd5 27 ♕xd5 ♖e1+ wins material. However, White is tempted to take the bait a few moves later.

26...♖d8 27 ♖ab1 ♗f4 28 ♘f5 ♕c7 29 ♘5d4 ♖c8 30 ♖b3 ♖ee8! 31 ♘e2 ♗e5 32 ♖c1 ♘e4! 33 ♕xd5?

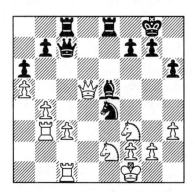

33...♗g3!!

A brilliant move which exploits the temporary disharmony in the white ranks.

34 c4

Other moves are also bad for White:

a) 34 ♘xg3 ♖cd8! 35 ♕f5 ♕c4+.

b) 34 fxg3 ♖cd8 35 ♕f5 ♕c4!

c) 34 ♖b2 is probably the best of a bad bunch, although 34...♗xf2 is still grim for White.

34...♖cd8 35 ♕f5 ♕xc4! 36 ♖e3

36 ♖xc4 ♖d1+ 37 ♘e1 ♘d2+ 38 ♔g1 ♖xe1 is mate.

36...♗b8 37 g3 ♕xb4 38 ♔g2 ♘d6

39 ♕d3 ♖xe3 40 ♕xe3 ♖e8 41 ♕d3 ♕xa5

The flurry of tactics is over and Black is completely winning. The rest of the game is of little note.

42 ♘f4 ♕f5 43 ♕b3 ♘b5 44 ♘d5 h5 45 h4 ♗d6 46 ♘g5 g6 47 ♕c4 ♔g7 48 f4 ♔h6 49 ♘c3 ♖c8 50 ♕b3 ♔g7 51 ♘xb5 ♖xc1 52 ♘d4 ♕f6 53 ♕xb7 ♗e7 54 ♕d5 ♖c8 55 f5 ♖d8 56 ♘de6+ fxe6 57 ♘xe6+ ♔h6 58 ♘xd8 ♗xd8 59 fxg6 ♔xg6 60 ♕d3+ ♔g7 61 ♕d1 ♕c6+ 62 ♔h2 ♗c7 63 ♕d2 ♕c5 64 ♔h3 ♕e5 65 ♕d7+ ♔f6 0-1

Game 68
Geller-Dreev
New York 1990

---

1 e4 e6 2 d4 d5 3 ♘d2 a6 4 ♘gf3 c5 5 exd5

Of course White is not obliged to capture on d5 here. The alternative 5 dxc5 is considered in Chapter 9, Game 77.

5...exd5

This position also frequently arises from the move order 3...c5 4 exd5 exd5 5 ♘gf3 a6. However, with this sequence Black can also play the slightly strange looking immediate 5...c4. The drawback to this idea is that after 6 b3 he is forced to exchange pawns, as 6...b5 walks into 7 a4. After 6...cxb3 7 axb3 ♗b4 8 ♘e5 ♘f6 9 ♗d3 0-0 10 0-0 ♗c3 11 ♖a4 ♗d7 12 ♘xd7 ♘bxd7 13 ♘b1! ♗a5 14 ♗d2 ♗c7 15 ♘c3 White has unravelled successfully and the bishop pair ensures an edge, as in Svidler-Korchnoi, Groningen 1996.

6 ♗e2

This move invites Black to claim space on the queenside with ...c5-c4 and ...b7-b5. Naturally Black could also continue in the normal fashion with ...♘c6 and ...c5xd4, but this would leave the move ...a7-a6 rather out of place.

The alternative 6 dxc5 is considered in Games 69 and 70.

6...c4 7 0-0 ♗d6 8 b3 b5 9 a4!?

The most critical response to Black's idea, attacking the pawn chain before Black has a chance to consolidate his development. White has to be willing to sacrifice material, as otherwise Black may just wind up with a crippling bind on the queenside. Two other moves are also worthy of consideration:

a) 9 ♖e1 (vacating the f1-square for the knight before starting queenside operations) 9...♘e7 10 a4 ♗b7! (10...c3 loses its appeal here: 11 ♘f1 b4 12 ♘g3 0-0 13 ♗d3 gave White the advantage on the kingside in Serper-Legky, USSR 1986) 11 ♘e5 0-0 12 bxc4 dxc4 13 ♗f3 ♘d5 with equality in Spasov-Dreev, Tunja 1989.

b) 9 c3 (physically preventing ...c4-c3!) 9...♘e7 10 a4 ♗b7 11 ♗a3 ♗xa3 12 ♖xa3 ♘d7 13 axb5 axb5 14 ♖xa8 ♗xa8 15 bxc4 bxc4 16 ♕a1 0-0 with equal chances in Ivanchuk-P.Nikolic, Moscow Olympiad 1994.

9...♗b7

Here 9...c3! is the most testing response. White can hardly contemplate locking in his entire queenside army with 10 ♘b1, so he must go 'all in' with 10 axb5 cxd2 11 ♗xd2 and now:

a) 11...♗b7 12 bxa6 ♘xa6 13 ♗xa6 ♖xa6 14 ♕e2+ ♕e7 15 ♕xa6!! ♗xa6 16 ♖xa6 ♕c7 17 ♖e1+ ♔d7 18 c4 dxc4 19 bxc4 f6 20 c5 ♗xc5 21 dxc5 ♘e7 22 ♘d4 1-0 was the brilliant game Geller-Kekki, CSKA-Matynkyla 1986. In the final position White's many threats include 23 ♖a7 ♕xa7 24 ♖xe7+ ♔xe7 25 ♘c6+.

b) 11...♘f6! 12 c4 dxc4! (12...0-0? 13 c5 ♗c7 14 b6 ♗xb6 15 cxb6 ♕xb6 16 ♗a5 was good for White in Dolgener-Liepold, Germany 1991) 13 bxc4 0-0 and although White obviously has some compensation for the piece, it is not clear whether it is really enough. Kr.Georgiev-P.Nikolic, Elenite 1993, supported this claim after 14 c5?! (weakening the d5-square) 14...♗e7 15 ♖e1 ♗e6 16 ♕b1 ♗d5 17 ♗a5 ♕c8 18

bxa6 ♗d8 19 ♗xd8 ♖xd8 20 a7 ♘c6 21 ♕b6 ♘d7 and, on realising that the a-pawn was lost, White abruptly resigned.

10 bxc4! bxc4

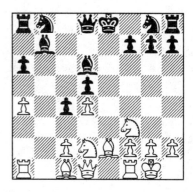

11 ♗xc4!

An inspired sacrifice which is not only good, but also quite necessary. If Black were able to complete his development then his clamp on the queenside would start to become a serious concern for White.

11...dxc4 12 ♘xc4 ♗e7

12...♘e7 runs into 13 ♘xd6+ ♕xd6 14 ♗a3!, after which Black is in grave trouble, e.g. 14...♕c7 15 ♖e1 ♘bc6 16 d5.

13 ♖e1 ♕c7 14 ♖b1

Threatening 15 ♖xb7 ♕xb7 16 ♘d6+. The white rooks really play their part in this game.

14...♕xc4 15 ♖xb7 ♘c6 16 ♘d2! ♕xd4 17 ♗b2! ♕xa4 18 ♖e4 ♕a2 19 ♗xg7 0-0-0 20 ♖b3

see following diagram

Black's position is beyond repair. Now 20...♘f6 loses after 21 ♖c4! ♖xd2 22 ♖xc6+ ♔d7 23 ♕xd2+ ♔xc6 24 ♕c3+! ♔d7 25 ♗xh8.

**20...&f6 21 &g4+ &c7 22 &f4+
&c8 23 &xf6 &xf6 24 &xf6 &xc2
25 &f5+! 1-0**

25...&c7 26 &e7+ or 25...&d7 26
&e8+ both win the queen. A powerful
performance by Geller, but we await
more tests with 9...c3!

Game 69
Donchev-Eingorn
Debrecen 1992

**1 e4 e6 2 d4 d5 3 &d2 a6 4 &gf3
c5 5 exd5 exd5 6 dxc5 &xc5 7 &b3
&a7**

Here Black utilises the a7-square
that was vacated by ...a7-a6. The retreat to this haven is obviously the
most natural move, but there is also
nothing wrong with 7...&e7, a favourite of Dolmatov. An example of
Black's chances is shown in the game
Einarsson-Dolmatov, Reykjavik 1988,
which went 8 &d3 &f6 9 0-0 0-0 10
&e1 &c6 11 c3 &g4 12 &g5 (12 h3
&h5 13 &g5 &d6 14 &e3 looks more
testing) 12...h6 13 &h4 &b6 14 &c2
&e4! 15 &xd5?! &xf3 16 gxf3 &xh4 17
&xe4 &xf2+ 18 &f1 g6 and White's
king didn't last many more moves.

8 &d3

8 &g5 is the subject of the next
game.

8...&e7+!

This annoying queen check is the
reason why 8 &d3 is not seen very
much. White has to choose between
losing a move with 9 &e2, or an un-
welcome exchange of queens.

9 &e2 &c6 10 c3

An early indication that Black has
no problems here was the game Mata-
novic-Korchnoi, Wijk aan Zee 1968.
After 10 0-0 &g4 11 h3 &h5 12 &f4
&xe2 13 &xe2 &f6 14 c3 0-0 15 &fe1
&fe8 16 g4 &g6 17 &f1 &e4 18 &xe4
&xe4 19 &g2 h5 20 g5 &d7 21 &d1
&f8 22 &e3 &xe3 23 fxe3 &e6 24 h4
&e8 Black had taken over the initiative
and went on to win.

10...&g4 11 0-0 &xe2 12 &xe2 &f6

This endgame holds absolutely no
worries for Black, whose active pieces
more than offset the weakness of the
d5-pawn.

**13 h3 &h5 14 g4 &g6 15 &fd4 h5
16 &g2 hxg4 17 hxg4 &e5 18 f3
0-0-0 19 &f2 &de8 20 &f4 &c4 21
&d1 &d7 22 &c2 &xc2 23 &xc2**

23...&b8!

From a very quiet-looking position, Black suddenly goes for a mating attack! 24 ♗xb8 ♘e3+ wins material, so the white king ventures into the unknown.

24 ♔g3 ♗xf4+ 25 ♔xf4 ♖h3! 26 ♖f2 ♘de5 27 ♖d1 ♘g6+ 28 ♔g5 ♖h6 29 ♖e2 0-1

Donchev didn't wait around to see 29...f6+ 30 ♔f5 ♘d6 mate.

♗d3 ♖e8 16 ♖he1 ♕d7 17 ♗xg6 ♘xg6 18 ♕g5 ♖xe1 19 ♖xe1 ♖e8 20 ♖xe8+ ♕xe8 21 ♕e3 ♕xe3+ 22 fxe3

The major pieces have been unceremoniously hoovered off and the only conceivable result is a draw.

22...♘e5 23 ♘f5 ♔f8 24 a4 b6 25 ♔d2 g6 26 ♘d6 ♘d7 27 ♘c8 ♔e8 28 ♔c3 ♔d8 29 ♘d6 ♔e7 30 ♘c8+ ♔d8 31 ♘d6 ½-½

Game 70
Van der Wiel-Seirawan
Biel 1985

1 e4 e6 2 d4 d5 3 ♘d2 c5 4 exd5 exd5 5 ♘gf3 a6 6 dxc5 ♗xc5 7 ♘b3 ♗a7 8 ♗g5 ♘e7 9 ♕d2

Planning both to castle queenside and exchange Black's most active minor piece with ♗e3.

9...♘bc6 10 ♗e3 ♗xe3 11 ♕xe3 0-0 12 0-0-0 ♗f5

The exchange of dark-squared bishops gives White a tiny edge in this position, but with careful play, as in this game, Black can often neutralise this completely. On the other hand, Black's winning chances are very slim.

Game 71
Rublevsky-Bareev
Rubinstein Memorial 1997

1 e4 e6 2 d4 d5 3 ♘d2 c5 4 exd5 exd5 5 ♗b5+ ♗d7

The alternative 5...♘c6 is seen in Game 73.

6 ♕e2+ ♗e7

The inferior 6...♕e7 is dealt with in the next game.

7 dxc5

Otherwise the queen check would have no point. White must now make his opponent work hard to regain the pawn.

7...♘f6 8 ♘b3 0-0 9 ♘f3 ♖e8 10 ♗e3 a6 11 ♗d3

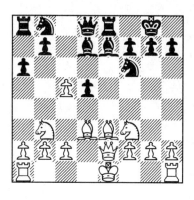

13 ♘fd4 ♘xd4 14 ♘xd4 ♗g6 15

11...♗a4

A very direct move. Black simply wishes to eliminate the knight on b3 and regain the c5-pawn. If Black prefers to play in sacrificial mode then 11...♘g4 is worth considering. In the game Van Wely-Ehlvest, Biel 1993, White quickly gained a substantial advantage after 12 0-0 a5 13 a4 ♗f6? 14 c3 ♘a6 15 ♗b5 ♘c7 16 ♘bd4 ♘xb5 17 axb5 ♕c7 18 b4 ♗xd4 19 b6 ♕b8 20 cxd4 axb4 21 ♕d2. However, 13...♘a6! is a stronger move. After 14 ♗xa6 ♖xa6 Black's two bishops give him definite compensation for the pawn.

12 ♘fd4 ♘bd7 13 0-0-0

The main move here, although the quieter 13 0-0 must not be underestimated. Here Black should probably continue with 13...♘xc5, as 13...♗xb3 was met by the zwischenzug 14 c6! in the game Kosashvili-Sjodahl, Arnhem 1989, when after 14...bxc6 15 axb3 ♗c5 16 ♕d1 ♕b6 17 ♖a4 a5 18 h3 ♘f8 19 ♕f3 Black's weak queenside pawns gave White an edge.

13...♗xb3 14 ♘xb3

Naturally 14 axb3 is also possible, although this may give Black more chances as the b3-pawn can be a target for the lunge ...a6-a5-a4. Van Wely-Brenninkmeijer, Holland 1993, continued 14...♗xc5 15 ♕f3 ♘e5 16 ♕h3 ♕b6 17 ♘f5 ♗xe3+ 18 ♘xe3 a5 19 ♘xd5 ♘xd3+ 20 ♕xd3 ♘xd5 21 ♕xd5 a4, when White is a pawn up but faces some tricky moments on the queenside.

14...a5

Or 14...♘xc5 15 ♘d4 (15 ♕f3 is probably stronger) 15...♘a4!? 16 c3 ♖c8 17 ♗c2 ♘b6 18 ♕d3 g6 19 ♘b3?!

♘c4 20 ♗d4? ♗a3!! 21 bxa3 ♕d6 22 ♘c5 ♘e4 with favourable complications for Black, as in Yudasin-Psakhis, Beersheva 1993.

15 a4 ♘xc5 16 ♗b5 ♘xb3+ 17 cxb3 ♕c7+ 18 ♔b1

White now has doubled pawns on the queenside, and the d5-pawn is also passed, as well as isolated. On the other hand, the white king is well protected now, and he can hope to use his two bishops in an open position.

18...♖ed8 19 ♗d4 ♘e4 20 f3 ♘c5 21 ♗e5 ♗d6

21...♕b6 allows 22 ♗xg7, so Black has to enter an inferior endgame, where the bishop is much stronger than the knight. Rublevsky, however, makes a few slight inaccuracies and this allows Bareev to hold the draw.

22 ♖xd5 ♗xe5 23 ♕xe5 ♕xe5 24 ♖xe5 ♘xb3 25 ♔a2

25 ♖e7 looks like a better winning try.

25...♘d4 26 ♖c1 ♖ab8 27 ♖c7 ♘e6 28 ♖d7 ♖dc8 29 ♖f5 f6 30 ♖d6 ♘c5 31 g4 b6 32 h4 ♔f7 33 g5 ♖d8 34 ♖c6 ♖dc8 35 gxf6 ♖xc6 36 ♗xc6 gxf6 37 ♖h5 ♖h8 ½-½

Game 72
Moya-Roldan
Correspondence 1984

---

1 e4 e6 2 d4 d5 3 ♘d2 c5 4 exd5 exd5 5 ♗b5+ ♗d7 6 ♕e2+ ♕e7?!

The endgame reached after this move is known to be comfortably better for White.

7 ♗xd7+ ♘xd7 8 dxc5 ♘xc5 9 ♘b3 ♕xe2+ 10 ♘xe2 ♘xb3 11 axb3 ♗c5 12 ♗d2

As well as the customary weakness of the d5-pawn, Black also has to worry about White's pressure on the semi-open a-file. All in all this makes the endgame unpleasant to defend.

12...♘e7 13 ♗c3 0-0 14 ♗d4 ♗xd4 15 ♘xd4 a6 16 ♔d2 ♖fe8 17 ♖he1 ♔f8 18 ♖e5 ♖ad8 19 ♖ae1 ♘c6 20 ♖xe8+ ♖xe8 21 ♖xe8+ ♔xe8 22 ♘xc6 bxc6 23 b4

An instructive position, where Black's weaknesses tell in the king and pawn endgame. Black has fewer 'passing' moves than White and consequently cannot prevent a decisive infiltration of the white king.

23...♔d7 24 ♔d3 ♔d6 25 ♔d4 f6 26 f3 h6 27 f4 g6 28 g4 h5 29 gxh5 gxh5 30 h4 ♔d7 31 ♔c5 ♔c7 32 f5 ♔d7 33 ♔b6 1-0

1 e4 e6 2 d4 d5 3 ♘d2 c5 4 exd5 exd5 5 ♗b5+ ♘c6

White can now obviously play 6 ♘gf3, transposing to lines in Chapter 7, while avoiding 5 ♘gf3 a6 and 5

♘gf3 ♘f6. In this game White keeps it independent with the queen check.

6 ♕e2+ ♗e7

6...♕e7 once again leads to an inferior endgame. For example, 7 dxc5 ♕xe2+ 8 ♘xe2 ♗xc5 9 ♘b3 ♗b6 10 ♗d2 ♘ge7 11 ♗b4 led to another grim, turgid defence for Black in Euwe-Botvinnik, World Championship 1948.

7 dxc5 ♘f6 8 ♘b3 0-0 9 ♗e3 ♖e8 10 ♘f3 a6 11 ♗d3 d4!?

An interesting attempt to liven the position up. Funnily enough, it seems to lead to a forced draw!

12 ♘fxd4 ♘xd4 13 ♘xd4 ♗xc5 14 c3 ♘g4 15 0-0 ♕h4 16 h3 ♘xe3 17 fxe3

17...♗xh3!

Striking before White can consolidate. Luckily for White he can steer the game to a drawn ending.

18 gxh3 ♗xd4 19 cxd4 ♕g3+ 20 ♔h1 ♖xe3 21 ♗xh7+! ♔h8

Or 21...♔xh7 22 ♕h5+ and 23 ♕xf7+.

22 ♕h5 ♕xh3+ 23 ♕xh3 ♖xh3+ 24 ♔g2 ♖xh7 25 ♖xf7 ♖d8 26 ♖xb7 ♖h4 27 ♖d1 ♖dxd4 28 ♖xd4 ♖xd4 29 ♔f3 ♔h7 ½-½

Summary

Despite a variety of attempts against 5 ♘gf3 ♘f6, Black's move has stood firm and the onus is clearly on White to produce something new. The variation 5...a6 6 ♗e2 c4!? is especially good for Black players determined to go for the full point, as many of White's most promising lines involve sacrificing material. 5 ♗b5+ continues to be less popular than 5 ♘gf3, as it seems that Black has sufficient resources after either 5...♗d7 or 5...♘c6 6 ♕e2+ ♗e7.

1 e4 e6 2 d4 d5 3 ♘d2 c5 4 exd5 exd5 5 ♘gf3

    5 ♗b5+ *(D)*

        5...♗d7 6 ♕e2+

            6...♗e7 – *Game 71*

            6...♕e7 – *Game 72*

        5...♘c6

            6 ♘gf3 – Chapter 7

            6 ♕e2 – *Game 73*

5...♘f6

    5...a6

        6 ♗e2 – *Game 68*

        6 dxc5 ♗xc5 7 ♘b3 ♗a7 *(D)*

            8 ♗d3 – *Game 69*

            8 ♗g5 – *Game 70*

6 ♗b5+ ♗d7 7 ♗xd7+ ♘bxd7 8 0-0 ♗e7 9 dxc5 ♘xc5 *(D)* 10 ♖e1

    10 ♘d4 – *Game 66*

    10 ♘b3 – *Game 67*

10...0-0 11 ♘f1 ♖e8 12 ♗e3 ♘fe4

    12...a5 – *Game 65*

13 c3 – *Game 64*

     5 ♗b5+   7...♗a7   9 ♘xc5

CHAPTER NINE

3...c5 4 ♘gf3

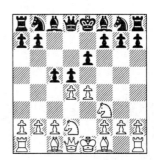

1 e4 e6 2 d4 d5 3 ♘d2 c5 4 ♘gf3

4 ♘gf3 is a sly transpositional move which White players often employ in order to direct the game into their opening terrain, rather than their opponent's. For example, after 4...cxd4 White need not play 5 exd5 ♛xd5, but can choose 5 ♘xd4, which gives an entirely different type of position (see Games 74 and 75). White also has other options against Black three main alternatives, 4...♘f6, 4...a6 and 4...♘c6, and Black needs to be prepared for all of these eventualities. The good news for Black is that none of these lines are particularly terrifying. In general White players straying from the main path are merely looking to reach a playable position rather than striving hard for a theoretical edge. Game 76 sees 4...♘f6, which together with the similar line 4...cxd4 5 ♘xd4 ♘f6 (Game 74), is probably Black's most reliable move. 4 ♘gf3 is a good idea against ...a7-a6 adherents, as White certainly has more options than simply transposing to Games 68-70 in the previous chapter with 4...a6 5 exd5 exd5, as we see in Game 77. After 4...♘c6 White normally plays 5 exd5, but in Game 78 we discuss the little played 5 ♗b5.

1 e4 e6 2 d4 d5 3 ♘d2 c5 4 ♘gf3 cxd4

Inviting the ...♛xd5 lines seen in Chapters 5 and 6 via 5 exd5 ♛xd5.

5 ♘xd4 ♘f6

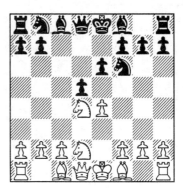

We will look at the alternative move 5...♘c6 in Game 75.

6 exd5

6 e5 looks quite tempting, but after 6...♘fd7 Black's position is extremely resilient. Svidler-Dreev, Rostov 1993, continued 7 ♘2f3 ♘c6 8 ♘xc6 bxc6 9 ♗d3 ♗a6! (this exchange of White's best bishop ensures Black a comfortable game) 10 0-0 ♗xd3 11 ♕xd3 ♗e7 12 c4 0-0 13 ♕c2 a5 14 ♖d1 a4 15 ♗f4 ♘b6 and Black was fully equal.

6...♕xd5?!

Black loses time after this move. 6...♘xd5 is stronger, when after 7 ♘2f3 ♗e7 the game transposed to Emms-Bronstein (see note to Black's sixth move in Game 76).

7 ♘b5! ♕d8 8 ♘c4 ♘d5

An exchange of queens brings no relief to the black camp, as 8...♕xd1+ 9 ♔xd1 leaves the squares c7 and d6 devoid of sufficient protection.

9 ♘e3 ♘c7

Levitt suggests 9...a6 10 ♘xd5 exd5 11 ♘d4, when White has an edge, but at least Black can reach a reasonable position.

10 ♗d2 ♘xb5 11 ♗xb5+ ♗d7 12 ♗xd7+ ♕xd7 13 ♕g4 ♘c6 14 0-0-0

Black is already in danger. White's development advantage is very serious, and Black has further problems developing the dark-squared bishop without losing the g7-pawn.

14...♕d4 15 ♕e2 ♕a4 16 ♔b1 ♗e7 17 ♗c3 0-0 18 ♖d7 ♘b4

This move loses, but it doesn't really deserve a question mark as it is probably Black's best practical chance and requires some quite brilliant play to refute it.

19 ♕g4 g6 20 ♕d4! ♕xa2+ 21 ♔c1 f6 22 ♗xb4 ♗xb4

In his book *Chess in the Fast Lane* Adams admits that he had intended 23 ♕xb4 ♖ad8 24 ♖xd8 ♖xd8 25 ♕a3 and White wins. Only here did he see that Black can play 24...♕a1+! 25 ♔d2 ♖xd8+ 26 ♔e2 ♕xh1 27 ♕e7 ♖f8 28 ♘g4 ♕c1 and Black is slightly better. Half an hour in the 'think tank' produced the answer.

23 c3!! ♕a1+ 24 ♔c2 ♕xh1 25 ♕xb4 ♖ad8

There is absolutely no way out. 25...♖ae8 allows 26 ♕h4 ♖f7 27 ♖d1! and the queen is neatly trapped on the h1-square.

26 ♖xd8 ♖xd8 27 ♕e7 1-0

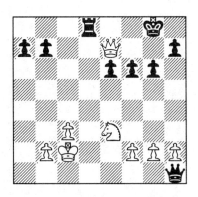

After 27...♖f8 28 ♘g4 White wins, the crucial difference being that there is now no ...♕c1 defence. A fantastic performance by Adams, but Black should certainly replace 6...♕xd5 with 6...♘xd5.

Game 75
Yudasin-Gulko
Biel 1993

---

1 e4 e6 2 d4 d5 3 ♘d2 c5 4 ♘gf3 cxd4 5 ♘xd4 ♘c6 6 ♗b5 ♗d7

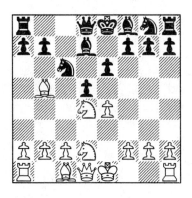

7 ♘xc6 bxc6

7...♗xc6 can lead to an endgame where Black's split pawns on the queenside give White a minute advantage, e.g. 8 ♗xc6+ bxc6 9 c4 dxe4

(9...♘f6!?) 10 ♘xe4 ♗b4+ 11 ♔e2 ♕a5 12 ♗e3 ♗e7 13 ♕d2 ♕xd2+ 14 ♗xd2, as in Van der Wiel-Ehlvest, Haninge 1990.

8 ♗d3 ♕c7 9 ♕e2 ♗d6

Black can also develop the knight first, which has the advantage of taking the sting out of White's e4-e5. For example, 9...♘e7 10 0-0 ♘g6 11 ♘f3 ♗d6 12 ♖e1 ♘f4 13 ♗xf4 ♗xf4 14 c4 0-0 15 g3 ♗h6 16 exd5 cxd5 was equal in Zakharov-Petrosian, USSR Championship 1976.

10 ♘f3 dxe4?!

This move, releasing the tension prematurely, is not to be recommended. In particular, Black now has real problems ushering his king into safety. A much better alternative is 10...♘e7 11 0-0 0-0 12 c4, when White is only slightly better.

11 ♕xe4 ♘f6 12 ♕h4 ♖b8

Black would like to play 12...0-0, but 13 ♗g5! is simply very annoying.

13 0-0 ♘d5 14 ♖e1 ♗e7 15 ♕g4 g6

Once again castling is out of the question: 15...0-0 16 ♗h6 ♗f6 17 ♕e4! and h7 is dropping.

16 c4 f5?

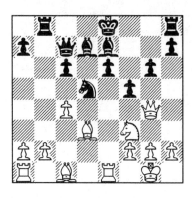

Things were already becoming

rather serious for Black, but this move allows White a pretty combination, which accelerates the end.

17 ♗xf5! ♘f6

17...gxf5 18 ♕h5+ ♔d8 19 cxd5 cxd5 20 ♘g5 and 17...exf5 18 ♕d4 ♖f8 19 cxd5 cxd5 20 ♗g5 are also very undesirable. Black seeks salvation in the endgame, but his airy king still causes too many problems.

18 ♕f4 ♕xf4 19 ♗xf4 ♖xb2 20 ♗xe6 ♗c5 21 ♗xd7+ ♔xd7 22 ♘e5+ ♔c8 23 ♘d3 1-0

After 23...♖c2 24 ♘xc5 ♖xc4 25 ♗e3 White is a clear piece up.

Game 76
Popovic-P.Nikolic
Yugoslavia 1991

---

1 e4 e6 2 d4 d5 3 ♘d2 c5 4 ♘gf3 ♘f6 5 exd5

Here 5 e5 ♘fd7 6 c3 ♘c6 7 ♗d3 transposes to lines considered in Chapter 3, Games 27 and 28. After 5 exd5 Black can obviously play 5...exd5, converting to Games 64-67, but here Black chooses another entirely playable move.

5...♘xd5 6 ♘b3

6...♘d7

6...cxd4 is probably more accurate. Emms-Bronstein, Maidstone 1994, continued 7 ♘bxd4 ♗e7 8 g3!? (8 ♗d3 is also possible) 8...0-0 9 ♗g2 b5! 10 0-0 (10 ♘xb5 ♕a5+ 11 ♘d2 ♕xb5 12 c4 ♕a6 13 cxd5 exd5 14 ♗xd5 ♘c6 gives Black excellent play for the pawn) 10...a6 11 ♕e2 ♕b6 12 c3 ♘d7 13 ♗g5 ♗xg5 14 ♘xg5 ♘7f6 and Black had equalised.

7 ♗g5! ♗e7 8 ♗xe7 ♕xe7 9 ♗b5 cxd4 10 ♕xd4 0-0 11 0-0-0 a6 12 ♗c4 ♘5f6 13 ♖he1 b5

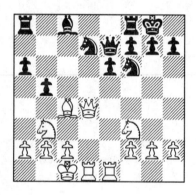

14 ♗d5!

14 ♗d3 ♗b7 would not have presented Black with any problems, but now White can steer the position into an endgame, where his control of the d-file will be the most important factor. Note that 14...♖b8 15 ♗c6 ♖b6 fails to 16 ♘e5!

14...♘xd5 15 ♕xd5 ♖a7 16 ♕d6 ♕xd6 17 ♖xd6 ♖c7 18 ♘e5 ♘b8

This looks rather ugly, but 18...♘xe5 19 ♖xe5, with the idea of ♖c5, also favours White.

19 ♘a5 f6 20 ♘d3 e5 21 ♘b4 ♔f7 22 ♖ed1 ♗e6 23 c3 ♗c8 24 g3 h5 25 h4 ♖e8 26 ♘d5 ♖a7 27 ♘b4 ♖c7

28 ♖1d2 ♖e6 29 ♖d8 ♖e8 30 ♖8d6 ♖e6 31 ♖d8 ♖e8 32 ♖xe8 ♔xe8 33 ♖d6 ♖a7 34 ♖b6 ♘d7 35 ♖e6+ ♔f7 36 ♖c6 ♖a8 37 ♘d5 e4?

Black has been forced to defend a grim endgame for quite a while, and finally cracks under the pressure. 37...♖b8 was the only way to hang on.

38 ♖c7

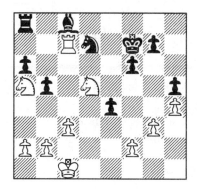

38...♔e6

This loses a piece, but 38...♔e8 fails to 39 ♖xd7, while after 38...♔f8 39 ♘c6 Black is completely tied up.

39 ♖xd7 1-0

White wins the rook on a8 after 39...♔xd7 40 ♘b6+ or 39...♗xd7 40 ♘c7+.

Game 77
Wolff-Yermolinsky
USA Championship 1993

---

1 e4 e6 2 d4 d5 3 ♘d2 a6 4 ♘gf3 c5

This position can also be reached via the move order 3...c5 4 ♘gf3 a6. If now 5 exd5 exd5 we have reached the standard position of the ...a7-a6 line (see Chapter 8, Games 68-70).

5 dxc5 ♗xc5 6 ♗d3 ♘e7 7 0-0 ♘bc6 8 c3 0-0

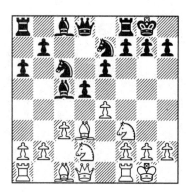

9 exd5

The other way to play this position is to maintain the pawn on e4. Rozentalis-P.Nikolic, Moscow 1994, continued 9 ♕e2 ♘g6 10 ♘b3 dxe4 (perhaps 10...♗a7!?, maintaining the tension, is more appropriate) 11 ♗xe4 ♗d6 12 ♗e3 ♕c7 (12...♘f4? loses 13 ♗xf4 ♗xf4 14 ♗xh7+ ♔xh7 15 ♕e4+) 13 ♖ad1 ♖d8 14 ♕c4! ♗d7 15 ♗xg6 hxg6 16 ♘g5! and White had drummed up a menacing initiative.

9...exd5

9...♘xd5 is also very reasonable, after which White should probably continue with 10 ♘e4. After 9...exd5 we have actually reached a position similar to that discussed in Chapter 7 (see Games 56-58). The difference here is that Black has committed himself to ...a7-a6, which is only a semi-useful move.

10 ♘b3 ♗d6 11 ♖e1 h6 12 h3 ♗f5

After 12...♘f5, which is normal procedure in Games 56-58, Black's ...a7-a6 proves to be a serious loss of time. White can simply play 13 ♗c2 ♗e6 14 ♕d3, when the threat of g2-g4 is hard to deal with.

13 ♗e3 ♖e8

14 ♘bd4

14 ♗c5!? ♕d7 15 ♗xf5 ♘xf5 16 ♕d3 is a sensible suggestion for White, when the pressure on d5 ensures a small edge.

14...♗e4 15 ♕c2 ♘g6 16 ♗xe4 dxe4 17 ♘d2 ♘xd4 18 ♗xd4 f5!

The nature of the position has suddenly changed. Black now has a potentially dangerous pawn roller on the kingside. Wolff now decided to grab a hot pawn on b7, but Alex 'the Yerminator' Yermolinsky utilised his initiative to the full.

19 ♕b3+ ♚h7 20 ♕xb7

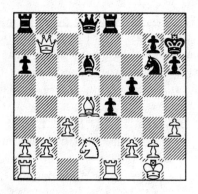

20...♗e5! 21 ♖ad1 ♗xd4 22 cxd4 ♕g5!

Now it is clear that White is in real trouble. 23 g3 ♘f4 24 ♚h2 ♘d3 is probably the best of a bad bunch, although Black's attack would still be serious.

23 ♘f1? ♘h4 24 ♘g3 f4 25 ♖xe4 fxg3 26 fxg3 ♖ab8 27 ♕c6 ♘f3+ 0-1

28 gxf3 ♕xg3+ 29 ♚f1 ♕xf3+ wins a rook.

Game 78
Kuijf-Uhlmann
Amsterdam 1990

---

1 e4 e6 2 d4 d5 3 ♘d2 c5 4 ♘gf3 ♘c6 5 ♗b5

An interesting bid to avoid the normal lines that arise after 5 exd5 exd5 (see Chapter 7).

5...dxe4

This is the theoretical choice, although 5...a6 also doesn't look bad, e.g. 6 ♗xc6+ bxc6 7 0-0 ♘f6 8 e5 ♘d7 9 c4 ♗e7 10 dxc5 ♘xc5 11 ♘d4 ♕b6 12 ♕g4 0-0 13 ♘2f3 f5 with an unclear position in Sutovsky-Psakhis, Haifa 1996.

Note that 5...cxd4 6 ♘xd4 simply transposes to Game 75.

6 ♘xe4 ♗d7

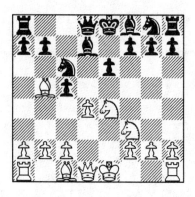

7 ♗e3

This doesn't really cause Black any problems at all. Black has to be more careful after the aggressive 7 ♗g5!? A typical Tal miniature concluded 7...♕a5+ 8 ♘c3 cxd4 9 ♘xd4 ♗b4 10 0-0! ♗xc3 11 bxc3 ♕xc3 12 ♘f5!! exf5 13 ♖e1+ ♗e6 14 ♕d6 a6 15 ♗d2! ♕xc2 16 ♗b4! axb5 17 ♕f8+ ♔d7 18 ♖ed1+! ♔c7 19 ♕xa8 1-0 Tal-Uhlmann, Moscow 1971. Instead of 8...cxd4, Black should play 8...a6 9 ♗xc6 ♗xc6, when his bishop pair off-sets White's slight development lead.

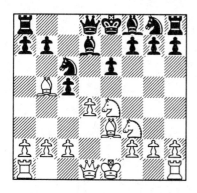

7...♕a5+ 8 ♘c3 cxd4 9 ♘xd4 ♗b4 10 0-0 ♗xc3 11 bxc3 ♘ge7 12 ♘xc6 ♗xc6 13 ♗xc6+ ♘xc6 14 c4 0-0 15 ♕b1 ♕c7 16 c5 ♖fd8

Black has no weakness, whereas White's doubled c-pawns are always a cause for concern. Optically things do not look too bad for White, who can use the d6-outpost. However, some extremely calm play by Uhlmann shows that Black holds all the positional trumps.

17 ♕b5 ♖d7 18 ♖ad1 ♖ad8 19 ♖d6 a6

19...♖xd6 20 cxd6 ♖xd6? fails to 21 ♗f4, as 21...e5 22 ♗xe5 ♘xe5 23 ♕e8 is mate.

20 ♕b2

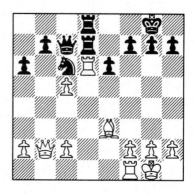

20...♘e7!

This regrouping manoeuvre spells the beginning of the end for White. Black wins a pawn after both 21 ♖fd1 ♖xd6 22 cxd6 ♖xd6 23 ♖xd6 ♕xd6 and 21 ♗d4 ♘f5 22 ♖xd7 ♖xd7 23 c3 e5, while White's chosen move also sheds a pawn.

21 ♗g5 ♖xd6 22 cxd6 ♖xd6 23 ♗f4 ♕b6! 24 ♕e5 ♖d7 25 ♗e3 ♕c7 26 ♕b2 ♘f5 27 ♗b6 ♕c6 28 g3 h5 29 h4 ♖d2 30 ♕b4 ♘xg3 0-1

A fine positional game from the French Defence stalwart.

Summary

As long as Black knows his stuff and doesn't get confused by any move order tricks, he should have nothing to fear from 4 ♘gf3. Black should avoid 4...cxd4 5 ♘xd4 ♘f6 6 exd5 ♕xd5?!, but all the other lines discussed in this chapter look quite playable.

1 e4 e6 2 d4 d5 3 ♘d2 c5 4 ♘gf3 cxd4

> 4...♘f6
>> 5 e5 ♘fd7 6 c3 ♘c6 7 ♗d3 – see *Games 27-28*
>> 5 exd5 *(D)*
>>> 5...exd5 – *Games 64-67*
>>> 5...♘xd5 – *Game 76*

> 4...a6
>> 5 exd5 exd5 – *Games 68-70*
>> 5 dxc5 – *Game 77*

> 4...♘c6
>> 5 exd5 exd5 – *Chapter 7*
>> 5 ♗b5 *(D)*
>>> 5...cxd4 6 ♘xd4 – *Game 75* (by transposition)
>>> 5...dxe4 – *Game 78*

5 ♘xd4 *(D)*

> 5 exd5 ♕xd5 – *Chapters 5-6*

5...♘f6

> 5...♘c6 – *Game 75*

6 exd5 – *Game 74*

5 exd5

5 ♗b5

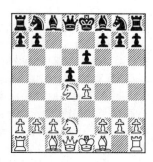

5 ♘xd4

CHAPTER TEN

Third Move Alternatives for Black

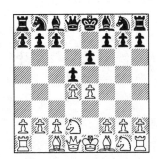

1 e4 e6 2 d4 d5 3 ♘d2

Although 3...c5 and 3...♘f6 continue to be the overwhelmingly popular choices at all levels, Black does have some playable alternatives, which we shall look at this final chapter. One option for Black is 3...♘c6 (Games 79-81), an unconventional move which to be honest has never really caught on. Black obstructs the c-pawn, so much of his typical queenside counterplay is eliminated, or at least delayed. Black often has to accept a passive, blocked position (see Game 81), but there are some positional ideas here that may appeal to certain players.

3...♗e7 (Game 82) is also seen infrequently, but it does seem more reliable than 3...♘c6. It is favoured by the Armenian GM Smbat Lputian, who has employed it with some success. In particular, White has to be quite mindful not to stumble into an undesirable transposition. In Game 83 we take a look at 3...a6 (which usually transposes to the 3...c5 variations that we have already discussed after 4 ♘gf3

c5) and some other unusual moves for Black.

The final two games are a bit of a bonus, as the Rubinstein Defence does not really belong to the Tarrasch proper. Even so, White players would do well to flick through the summary of main lines. The introduction of some new ideas for Black, such as the aptly named 'Fort Knox Defence' (Game 84), has given the Rubinstein a new lease of life. The classical 4...♘d7 is seen in Game 85.

Game 79
Xie Jun-Brunner
Shanghai 1995

---

1 e4 e6 2 d4 d5 3 ♘d2 ♘c6 4 c3

This tricky line generally leads to very open positions. The more common 4 ♘gf3 is considered in Games 80 and 81.

4...e5!

Black does best to strike immediately in the centre here. This outwardly extravagant second move of the e-pawn is warranted by White's non-developing 4 c3.

5 exd5 ♕xd5 6 ♘gf3

6...exd4

The natural looking 6...♗g4? is actually a blunder here. After 7 ♗c4! ♗xf3 8 ♕b3! Black is in difficulty, e.g. 8...♕d7 9 ♘xf3 ♘a5 10 ♗xf7+! ♕xf7 11 ♕b5+, regaining the knight with a pawn to boot.

7 ♗c4 ♕h5!

With 7...♕h5 Black is ready to sacrifice a pawn. In my opinion this move is stronger than 7...♕f5, when after 8 ♘xd4 ♘xd4 9 cxd4 ♗d7 10 0-0 0-0-0 11 ♕b3! White has annoying pressure on the f7-pawn. Emms-Crouch, Isle of Man 1993, continued 11...♘h6 12 ♘f3 ♗d6 13 ♖e1 ♖df8 14 ♗xh6 gxh6 15 ♘e5 ♗e8 16 ♖e3 ♖hg8 17 ♖f3 ♕h5 18 ♗d5 with a clear advantage to White.

8 cxd4 ♗e6 9 ♗xe6 fxe6 10 ♕b3 0-0-0 11 0-0 ♘f6

This looks like the most natural move, but also playable is 11...♘h6, intending to put pressure on d4 with ...♘f5. After 12 ♘e4 ♘f5 13 ♕xe6+ ♔b8 14 ♗g5 ♘fxd4 15 ♘xd4 ♖xd4 16 ♗e3 ♕d5 17 ♘g5 ♕xe6 18 ♘xe6 ♖d7

19 ♘xf8 ♖xf8 an equal position was reached in Lane-Landenbergue, Zug 1989.

12 ♕xe6+

After 12 ♘e4 Black can shield his weak e6-pawn with 12...♖d5. An example of Black's chances in this line is illustrated by this following horror story for White: 13 ♖e1 ♘xe4 14 ♖xe4 ♗d6 15 h3 ♖f8 16 ♖xe6 ♖df5 17 g4?? ♕xh3! 18 gxf5 ♘xd4 19 ♘g5 ♕h2+ 20 ♔f1 ♕h1 mate 0-1 Lawson-Landenbergue, Haifa 1989.

12...♔b8 13 ♘e4 ♘xe4 14 ♕xe4 ♖e8 15 ♕d3 ♗d6 16 ♗d2 g5!

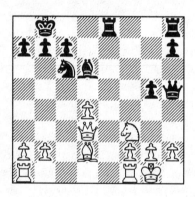

After this lunge Black manages to create sufficient counterplay to compensate for the sacrificed pawn. The greedy capture on g5 would of course lead to a disaster for White: 17 ♗xg5? ♖ef8 18 h4 h6 19 ♗d2 ♖hg8 20 ♔h1 ♖xg2 21 ♔xg2 ♕g4+ 22 ♔h1 ♖xf3 and White can safely resign.

17 g3 g4 18 ♘h4 ♖hf8 19 ♗c3 ♖d8 20 ♖ae1 ♗e7 21 ♘g2!

Preparing to offload an exchange, which releases much of the pressure on the white kingside. Black still has to play carefully to maintain the balance.

21...♘e5 22 ♖xe5 ♕xe5 23 ♕xh7 ♕d6 24 ♘e3 ♗f6 25 ♖d1 ♖g8 26 ♕f5 ♖g5 27 ♕e4 ♖dg8 28 ♖e1 a6 29 ♘c4 ♕d7 30 ♕e6 ♕g7 31 ♘e5 ♗xe5 32 dxe5 ♖g6 33 ♕c4 ♖e8 34 ♖e4 ♕d7 35 ♔g2 ♕d1

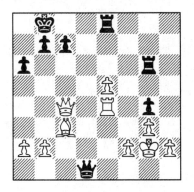

The g4-pawn gives Black just enough counterplay to ensure the draw.

36 ♕e2 ♕d5 37 ♕c4 ♕d1 38 ♕e2 ♕d5 39 ♕c4 ½-½

Game 80
Krishilovsky-Doroshkievich
Novgorod 1997

---

1 e4 e6 2 d4 d5 3 ♘d2 ♘c6 4 ♘gf3 ♘f6 5 e5 ♘d7 6 ♗b5

By putting pressure on the a4-e8 diagonal, White discourages his opponent from playing the desirable ...f7-f6 advance.

Of course the natural 6 ♗d3 is also important here. After the critical 6...f6 White can simply capture, but the real fun starts after 7 ♘g5!? Now 7...fxg5? actually loses after 8 ♕h5+ g6 9 ♗xg6+ hxg6 10 ♕xg6+ ♔e7 11 ♘e4!! ♗h6 12 ♗xg5+ ♗xg5 13 ♕g7+ ♔e8 14 ♕xh8+ ♘f8 15 ♕h5+. Fortunately for Black he can play 7...♘dxe5! 8 dxe5 fxg5 9 ♕h5+ g6 10 ♗xg6+ ♔d7 with a very messy position. Note that 11 ♘f3 is a blunder here due to 11...hxg6, when 12 ♕xh8 fails to 12...♗b4+.

The other main alternative, 6 ♘b3, is the subject of Game 81.

6...a6

Another option for Black is the strange looking 6...a5!?, which prepares ...♘a7, hitting the bishop on b5 and preparing ...c7-c5. Nevertheless, this all sounds rather time-consuming, just to play something which could have been played at move three! After the simple 7 0-0 ♘a7 8 ♗d3 White must be better.

7 ♗xc6 bxc6 8 ♘b3! c5

The game A. Rodriguez-Pecorelli Garcia, Cuba 1997, went instead 8...a5 9 ♗d2! a4 10 ♘a5 ♘b8 11 c4 a3 12 b4 dxc4 13 0-0 ♗a6 14 ♖e1 ♗b5 15 ♕c1 ♕d5 16 ♕xa3 ♘d7 17 ♕c3 ♘b6 18 a3 h6 19 ♕c2 ♗a4 20 ♕c1 ♗e7 21 ♗e3 ♗b5 22 ♘d2 0-0 23 ♘b1! f5 24 exf6 ♖xf6 25 ♘c3 ♕h5 26 ♗f4! and Black was in a massive bind. After 8...c5 Black plans to exchange off his doubled c-pawn.

9 ♗g5 ♗e7 10 ♘a5!

The point to White's previous play. Now 10...♗xg5 11 ♘c6 traps the queen, so Black is forced into contortions.

10...♘b8

The other try is 10...♘xe5 11 dxe5 ♗xg5 12 ♘c6 ♕d7 13 ♘xg5 and now:

a) 13...♕xc6 14 ♕h5 ♕d7 (14...g6 15 ♕h6 ♗d7 16 ♕g7 0-0-0 17 ♘xf7 is very good for White) 15 ♘xh7, when Black has to deal with the menacing threat of ♘f6+.

b) 13...h6 14 ♘xf7 ♕xf7 15 0-0 0-0 16 ♕d2 ♗d7 17 ♘a5 ♖ab8 18 c4 ♕f4 19 ♕e2 and Black's weak pawns give White the advantage, as in Yudasin-Drasko, Tbilisi 1987.

11 ♗xe7 ♕xe7 12 c3 0-0 13 0-0 cxd4

White also holds the advantage after 13...c4 14 b4 cxb3 15 ♕xb3!, as 15...c5 runs into 16 ♕a3!

14 cxd4

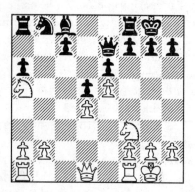

A very pleasant position for White. Black is forced to play ...c7-c5 before it is prevented forever, after which White is ahead in development, has nice outposts for his knights, and can utilise the c-file with his rooks. Meanwhile, Black has problems finding a useful square for the bishop on c8.

14...c5 15 dxc5 ♕xc5 16 ♕d2 ♘c6 17 ♘xc6 ♕xc6 18 ♖ac1 ♕b6 19 ♖c3 ♗d7 20 ♖fc1 ♖fb8 21 b3 h6 22 ♘d4 a5 23 a4?!

Around here White starts to drift slowly but surely, until the players agree a draw in a virtually level position. 23 a3 a4 24 b4!, securing a protected passed pawn, would have been preferable.

23...♕b4 24 ♕f4 ♖c8 25 ♖xc8+ ♗xc8 26 h3 ♗d7 27 ♖c7 ♗e8 28 ♕e3 ♖b8 29 f4?! ♕a3 30 ♕c3 ♕a2 31 ♖c8 ½-½

Game 81
Spassky-Drasko
Sarajevo 1986

---

1 e4 e6 2 d4 d5 3 ♘d2 ♘c6 4 ♘gf3 ♘f6 5 e5 ♘d7 6 ♘b3

This is the theoretical recommendation for an advantage against 3...♘c6. White lets the c1-bishop out and prepares for action against Black's ...c7-c5.

6...a5 7 a4 b6 8 ♗f4 ♗e7 9 h4 ♗b7 10 c3 ♕c8 11 ♗b5 ♘d8

We are now treated to a bout of

heavy duty manoeuvring from both sides. The assessment of the position doesn't change. White has a nice, healthy space advantage.

12 ♗g5 ♗f8 13 h5 h6 14 ♗h4 c6 15 ♗e2 ♗a6 16 0-0 ♗xe2 17 ♕xe2 ♕a6 18 ♕d1 c5 19 ♗xd8 ♖xd8 20 ♘e1 ♗e7 21 f4 f5 22 ♘c2 ♖g8 23 ♘e3 ♘f8

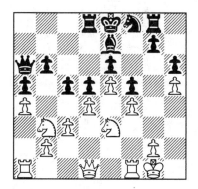

24 ♔h2?

24 ♔f2 is more accurate. The white king may find itself surprisingly exposed on the h-file.

24...g5 25 hxg6 h5!

Now 26 ♕xh5 ♘xg6 27 ♔g1 ♔f7 allows Black to take over operations on the kingside, so Spassky bailed out with a timely draw offer.

26 ♘c1 ½-½

Game 82
Adams-Lputian
Manila Interzonal 1990

---

1 e4 e6 2 d4 d5 3 ♘d2 ♗e7

see following diagram

---

4 ♗d3

One of the ideas behind the 3...♗e7 line is seen after the normal 4 ♘gf3.

After 4...♘f6 5 e5 ♘fd7 6 ♗d3 c5 7 c3 ♘c6 White has slipped into a ♘gf3 line against 3...♘f6, which is not everyone's cup of tea.

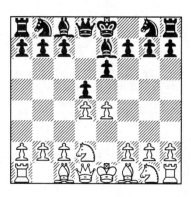

4...c5 5 dxc5 ♘d7!

With the bishop already having moved to e7, this is the most favourable way of recapturing on c5. We now reach a position similar to those that arise after 3...c5 4 exd5 exd5 5 ♘gf3 ♘f6 (Games 64-67), the only difference being that the light-squared bishops remain on the board. In any case, Black's position looks perfectly playable.

6 exd5 exd5 7 ♘b3 ♘xc5 8 ♘f3 ♘f6 9 0-0 0-0 10 ♗e3 ♘ce4!

10...♘xd3 11 ♕xd3 nets a bishop for a knight, but helps White to coordinate his remaining pieces. As is normal in these IQP positions, it is generally useful for Black to keep the pieces on.

11 ♗e2 ♗d6 12 ♖e1 ♖e8 13 ♗d4 ♘h5?!

Here Black starts to go somewhat astray, weakening his position without any provocation. The simple 13...♗f5 would have been perfectly acceptable.

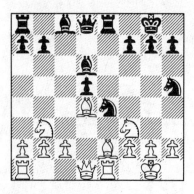

14 g3 f5 15 ♗f1 ♗e6?! 16 ♗e5!

Adams is at his best in these type of positions. Here he offers an exchange of dark-squared bishops, which would emphasise Black's newly formed weaknesses.

16...♘hf6 17 ♕d4 ♗e7 18 h3 ♖f8 19 ♗g2 ♕e8 20 ♕d3 ♘d7 21 ♗f4 ♘dc5 22 ♘xc5 ♗xc5 23 ♖e2 ♕a4? 24 ♘g5! ♕c6 25 ♘xe6 ♕xe6 26 ♔h2 ♕f7

Visually Black's position looks okay, but in fact it is about to fall apart at the seams. Note that 26...♗xf2 27 ♖xf2 ♘xf2 28 ♗xd5 wins for White.

27 f3 ♘d6

28 ♖ae1

28 ♗xd6 ♗xd6 29 f4 is also very strong, but the game move is even more telling.

28...♘c4 29 c3 ♖ad8 30 b4 ♗b6 31 ♖e7 ♕f6?

31...♕h5 32 ♖xb7 leaves White in a position of total dominance. After 31...♕f6 the end is accelerated, as Black's queen goes west.

32 ♖1e6 1-0

Game 83
Oll-Topalov
Zaragoza 1992

1 e4 e6 2 d4 d5 3 ♘d2 a6

Here is a quick look at two rare moves:

a) 3...f5 has been played from time to time, but it looks rather ugly and gives White a nice juicy outpost on e5. The game Karpov-Enevoldsen, Skopje Olympiad 1972, which went 4 exf5 exf5 5 ♘df3 ♘f6 6 ♗g5 ♗e7 7 ♗d3 ♘e4 8 ♗xe7 ♕xe7 9 ♘e2 ♕b4+ 10 c3 ♕xb2 11 0-0 0-0 12 c4 dxc4 13 ♗xc4+ ♔h8 14 ♖b1 ♕a3 15 ♘e5 with a clear advantage to White, has put most people off this line.

b) 3...♘d7 4 ♘gf3 ♘e7!? is an unusual idea of Petrosian. Now after 5 c3 c5 6 e5 ♘c6 we have suddenly reached a main line 3...♘f6, with White's king's knight committed to f3. Instead White can consider keeping the tension with 5 g3 c5 6 ♗g2 cxd4 7 ♘xd4, or 5 ♗d3 c5 6 c3, both of which look slightly better for the first player.

After 3...a6 most White players continue with 4 ♘gf3 c5, transposing to lines considered in Chapters 8 and 9. Here we look at another possibility.

4 e5 ♗d7!

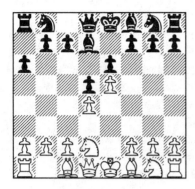

A cute idea. Black's notorious problem child will pop out at b5, where it can exchange itself for one of White's minor pieces. This move seems to secure a comfortable game for Black.
5 ♘e2 c5 6 ♘f3 ♗b5 7 c3 ♘c6 8 ♗e3 cxd4 9 ♘exd4 ♗xf1 10 ♔xf1 ♘ge7 11 g3 ♘xd4 12 cxd4 ♘c6 13 ♔g2 ♗e7 14 ♖e1 ♕b6 15 ♖e2 ♖c8 16 ♖c1 0-0 17 h4 h6

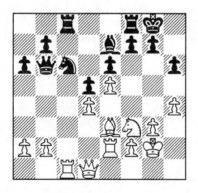

White has the normal space advantage, but with the exchange of two sets of minor pieces, this becomes rather insignificant. Now the game heads for a predictable draw as all the rooks are hoovered off.
18 h5 ♕b5 19 ♖ec2 ♘a7 20 ♘h2

♖xc2 21 ♖xc2 ♖c8 22 ♖xc8+ ♘xc8 23 b3 ♘a7 24 ♘g4 ♘c6 25 ♕d2 ♕b4 26 ♕c1 ♕a3 27 ♕c2 ♕b4 28 ♕c1 ♕a3 29 ♕c2 ♕b4 ½-½

4...♗d7 looks like a complete answer to 4 e5.

> ### Game 84
> ### **Shirov-Hübner**
> *Munich 1993*

1 e4 e6 2 d4 d5 3 ♘c3 dxe4 4 ♘xe4 ♗d7
The classical 4...♘d7 is considered in the next game.
5 ♘f3 ♗c6 6 ♗d3 ♘d7

This is the 'Fort Knox Defence', so-called because Black achieves a super solid structure, albeit with a rather passive position. This line has found some distinguished advocates, including FIDE World Champion Anatoly Karpov.
7 0-0 ♘gf6 8 ♘g3
8 ♘xf6+ ♕xf6 is fine for Black, who has some annoying pressure on f3. However, Black must beware after the enterprising 8 ♘eg5, e.g.
a) 8...h6 9 ♘xe6! fxe6 10 ♗g6+ ♔e7 11 ♖e1 with a very strong attack.

b) 8...♗d6! is more accurate. Korchnoi-Dreev, Brno 1992, continued 9 ♖e1 h6 10 ♘h3 ♗xf3 11 ♕xf3 c6 12 ♘f4, and now instead 12...0-0 13 ♘h5, which gave White a promising attack, Black should have played 12...♕c7 or 12...♕a5, followed by ...0-0-0, with about equal chances.

8...♗e7 9 b3 0-0 10 ♗b2 ♗xf3 11 ♕xf3 c6

This is all very typical of the Fort Knox. White has the bishop pair and extra space, but it is still difficult to break down Black's position.

12 c4 ♖e8 13 ♖fe1 ♘f8 14 h4!? ♕c7 15 ♖ac1 ♘g6!

Good defence. Against 15...♖ad8 Shirov had planned 16 d5! cxd5 17 cxd5 ♕d7 18 d6! and now:

a) 18...♗xd6 19 ♗xf6 gxf6 20 ♘h5 ♗e5 21 ♖xe5 wins for White.

b) 18...♕xd6 19 ♗b5 ♘8d7 20 ♖ed1 ♕b6 21 ♗xf6 ♕xb5 22 ♗xe7 ♖xe7 23 ♖c7! and the pinned knight on d7 causes Black all sorts of problems.

16 h5 ♘h4 17 ♕e3 ♗d6! 18 ♘e4!?

An enterprising idea. Initially White gives up the exchange, but later he wins Black's knight on h5, which runs out of squares. However, the position

still remains quite unclear, as Black picks up a couple of pawns while the white king rushes to safety.

18...♗f4 19 ♘xf6+ gxf6 20 ♕e4 f5 21 ♕e2 ♗xc1 22 ♖xc1 f6! 23 g3 ♔f7! 24 gxh4 ♕f4 25 ♖e1 ♖g8+! 26 ♔f1 ♖ae8 27 ♕e3 ♕xh4 28 ♔e2! ♕xh5+ 29 ♔d2 ♖g2! 30 ♖e2 ♕g5 31 f4 ♖xe2+

Shirov gives 31...♕g3!? 32 ♕xg3 ♖xg3 33 ♖h2 ♔g6 as unclear.

32 ♗xe2 ♕g2 33 ♕f3 ♕xf3 34 ♗xf3

The two bishops give White a small edge in this tricky endgame, but Hübner now starts to make some serious inaccuracies, which make Shirov's task much easier.

34...♔g6?! 35 ♔e3 ♖d8?! 36 ♗c3 ♔f7 37 a4 ♔e7 38 a5 ♔d7?! 39 d5! exd5 40 cxd5 cxd5 41 ♗xf6 ♖f8 42 ♗h4! ♔c6 43 ♔d4 ♔b5 44 ♗xd5 ♔xa5 45 ♗xb7 ♖b8 46 ♗d5 h5 47 ♗e6 ♔a6 48 ♗c4+ ♔b6 49 ♔e5 a5 50 ♔xf5 ♔c5 51 ♔e5 1-0

Game 85
Aseev-Nevostrujev
St Petersburg 1994

---

1 e4 e6 2 d4 d5 3 ♘c3 dxe4 4 ♘xe4

♘d7 5 ♘f3 ♘gf6 6 ♘xf6+ ♘xf6

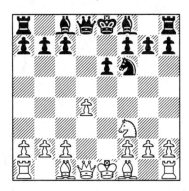

7 ♗b5+

A small refinement, which doesn't make much difference, apart from adding an extra move to each player's scoresheet. The normal move order is 7 ♗d3 c5.

7...c6 8 ♗d3 c5 9 dxc5 ♗xc5 10 0-0

10 ♕e2!?, retaining the option of castling either side, is an ambitious alternative to 10 0-0. Here are a couple of examples:

a) 10...0-0 11 ♗g5 ♕a5+ 12 c3 ♗e7 13 ♘e5 h6 14 ♗h4 ♖d8 15 0-0 ♕c7 16 ♖ad1 b6 17 ♖fe1 ♗b7? 18 ♘xf7! and White was clearly better in the game Karpov-Speelman, Reykjavik 1991, as 18...♔xf7 fails to 19 ♕xe6+ ♔f8 20 ♗xf6 ♗xf6 21 ♗c4.

b) 10...♕c7 11 ♗d2 ♗d7 (11...0-0 looks quite sensible and may well be stronger than 11...♗d7) 12 0-0 ♗d6 13 ♖fe1 0-0-0?! (Nunn gives 13...♗c6 14 ♘e5 ♗xe5 15 ♕xe5 ♕xe5 16 ♖xe5 as just slightly better for White) 14 ♖ad1 ♗c6 15 h3 h6?! 16 b4! and White's offensive on the queenside will be first, as in Nunn-Korchnoi, Amsterdam 1990.

10...♕c7

Also possible is 10...0-0 11 ♕e2 (11 ♗g5!?) 11...h6 12 b3 b6 13 ♗b2 ♗b7 14 ♖ad1 ♕e7 15 c4 ♖fd8 16 ♘e5 ♖d6 and Black had equalised in I. Rogers-Vaganian, Manila Interzonal 1990.

11 ♗g5 b6 12 ♕e2 0-0! 13 ♘e5

13 ♗xf6 gxf6 14 ♕e4 looks tempting, but the rook is poisoned! 14...f5 15 ♕xa8 ♗b7 16 ♕xa7 b5 traps the queen.

13...♘d7?

A blunder which immediately decides the game. Black should have played 13...♗b7, not fearing 14 ♗xf6 (14 ♖ad1 is less committal) 14...gxf6 15 ♕g4+ ♔h8 16 ♕h4 f5, when White should probably take the perpetual, otherwise he is likely to stand worse.

14 ♗f4 ♗b7

Or 14...♘xe5 15 ♗xe5 ♕e7 16 b4! ♗xb4 17 ♕e4 and White wins.

15 ♗xh7+! ♔xh7 16 ♘g6!

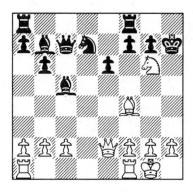

Black has only one way to deal with the two threats.

16...♗xf2+ 17 ♖xf2 ♕c5 18 ♗e3 ♕a5 19 b4! 1-0

After 19 b4 ♕d5 20 c4 Black cannot cover h5 any longer.

Summary

Out of all of Black's third move alternatives, 3...♗e7 looks to be the most underrated and it is surprising that it is not seen more often. After this move Black often reaches uncharted positions similar to those that arise after 3...♘f6 and 3...c5. On the other hand, 3...♘c6 should cause well prepared White players no problems whatsoever.

1 e4 e6 2 d4 d5 3 ♘d2

3...♘c6
>   3...♗e7 – *Game 82*
>   3...a6 *(D)*
>>   4 ♘gf3 c5
>>>   5 exd5 exd5 – *Games 68-70*
>>>   5 dxc5 – *Game 77*
>>   4 e5 – *Game 83*
>   3...dxe4 4 ♘xe4 *(D)*
>>   4...♗d7 – *Game 84*
>>   4...♘d7 – *Game 85*

4 ♘gf3
>   4 c3 – *Game 79*

4...♘f6 5 e5 ♘d7 *(D)* 6 ♘b3
>   6 ♗b5 – *Game 80*

4...a5 – *Game 81*

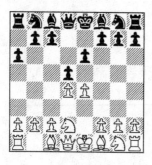

3...a6

4 ♘xe4

5...♘d7

INDEX OF GAMES